THE GOD

CONCLUSION

Charles S. Taylor

Published by Accent Press Ltd 2018

ISBN 9781786156402
eISBN 9781786156396

Accent Press Ltd
Octavo House, West Bute Street, Cardiff CF10 5LJ

Thank you for the encouragement and suggestions:

Andrew F

Anna W

Duncan S

Penny T

Graham H

Hazel C

Michael B

David P

Contents

Introduction

When you buy a book and you want to get on and read it, the book should speak for itself. An Introduction can do little more than spoil any surprise ending. However, some readers do like introductions, so I have written a short one just for you.

I am not a priest, professional theologian, or a spiritual adept. I practised as a barrister for forty years and my expertise is in assessing evidence, spotting contradictions and errors in statements and in – hopefully – presenting an analysis of what the evidence suggests, in a way which a jury can understand and even enjoy. 'The Legal 500' kindly described me as "… very knowledgeable, incisive and determined." I have tried to bring these characteristics to bear on a subject about which I have pondered for a lifetime. I am now not that far away from finding out whether I am right.

Like you, I have always wondered about the meaning of life. I have had the good fortune to meet many wonderful people and even a few sages. I began life as quite an earnest Christian and enthusiastically attended Sunday school and church. As I grew older I began to detect inconsistencies and improbabilities in what I was being told. Indeed, I started to view some passages in the Bible as quite horrid.

As a teenager I looked about at other religions and after initial flirtations they equally failed to satisfy my reason and instinct. Most religions advertise a God who answers prayers and intervenes to help humanity. In reality God clearly fails to do either. In reaction to these sadly false promises of God's active interest, I then toyed with atheism and even materialism, which supposes that we are mere automata reacting to chemical brain reactions with no free will, consciousness or soul. The muddled thinking and smug superiority of some vocal evangelicals seems to make materialism look attractive. Unquestioning belief that scripture contains literal truth is as ludicrous as it is dangerous.

Scripture, if read figuratively, can hold much wisdom. All books, even thrillers, may contain something enlightening.

For instance, one charming old 'who-done-it?' contains a guiding principal for the seeker after spiritual truth. The detective hero, Albert Campion, is listening to a beautiful actress trying to justify her past life. He is deeply upset by her self-serving distortion of the facts: "Mr Campion was shocked." There are some people to whom muddled thinking and self-deception are the most heinous sins in the world.[1] In any spiritual search muddled thinking and self-deception are indeed mortal sins. A theological Campion would be equally shocked at the muddled thinking and self-deception to be found in both religion and materialism. Each side seems determined to maintain belief at all costs. This book is an attack on muddled thinking and self-deception. If, having read it, you conclude that I am equally guilty, I shall still have proved my point.

As I have grown older and experienced the great joys and sorrows of life, I have become increasingly sure that fundamentalist religion and materialistic atheism are opposing extremes and that the answer to the Great Mystery is somewhere in between. As you may have done, I have always perceived within myself a spiritual element together with a sense of some Great Mystery beyond. The more I have read and the more I have listened to others the clearer it has become that there is evidence supporting our instinctive sense of a spiritual dimension.

Evidence, instinct and logic combine to challenge the fundamental concepts of religion and materialism and so both camps try to dismiss summarily all facts and thoughts

---

[1] Margery Allingham, *The Fashion in Shrouds*.

incompatible with their own belief systems. Sadly, most religions, which rightly recognize the essential importance of the spirit, bury this central truth under a mass of dubious detail about the deity they worship.

This book reflects the pattern of my own spiritual path through life. The first five chapters deal with the problems of religion and, in particular, Christianity. The second five chapters grapple with evidence tending to cast doubt on materialism and suggesting that materialists have equally closed minds, despite their claim to a monopoly of reason.

Richard Dawkins' *The God Delusion* is presently the most popular statement of materialism. Despite being published as far back as 2006, this book is a very important contribution to the debate. It has recently been discovered that over 30 million copies have been illegally downloaded – three million of them in Saudi Arabia alone. There are many religious books challenging Dawkins' powerful conception of a materialist world empty of any spiritual dimension. The most widely read of these religious counter-arguments is currently Timothy Keller's *The Reason for God*, in which the writer himself appears to have lost all sense of reason. One purpose of the book you are about to read is likewise to challenge Richard Dawkins' simplistic dismissal of God and the spirit within us, but it is written from an anti-religious perspective and challenges materialism not with the tools of scripture and blind faith, but with the materialists' own weapons of choice, namely logic and reason. Neither materialists nor religionists seem particularly interested in evidence, but I hope that you are.

Religions have made *some* positive contributions, but they should accept that they have also done great harm. Leo Tolstoy, in his search for God and 'the meaning of life' was appalled both by the way religions violently disagreed with each other and by the violence done in the name of Jesus.

Religions have been responsible for bigotry, violence and persecution. Even now there are religious wars and widespread acts of religious terrorism throughout the world.

On the other hand, for over two centuries following 'The Enlightenment', we in the West have purported to revere 'Reason' and yet we have inflicted upon ourselves numerous wars, including, still just in living memory, the two World Wars and the Holocaust. Our world is now threatened by climate change, overpopulation and grotesque inequality. We have filled our oceans with plastic and chemicals.

In the United Kingdom's last National Census about half the population declared no religion, but most were not atheists. Many people throughout the world are no longer satisfied by religion and yet find materialism dispiriting.

Individuals are confused and depressed by the way the world continues to slide downwards under the weight of human anger, violence and greed. The solution is not a populist movement. Our great problems cannot be solved by the miracles promised by populists and priests alike. The solution is for each of us to reawaken our own personal sense of spiritual awareness and purpose. We must all think for ourselves and we must feel for ourselves too.

"They would not listen, they did not know how
Perhaps they'll listen now ...

"They would not listen, they're not listening still
Perhaps they never will"

Don McLean's "Vincent"

Songwriters: Don McLean
Vincent (Starry, Starry Night) lyrics © Universal Music
Publishing Group

Chapter One

The Origin of Something

In 1953 an American housewife predicted that the world would end on 20th December, 1954. Her name was Dorothy Martin and she was interested in Scientology, science fiction and aspects of the occult. She believed she was receiving messages from a supreme being, who had promised that a flying saucer would save her and her followers from the earthquake and tidal wave ordained to destroy America. Some 'Martinites' gave up their homes and sold their belongings in reliance on this doomsday prophecy.

As the more perceptive reader will already have begun to suspect, the world did not end as Mrs Martin had predicted.

On the day appointed for universal destruction her disciples became impatient at the delayed arrival of the flying saucer. She then announced that she had received a further message from the 'supreme being.' He was, she said, so pleased by their devotion that the world had been saved.

Astonishingly, as undercover researchers who had infiltrated the group discovered, the cult members believed even more strongly in their leader after her fundamental prophecy had failed. The conclusion of the researchers was that the Martinites were, like most of us, suffering from "cognitive dissonance."[1] That is, when our beliefs conflict with clear facts our inclination is to deny and disregard inconvenient evidence rather than to reassess our faith.

That the Martinites should have been quite so credulous seems even more surprising, because there have been *so many* failed predictions of doom being nigh. For instance, there was more widespread hysteria in 1844, when Baptist preacher, William Miller, predicted the destruction of the world as a precursor to the second coming of Jesus. God's disobliging failure to destroy the world was without irony called 'The Great Disappointment' by Miller's followers.

Regardless of this disappointment the majority of 'Millerites' still clung to religion, many joining the Shakers or Jehovah's Witnesses.

Most of us rightly sense there is a spiritual element in life and this makes us dangerously open to religious claims of divine revelation, which claims usually define that spiritual element with comforting certainty. Comforting certainty proclaimed by a group can be seductively attractive, but in any

---

[1] Leon Festinger and others, *When Prophecy Fails*.

worthwhile search for this spiritual element it is vital to examine the facts for ourselves.

Religious faith is a simple solution, which has the potential both to abbreviate our personal quest for spiritual truth and to replace reason. In the case of the Martinites the complete and undeniable failure of the key part of their credo should surely have triggered some scepticism, but we must face the depressing truth that it had precisely the opposite effect. Nor did believers appear to have had any misgivings as to the morality of a supreme being proposing to destroy the world and many good people who, due to no fault of their own, remained unaware of 'Martinism'. Indeed, I suspect that many Martinites and Millerites took perverse pleasure both in the terrible fate awaiting their fellow countrymen and in their own spiritual superiority. The Martinites were comparatively harmless, but people can be induced by religion to act violently. Members of the Branch Davidian Sect in Waco, Texas, felt that their religion necessitated 104 semi-automatic AR-15 rifles as well as machine-guns and explosives. This sect ended in 1993 with some adherents being shot by 'law enforcers', some ending their own lives and others being helped along to death by their own co-religionists.

The dangers of religion prompted John Lennon to 'Imagine' a more peaceful and loving world with "no religion," "no heaven" and "no hell below us." In *National Brotherhood Week* Tom Lehrer humorously highlighted religionists' hostility towards each other.[2] Lehrer was optimistic, because the conflict is not just between different faiths. Each religion is split into groups, or sects, which particularly detest each other and regard themselves as superior by reason of their particular brand of belief. This superiority can express itself in violence towards those not sharing the chosen religion, or, worse still, not sharing the precise beliefs of a sect of that religion.[3] In the first part of *Gulliver's Travels* humanity's inclination to violence based on trivial doctrinal disagreement is satirised in the form of the Lilliputians, who fight destructive wars over the correct end to be used to open an egg.[4]

At an airport, this disdain for those with different beliefs can range from being rudely shoved aside by an Hasidic Jew

---

[2] " ...Oh, the Protestants hate the Catholics, And the Catholics hate the Protestants, And the Hindus hate the Muslims, And everybody hates the Jews ... "

[3] For example, the Plymouth Brethren have splintered into a number of mutually hostile sects, including The Open Brethren and The Exclusive Brethren; the latter will not even eat with those not of their sect, even if related.

[4] Jonathan Swift (1667-1745).

to being blown up by a Muslim terrorist. Any good God would surely want the people of the world to come together in love rather than killing each other over religious differences.

"We have just enough religion to make us hate, but not enough to make us love one another."[5]

The many horrific acts of violence purportedly committed in the name of Islam are current and continuing. It is easy to pass over accounts of religious atrocities as mere impersonal reports and statistics, but each person killed or wounded is like us, a person with friends and family.[6] Religion has the potential not only to create violence but also to dehumanize non-believers in the eyes of the devout. St Paul saw those who were not Christian as being, for that reason alone, 'wicked and dark.'

In 2016 there were terrorist atrocities in the name of Islam ranging from blowing up small children on swings in Lahore to the murder in Scotland of a Muslim shopkeeper,

---

[5] Jonathan Swift, *Thoughts on Various Subjects*.

[6] In the 2015 terrorist massacre at the Bataclan theatre in Paris, Nick Alexander was shot five times and died at the scene. His devoted partner, Polina Buckley, recalled at his inquest, 'He told me he had been shot ... I asked him if he could breathe. We were holding hands the whole time. He told me it was hard to breathe so I told him to stay with me. I was telling him I loved him.'

Asad Shah, who had lapsed so far from his faith as to wish his customers a Happy Easter.[7] One Muslim calling for this murder to be condemned himself received death threats.

Historically, however, Islam is *not* exceptionally violent[8] and in earlier times it was comparatively tolerant of other beliefs. Many adherents of other religions also believe, or have believed, that their God ordains violence towards others. I particularly remember the beginning of the modern IRA bombing campaign in 1973, because I had rented a room above the NatWest bank in Solihull and the first real bomb of the modern campaign exploded there a few days after I had left. I was always surprised not to have been questioned.

---

[7] His message on the Internet was, 'Good Friday and very Happy Easter, especially to my beloved Christian nation.' There were other complaints of apostasy against him, including his sect and even suggestions that he was the/a Prophet. When sentenced, the murderer shouted, 'Praise for the Prophet Muhammad, there is only one prophet,' with his supporters echoing him.

[8] Ken Livingstone, who has great experience of large Muslim communities in the UK, in his autobiography, *You Can't Say That*, points out that the large majority of Muslims are peaceful and law-abiding and I would endorse that view. The point here is that religion can make people do terrible things and *currently* some Muslims are sadly a conspicuous example of this.

This bombing campaign – there had been a previous one ending in 1938 – continued for about twenty-five years till the Good Friday Agreement in 1998 and was, of course, an offshoot of the civil war in Ireland between those identifying themselves as Protestant Christians and those identifying themselves as Catholic Christians. Both ostensibly Christian sides demonstrated a great capacity for violence and evil.

This was nothing new. Under Queen Mary Tudor, Catholics murdered and persecuted Protestants and under Queen Elizabeth Tudor the Protestants more than got their own back. The Thirty Years' War (1618-1648) in Europe was essentially a religious one between Protestants and Catholics and resulted in up to eleven million deaths. A mere appetizer to this was the St Bartholomew's Day Massacre of 1572, in which Catholics murdered over five thousand Protestant Christians. The Pope celebrated this atrocity with prayer services and commissioned a commemorative fresco in the Vatican, which, perhaps understandably, is not now on public view.

Presently, Christians in South Sudan are waging a bloody civil war during which their fellow believers are dying of starvation.

The division between Sunni and Shi'a Muslims, originating over the identity of the true successor to the

Prophet, has led to much historic and current bloodletting. Sunni Muslims favour a line going to the father-in-law and Shi'a favour a line going to a son-in-law. This divide, now essentially between Sunni Saudi Arabia and Shi'a Iran, is worsening catastrophically. Nor should it be overlooked that the dishonest and ill-considered invasion of Iraq by the zealous Christians, President George W. Bush and Prime Minister Tony Blair, is still a big factor in sectarian violence in the Middle East and elsewhere. Renunciation of violence is ostensibly at the heart of Buddhism yet, in Thailand, nationalist Buddhist monks formally declared that this message of peace did not include communists. Buddhists in Myanmar – formerly Burma – having historically persecuted Rohingya Muslims, are now committing genocide. In Sri Lanka, the Sinhalese Buddhist majority has been far from non-violent towards the Muslim and Tamil minorities.

Although in many parts of the world Muslim atrocities are current, Islam is a comparatively young religion. Christianity in its earlier history was arguably much more destructive. In the 4th and 5th centuries many thousands of quasi-Christians – with elements of Zoroastrianism and Gnosticism – were killed in the name of Jesus for Manichaean heresy, which in brief was a belief that matter was evil and the mind good.

The Cathars, who had similar dualist beliefs as well as a dangerous inclination to treat women as equals, were exterminated with the encouragement and blessing of a number of Popes, including the inappropriately named Innocent III. At least half a million people perished in this religious pogrom. Those carrying out this holy extermination were assured of God's blessing, in addition to enjoying the earthly benefit of being permitted to steal the victims' land and wealth. This was not religious violence by "defiantly unorthodox fundamentalists",[9] but mass murder by orthodox Christians of the time. There was usually a profit in piety: the priceless contents of pagan temples destroyed as a demonstration of faith could be pillaged; the possessions of those executed as pagans under the laws of Justinian were forfeit; and those joining monasteries were, like Moonies today, obliged to sign away their estate to the Church.

The first Christian crusade of 1095 was ordered by Pope Urban II. In 1098 a single Christian victory cost around fifty thousand Turkish lives. After the battle the Christian soldiers were commended by Christian chronicler, Fulcher of Chartres, for doing "no other harm to the women found in the tents, save that they ran their lances through their bellies." In the

---

[9] Karen Armstrong, *The Case for God*, page 7.

following year, Jerusalem fell and about sixty thousand Muslim and Jewish men, women and children were killed. Reasonable estimates of around twenty million are given as the total death toll for all the Crusades. From the 12th century onwards there were also Crusades around the Baltic, in which pagans in northern Europe were also massacred.[10] The sad irony inherent in 'killing for Jesus' was overlooked. Seemingly nobody involved gave thought to the propriety of giving service to a God who, according to his priests, blessed murder, massacre, rape, pillage and impaling women with lances.

Things have not changed that much. The Rwandan genocide in 1994 had a strong religious element. Some Hutus reportedly styled themselves as "The Army of Jesus" and both Protestant and Catholic churches were implicated.[11] In 2017 in Nigeria Apostle Johnson Suleman, leader of the Omega Fire Ministry, called for reprisal killings by Christians against Muslims. On a more domestic scale, in October, 2015, the *Daily Express* reported that "CHRISTIANS in Syria overwhelmingly SUPPORT Vladimir Putin's aerial bombing

---

[10] The Christian *Livonian Rhymed Chronicle* contains praise of killing in the name of Mary almost as if she were a goddess of war rather than the mother of a prophet of peace and love.

[11] Timothy Longman, *Christianity and Genocide in Rwanda*.

campaign of ISIS and rebel strongholds, a church leader from the embattled city of Aleppo has claimed." In November, 2015, the Church of England passed a motion seeming to support military action in Syria and the Archbishop of Canterbury commented that armed action was "almost inevitable". In 2017 Donald Trump concluded his announcement of a missile strike on Syria with the words, "God bless America and the entire world", which must have greatly comforted those killed and injured by those missiles.

I can remember, when I was young and pious, being dumbfounded when the then Archbishop of Canterbury, subsequently known as 'Bomber Ramsey', called for the bombing of Ian Smith's Southern Rhodesia. Special mention is earned by Jair Bolsonaro in Brazil. In 2018 he is running for President. In 2015 he declared that Brazil was a Christian country and that non-Christians were not 'true citizens.' This progressive Christian is also against black people, women's rights and homosexuality, while declaring approval of sterilisation of the poor, guns and torture. All this support for violence is from Christians purportedly following Jesus, who declared in his Sermon on the Mount, 'Blessed are the peacemakers: for they shall be called children of God.'[12]

---

[12] *Matthew* 5:9

Modern Christianity tends to ignore its own history. Without dwelling on the litany of historic violence and modern abuse attributable to Christianity, evangelical Christian, Timothy Keller, in his riposte to Dawkins' *The God Delusion*, writes, "We cannot skip lightly over the fact that there have been injustices done by the church in the name of Christ, yet who can deny that the force of Christians' most fundamental beliefs can be a powerful impetus for peacemaking in our troubled world?"[13] All those with a reasonable grasp of history must surely deny this claim. Certainly, Mr Keller and his fellow evangelists habitually *skip lightly* over the inconveniently violent history of Christianity.

Christians have been responsible for the persecution and massacre of Jews, often fuelled by fake news that Jews ritually killed Christian children. Sadly, many other brands of religionists have also persecuted the Jews. From 167 BC the Seleucids imposed the Greek gods on the Jews with much cruelty. Likewise the Muslims: even though Muhammad had been given sanctuary by the Jews of Medina, he later expelled some Jewish tribes. Muslim pogroms against Jews occurred regularly in the last two centuries, ending with a comparatively modest massacre in Baghdad in 1941. All this

---

[13] *The Reason for God*, page 21

killing was in the name of God. It must, in fairness, be repeated that, in earlier times, Jews, Christians and others were often tolerated in Muslim countries. They usually had fewer civil rights and paid higher taxes, but were allowed a reasonable degree of freedom. In 1492, Christian monarchs, Ferdinand and Isabella, finally conquered Granada, the last Spanish territory held by the Muslims. The Jews, who had enjoyed a peaceful life under their Islamic rulers, were then given the option of converting to Christianity, or exile and about eighty thousand went to Portugal and fifty thousand to the Ottoman Empire. The remaining Spanish Jews and Muslims were soon given the same choice. Sadly for those Jews and Muslims remaining in Spain, they 'did not expect the Spanish Inquisition' and many suffered persecution, torture and death. History seems to be cyclical, because the myth of ritual murder by Jews is now being regenerated by highly placed priests in the Russian Orthodox Church: according to this modern fake news Tsar Nicholas II – canonised in 2000 – and his family were not executed by the Bolsheviks on the order of Lenin, but were the subject of ritual killing by the Jews.

Michel de Montaigne's old chestnut still says a lot: 'Man is certainly stark mad; he cannot make a worm, and yet he makes gods by the dozen.'[14] Because we humans make God in our own image, we seem to attribute to God many of our own most unattractive characteristics, including anger, malevolence and intolerance. Once people believe that they can converse with God, their personal prejudices will inevitably colour their perception of this dialogue. Many human beings like to control others and what better way, as the example of Mrs Martin shows, than by claiming direct contact with a divine being, or by asserting a superior interpretation of divine writings. So religionists have many primitive rules such as these parts of the body must be chopped off our children[15], only these things may be eaten, only these garments shall be worn, people must fast, people

---

[14] *The Complete Essays*

[15] Female Genital Mutilation is carried out by some Muslims, especially in Egypt, and to a lesser extent by some Christians, Jews and Animists. There is no clear authority for this in the Qur'an, or in the Jewish and Christian Bibles. There is, however, religious authority for circumcision, which is a brutal experience for a baby. Some rabbis – more precisely *mohels* – still suck and bite off the foreskin orally by the practice of metzitzah b'peh. In New York City 11 infants have contracted herpes from this operation and two have died since 2000: *Haaretz*, 23rd June, 2016. Iceland is considering whether circumcision is a breach of the baby's human rights.

must confess, or kneel, of go on crusades and jihad, women should be regarded as inferior, polio vaccine is really a devilish plot, condoms may not be used even in areas where Aids, Ebola or Zika viruses are endemic. So it is that religions tend to control and damage their adherents, and usually non-believers suffer collateral damage. Most religious rules tend to be negative and repressive.

Why is a good virtuous life assumed by many religionists to be a life of denial and misery? In the West, this negative philosophy of salvation through self-torment was magnified by St Paul (5-67AD) to set the tone for Christianity, or Paul's 'Cross-tianity' as others put it. By the 3rd century, Clement of Alexandria in his definitive guide to Christian conduct asserted that, "Unblushing pleasure must be cut out by the roots." Most religious rules of behaviour reflect a mistrust of pleasure and joy. I know a distinguished practitioner in alternative medicine, whose mother was afflicted by a serious illness. He provided treatment, which satisfactorily controlled her condition. She had been raised in a Catholic institution and such was her ingrained religiosity that she subsequently refused treatment saying that she should suffer God's will. She appeared to relish an agonizing death as a form of Christian virtue. How could anybody be led to believe that her God wanted her to suffer at all, let alone unnecessarily? It is a

23

warped message that causes people to take comfort in suffering and to recoil from happiness and pleasure. We may be "born to trouble,"[16] but we are not born *for* trouble. At least some religious leaders can be positive. Just three years after St Paul's death, when looking upon the final destruction of the Temple in Jerusalem, the great Rabbi Yohanan, leader of the Pharisees, did not yield to the dark side, but reaffirmed the text, "I desire love not sacrifice." There is nothing inherently good in sacrifice and nothing inherently sinful in pleasure. We should better trust our conscience. Although not conspicuously keen on women, St Paul, being a Pharisee himself, must have believed that God had created Eve. If alive today, as a self-denial enthusiast, he would be particularly infuriated by modern research showing that women have more orgasms if they perceive pleasure as good and positive.[17] Self-denial for its own sake is quite poisonous.

Religion does not harm everybody, because not all religious leaders practice the self-denial they preach. In about 1830 Joseph Smith was able to give up his profession of finding objects by using 'mystic powers' to search for them in

---

[16] *Job* 5:7.

[17] Dr Nicole Prause, neuroscientist, "Generally women who orgasm consistently tend to be erotophilic; that is, they see pleasure as something that's good and positive." – *Times*, 10th April, 2017.

a mirror, because he had founded The Church of Jesus Christ of Latter-day Saints. In 2012 there was a scandal, when Russian Patriarch Kirill was photographed wearing a $30,000 Breguet watch. After the outcry began, the Russian Orthodox Church's reaction was not to give an honest explanation and apology. Instead, the image of the watch itself was deleted from the photograph, but leaving its reflection in the polished table below. The late Bhagwan Shree Rajneesh collected between 74 and 93 Rolls-Royce cars. More recently Indian guru, Gurmeet Ram Rahim Singh, amassed a huge portfolio of investments and enjoyed the extra perk of a secret passage to the dormitories of his female followers. After he was convicted of rape, his devotees rioted causing 39 deaths. Amazingly, the infamous sex scandal which embarrassed the television evangelist, Jimmy Swaggart, caused only a moderate setback to his lucrative enterprises. The Internet contains rich lists of American Pastors. In May 2018, televangelist, Jesse Duplantis, asked his followers to find over $50 million to fund his fourth jet, so that he could be saved the inconvenience of refuelling: 'If Jesus were alive today, he'd be in an airplane preaching the gospel.' The late L. Ron Hubbard, founder of Scientology, was alleged to have said, 'If you really want to make a million ... the quickest way is to start your own religion.'[18] I suspect that Saul of Tarsus did not have a divine experience on the road to Damascus, but his vision was a realization that Christianity was better business and that is why he turned from persecutor to proselytizer. Likewise Emperor Constantine claimed a convenient vision of a giant cross in the sky just at the time when he needed to win Christian support to bolster his military position. The Catholic Church has amassed a fortune on Earth in cash, investments, fine art and real-estate. In 2015, Pope Francis, who appears to have many excellent qualities, formally declined to sell 'the riches of the Church' because this treasure 'belongs to humanity.' Those dying of poverty may fail to draw comfort from the knowledge that religions preserve their great wealth for humanity.

Despite the more absurd aspects of religion, there is evidence suggesting that a God exists, but not a God wanting to be a profitable commodity, or a violent one demanding suffering and terror. God is not a vengeful and spiteful old misogynist in the clouds, but rather is a universal and loving force. We do not need 'faith', because the evidence shows that

---

[18] The attribution of this quotation has not surprisingly been challenged by L. Ron Hubbard Junior – *Oxford Dictionary of Quotations*.

we have been given free will, free destiny and a conscience by which to navigate through life. I must, however, be sadly deficient in devotion to my own conclusions, because I do not want to injure any other person for not sharing them. I do, though, very much care that religions continue to cause so much harm both to the world generally and to the spiritual awareness of people individually. Religion tends to block free will, to impede logical thought and to act as an easy substitute for the often uncomfortable demands of a person's own conscience. Although I believe in a force, which I call God, I strongly challenge the idea that faith in God is essential to eternal salvation. The majority of people are good. Most religionists are well intentioned and act well. Most atheists, who reject religion and God with it, are equally good people. Presently the proportion of atheists is dwindling.

Research shows that religionists now have a significantly higher birth rate than secularists.[19] Although the

---

[19] Ellis, L. et al., *The Future of Secularism: a Biologically Informed Theory Supplemented with Cross-Cultural Evidence. Evolutionary Psychological Science* (2017) 3:224–242 (doi:10.1007/s40806-017-0090-z): "It is ironical that effective birth control methods were developed primarily by secularists, and that these methods are serving to slowly diminish the proportional representation of secularists in forthcoming generations."

biological future of secularism is comparatively poor, it is fair to say that the peace of the world is not presently threatened by the non-belief of fundamentalist atheists. Religion and materialism are at the extremes of the spiritual spectrum. Like infrared and ultraviolet the supporting evidence for their positions is invisible. The truth is at neither extreme, but, in trying to find the truth, the starting point must be to question religionists' absolute certainty that they have found the ultimate truth. Andy Hamilton detests the certainty at the extremes and rightly suggests that, "Nobody ever died following the banner of mild conjecture." Nor has mild conjecture ever caused killing and persecution.

Most religions have some profound spiritual truth at their core. Sadly, the power of this truth has been hijacked and embroidered by men to promote a picture of a God they would like to exist and to control others by writing scripture, which they claim has somehow been revealed to them by that God. An obvious objection to any religion based on 'revelation' is that God delayed so long before revealing the true path to salvation. My smugness in having perceived this logical flaw in most religions was marred by later discovering that many others have already noticed it, beginning in 170 AD with

Celsus, a Greek critic of Christianity.[20] Our world is more than four and a half billion years old. Just about six million years ago hominids appeared. Did God create these early hominids sharing our genus – Latin homo, "human being" – such as *Homo habilis* and the schoolboy's favourite, *Homo erectus*, or was his favour exclusively reserved for us? Why did he delay so many eons before creating modern man? Much to the Earth's disadvantage, *Homo sapiens* first appeared only about two hundred thousand years ago. How does our subsequent interbreeding with Neanderthals square with divine creation? The average human still retains 2 per cent Neanderthal DNA. The Sphinx in Egypt was constructed between 10,000 and 2,500 BC. Records of Chinese culture date back about four thousand years. Modern revelatory religions, that is, religions based on revelation by God himself of his existence, face a real problem in accounting for God's extreme delay in revealing the true faith. So Christianity is only about two thousand years old. Christians say that without letting Jesus into your heart you cannot be saved. Either this is a marketing ploy, or it poses a significant problem for all those born before

---

[20] Celsus' book was called, *On the True Doctrine*. A century later another philosopher, Porphyry of Tyre, dissected the absurdities in Christianity in some 15 books. These, like the biographical details of both critics, were eradicated by the Church and Christian rulers.

Jesus, including a great number of revered characters in the Old Testament, who had not heard the message of Jesus. The rather unconvincing answer to this is that Jesus went down to Hell[21] and led out all good people after his resurrection. Hell must have been most unjustly overcrowded for more than a hundred and fifty thousand years. Islam is an even younger religion, being a bit over fourteen hundred years old. Extreme Islamists – ISIS etc. – destroy historical monuments, like sites in Syria and the great statues of the Buddha in Afghanistan, primarily because the historical evidence contradicts the version of Islamic history they want to believe in: 'alternative facts'; 'cognitive dissonance'.[22] God waited till about 1830 before allegedly revealing Mormonism to Joseph Smith. In

---

[21] *Ephesians* 4:9 appears to suggest that Jesus visited "the lower parts of the earth" and the Apostles' Creed is more specific.

[22] This is not peculiar to Islam. Christians systematically destroyed temples, pagan art works and books worldwide and in 391 AD Pope Theophilus ordered the destruction of the great library in Alexandria. When Caliph Omar conquered Alexandria in 641 AD he likewise burned the great library saying, 'If these writings of the Greeks agree with the Book of God, they are useless and need not be preserved; if they disagree, they are pernicious and ought to be destroyed.' (Edward Gibbon, *The Decline and Fall of the Roman Empire*, chapter 51).

about 1881, much influenced by Miller, the failed doomsday predictor, Pastor Charles Taze Russell (1852-1916) effectively created the Bible Student Movement, part of which later became the Jehovah's Witnesses. Four times in thirty-five years he erroneously forecast the end of world, but still the movement thrived. More recently the end of the world has been predicted for 1975[23] – said to be six thousand years from Creation – and 2015. Despite these repeated 'disappointments', the faithful remain confident that they will imminently be beamed up by 'The Rapture'. It was as recently as 1954 that Scientology was created by L. Ron Hubbard.

This hiatus between creation and revelation would be unacceptably unjust to those who lived before the invention of each religion and it was surely somewhat remiss of God to have delayed so long both in creating *Homo sapiens* and in disclosing the true path to us, whichever path that is. Baptists, for example, have told me that it is only through the Baptist Church – created circa 1612 – that salvation can be found. Other Christian churches similarly view themselves as having the monopoly on God. Even G. K. Chesterton's kindly Father Brown believed that only Catholicism could offer salvation.

---

[23] This failed prediction is now usually denied, but please see for instance pp 622-3 of *The Watchtower*, 15th October, 1969, and for a more readable reference, *White Teeth* by Zadie Smith.

We are given a very odd picture of God, who says to those after death, 'Sorry, you were a very good person and lived a good life with a generous open heart but, regrettably for your salvation, you worshipped in the wrong religion.'! Is it only a Muslim of the right brand, or only a Jew of the right type, or maybe a Presbyterian – anagram of 'best in prayer' – who hold the key to the afterlife? Can it be right that a person's salvation should depend not on true goodness, but on punctilious observance of the rules of the correct religion? This would seem remarkably cruel for those who have not had the opportunity to hear the *correct* message, or who, like most of us, have been brought up in a particular religion from birth. A really good person, who had loved his fellow man, but worshipped in the wrong place, would have no prospect of salvation, whereas a quite unpleasant member of the correct religion would at least have a ticket in the afterlife lottery. How can any sensible person believe in a deity capable of making such preposterous distinctions?

Each religion has a vested interest in claiming that it has God's especial favour. How can religions be so certain about what God is like and what highly specific devotional acts he requires? In one breath, religions describe God as too great for description in words – ineffable – and in the next they present a detailed set of 'revealed' certainties. The spiritual realm is no place for absolute certainty, let alone rigid prescriptive rules. Any human claiming spiritual certainty and applying that certainty for the purpose of directing others how to act should be viewed with the greatest suspicion. I have always loved Frank Muir's witticism, 'I used to be an agnostic, but now I am not so sure.' There is every reason for doubt. However, if God *does* exist, one sad probability is that the 'superman' God of most religions does not; that is, a God who, like Superman, actively intervenes in the world. Standard religion assures its adherents that if they follow the precepts of their religion devoutly, if they worship precisely in the correct manner, if they pray with sufficient faith and piety, if they make the appropriate sacrifices like giving money, then God will intervene to smite enemies, to prevent or abate a plague, to ensure that an exam is passed, or to give victory in wars and football matches. These systems cunningly attribute all things good to God and anything bad both to the Devil – or the equivalent – and also to the insufficient piety of the disappointed believer. It really is a clever system: if it is good, it's God; the bad is down to you and Satan. So, Wilbert Jones of Louisiana was freed after being in jail for forty-five years for a crime he had not committed. Upon his release, he did not ponder on how his God had allowed his life to be ruined and the true offender to escape, but thanked God for his eventual intervention, declaring, 'Through God all things are possible.' I remember hearing on the radio an unconvincing attempt by the admirable John Sentamu, Archbishop of York, to explain how God could have caused or permitted the earthquake, which shattered Haiti. While, of course, God did neither, this is the unanswerable question for proponents of an interventionist God.

A religion with a superman God has a lot more pulling power, when it comes to recruiting followers. After all, as the modern prince of materialism, Richard Dawkins, writes, "... what is the use of a God who does no miracles and answers no prayers?"[24] It is no coincidence that 'prayer' in most languages also means 'request.' Many religious devotees expect reward in material form for their religious devotion. "They make their religion into an attempt to get what they want from the 'Great Vending Machine in the Sky.'"[25] The problem is that once you create the image of an interventionist God, then you do have to explain and justify God's many conspicuous failures to intervene. If God will really help to win a battle, or a football match, what was he doing during the earthquake in Haiti, or during the Holocaust, or when the H-

---

[24] *The God Delusion*, page 84.

[25] Tony Campolo, *Choose Love Not Power*, pages 73-74.

bomb was created and dropped, or in earlier times during the Catholic genocide of the Cathars? What is God doing when our loved ones die unnecessarily early and cruel deaths? Why do some self-evidently horrible people reach positions of power and influence, or have lives of apparent comfort, whereas some conspicuously good people suffer poverty, ill fortune and wretchedness? With the possible exception of reincarnation and karma, which suppose that present existence has been affected by conduct in previous lives, this cannot be easily rationalized in spiritual terms. The explanation that 'God moves in mysterious ways his wonders to perform' does not begin to answer the question. The late Billy Graham (1918-2018) in his 9/11 address said, 'I have been asked hundreds of times why God allows tragedy and suffering. I have to confess that I do not know the answer. I have to accept, by faith, that God is sovereign, and that He is a God of love and mercy and compassion in the midst of suffering.' This will not do to explain the self-evident passivity of an interventionist God, unless 'faith' really means a willingness to believe something unquestioningly, which is clearly dissonant with the evidence. The late Sir Terry Wogan lost his faith by reason of his daughter's early death. Two of my most beloved friends – a Christian and a Jew – lost their faith when those close to them suffered badly without the sort of intervention from God which their religions had encouraged them to expect. Loss of faith in such circumstances results from a justifiable rejection of a deity who has been advertised as an interventionist, but who refuses to intervene in circumstances where any humane person, who could do something, *would* do something. Indeed, why has God not prevented the cruel event in the first place? Also, why should an interventionist God really require prayers and sacrifices to be prompted to do what is right? Would you require worship before trying to save somebody from drowning? God did not 'die in Auschwitz',[26] but for any reasonable person the concept of an interventionist God cannot have survived the Holocaust, or the many other terrible events in our history.

Another type of interventionist God is the one referred to as a 'personal' God. Most religions are certain theirs is a personal God. Such a God pays particular attention to overseeing our own personal needs and conduct. A personal God is aware of our very thoughts and some religionists, like President Carter, follow Biblical text and suggest that an evil thought is as bad as an evil deed. This seems twice wrong. Firstly, a person who resists an evil thought and acts well,

---

[26] Eli Wiesel, Holocaust survivor and Nobel Laureate, in her book *Night* describes how God died for her as she watched terrible violence being done.

arguably deserves more credit than somebody free of that temptation. Secondly, the idea suggests that, having had the thought, the guilty person may as well do the deed with no further moral culpability. For humans to imagine a God interested in our every thought and action is surely a great conceit.

For humans to imagine that God could be so deeply interested in our personal lives also seems a matter of self-deception, because for there to be violence and evil in the world, or great suffering or injustice in the personal lives of individual believers, is surely compelling evidence that no personal God really exists. Timothy Keller attacks this reasoning as "fallacious"[27] and writes, "Just because you can't see or imagine a good reason why God might allow something to happen doesn't mean there can't be one." This sort of fuzzy-minded evasion makes it all the more important for Mr Keller and other zealots to produce real evidence of the personal God they describe. The impossibility of proving that God does not exist is not positive proof that God does exist. Mr Keller moves on to a proposition, which is similar to that debunked by Bertrand Russell's example of a teapot in

---

[27] *The Reason for God*, page 23.

space.[28] Mr Keller says that if you look into a kennel for a St Bernard and one is not obvious then it is reasonable to presume that the dog is not there. If, however, you are looking into the kennel for a microscopic bug with an unpleasant bite, called a 'no-see-um', and you do not see one it is unreasonable to assume that they are not present. His argument is that the 'no-see-um' is there and yet not readily visible to us in just the same way as his God is present yet invisible. God, if the powerful personal God depicted by the main monotheistic religions, should surely be far more conspicuous in the world than a St Bernard in a kennel. According to the Bible, God frequently manifested himself for the purposes of causing floods, wiping out towns, winning battles, exterminating nations, parting the Red Sea, ordaining Commandments and laws and much more. As we have been given powers of observation and reason either by God, or by Natural Selection, or by both, then it would be quite wrong for us not to use those powers to recognize that in more modern times there have been no such divine manifestations.

Does the great suffering in the world tend to support or refute the existence of an interventionist and personal God? Given that belief in God is usually based on ancient scripts

---

[28] Please see chapter 4.

claiming to depict observable interactions between God and man, does the absence of any modern manifestation, even when failure to intervene seems quite unjustifiable, tend to support or refute the existence of an interventionist God? Also, why does God have to be relegated to the magnitude of a 'no-see-um' to be believed in? Mr Keller's analogy fails on a more practical level too. I could, of course, use a microscope to ascertain the presence of minute insects in Mr Keller's kennel. More simply still, if I were to crawl into the kennel, supposing no 'no-see-ums' to be present, I should soon experience proof of their existence in the form of their bites. Where in modern history do we find compelling evidence of God intervening, interacting, or even leaving humanity with some divine bites? "But the God of Theologians is incapable of local visibility."[29]

One believer in a personal God is Israeli, David Shoshan, who brought a legal action against God. He wanted a restraining order because God had 'treated him harshly'. The

---

[29] Percy Bysshe Shelley (1792 1822), *The Necessity of Atheism*. Desmond Morris notes that a visiting alien would wonder about our large religious buildings: "These – the houses of the gods – the temples, the churches and the cathedrals – are buildings apparently made for giants, and the space visitor would be surprised to find on closer examination that these giants are never at home." (*Manwatching*, page 152)

Haifa Magistrates' Court dismissed his claim as "ludicrous." This kind of human egocentricity was once reflected in the belief that our world was the centre of the universe. Contrary to ancient learning, religions fostered the idea that mankind is central and foremost in the universe and that our planet with everything on it was directly created by God. According to this obligatory view, everything was centred on our tiny planet, just as everything on it was to be viewed as being centred on man. In the face of violent resistance from the Church,[30] it took Galileo and others, after he was tortured into recantation, bravely to prove that our tiny sphere is just an insignificant speck in the Universe. It was only in 1822 that the Catholic Church formally decided to relax its absolute ban on any suggestion that the sun was the centre of the Solar System. Even then the Church could not bring itself fully to accept the Earth's subordinate position. It took till 1992 for Pope John Paul II to acknowledge the wrongfulness of Galileo's forced recantation due to what he described as a "tragic mutual misunderstanding." Even now some extreme Protestant sects still insist that Galileo was wrong. There are more than ten billion planets in the Milky Way alone, which are capable of

---

[30] In 1600 the Church burned Giordano Bruno alive for, amongst other things, supporting the view that the sun was the centre of the solar system.

sustaining life within the terms of our limited understanding. There must be an abundance of life throughout the Universe. If there is life elsewhere then it makes it harder still to believe in a God concerned for mankind alone. Unlike the mechanism of the Solar System, the relationship of God to humanity cannot be a matter of scientific certainty, but both evidence and reason suggest that belief in a God who, in our own form, takes infinite interest in the thoughts and deeds of each of us, is as ludicrous and egocentric as David Shoshan's legal action.

In his argument for a personal God, Mr Keller passes on to the proposition that good comes out of suffering. Sadly, very much more often than not, *misery* comes out of suffering. Mr Keller uses the example of Joseph of the Coat of Many Colours, whom he describes as an "arrogant young man". Certainly Joseph was hated by his brothers for being favoured by their father and he aggravated this dislike by rather tactlessly relating dreams, which implied his superiority, but I am doubtful that the text of Genesis[31] really sustains the adjective 'arrogant'. He points out that Joseph was cast into the pit then into slavery, but "through his suffering, he achieved power and saved many from famine." This is false reasoning. Joseph's suffering was not a prerequisite either of

---

[31] *Genesis*, 37:1-14.

41

Joseph's later power or of the prevention of the famine. God could simply have ordained that there would be no famine, or that Joseph, or if not he, the person then in charge of Egypt's food supply, had the dreams about fat cows and wheat ears – it seems odd that divine messages in scripture tend to be so unclear[32]. The fact that very occasionally some good comes out of bad does not prove God's existence, or excuse his failure to prevent bad things. Reality, which is that the world contains much terrible and unresolved suffering with no good coming out of it at all, tends strongly to contradict the evangelical message.

When it suits, religionists do not see the ways of God as mysterious. They are often certain about God's displeasure. "When the vines in my village are nipped by frost, my priest

---

[32] In Robert Graves' *I, Claudius*, Claudius tells the Empress Livia that a lightning strike on the Temple of Jove has transformed an inscription into a message in Etruscan, an ancient and now totally lost language. The Empress calls Claudius an idiot and rightly observes that if God wanted to communicate with the Roman people he would use Latin not Etruscan. There is no reason why, if God wished to communicate with us, he could not do so in clear unambiguous terms, as he is alleged to have done in the early days of most religions. Any alleged divine communication, which is obscure, or requires interpretation by an intermediary, is highly dubious.

immediately argues that God is angry with the human race …"[33] The 9/11 terrorist attacks were described by Anne Graham Lotz, Billy Graham's daughter, with confident certainty as a "Wake-up call from God." Another leading American evangelist, Jerry Falwell, asserted on television that, '… the pagans, and the abortionists, and the feminists, and the gays and the lesbians who are actively trying to make that an alternative lifestyle, the ACLU, People For the American Way, all of them who have tried to secularize America. I point the finger in their face and say "you helped this happen."'[34] Although Falwell apparently recanted later, this typifies the way religionists attribute natural and man-made horrors to divine punishment by their God for mankind's failure to observe their own particular beliefs. The great tsunami of 2004 was attributed by representatives of all faiths to a judgement by God. For instance, Muslim clerics in Indonesia blamed the event on failure by the faithful to pray sufficiently and some Hindus blamed it on the wrongful arrest of an activist called Jayendra Saraswathi, the Kanchi Shankaracharya.

Faith in God is often rejected when the absurdity of a

---

[33] Michel de Montaigne, *Essays*, book one, chapter 6.

[34] *Jerry Falwell and Pat Robertson Blame 9/11 on Organizations Like People For the American Way*, PFAWdotorg, www.youtube.com, 2nd April, 2010

particular religion dawns on the devotee. If a preacher declares that the Bible is the absolute word of God, then the thinking religionist would surely have serious doubts, because the Bible contains major factual and doctrinal contradictions and approves objectionable concepts like slavery[35], murdering homosexuals and specified ritual animal sacrifices.[36] Who was the observer who chronicled *Genesis* and why is there no mention of dinosaurs, or kangaroos, or other creatures unknown to ancient Hebrews? How does the Creation square with the 'Great Dying' about two hundred and fifty million years ago, when global warming killed over 90 per cent of species of all living things, or the later extinction of the dinosaurs by a random asteroid? Incidentally, thanks to us, who are supposedly the 'divine creation', the number of wild living things in the world more than halved between 1970 and 2012 and this is generally referred to by scientists as the 'Sixth

---

[35] e.g. *Leviticus* 26:44 et seq.

[36] *Leviticus* 12:3-6

Great Extinction'.[37] A friend reminded me that on a sunny day in the 1950s, if you sat in or near an area of long grass, even on an urban bomb-site, the noise made by the insect life was incredibly loud. Now, in a mere sixty years, our grass has fallen silent. Whatever doubt there may be about the creation of the world, it is certain that we are destroying it.

Also, why do religionists not claim *full* credit for their God's creation, so as to include as part of that divine creation such things as parasites, leprosy, bubonic plague and polio? Once God is enmeshed in a religion then the concept of God can so easily be rejected along with the religion itself. Of course, *Genesis* is really a creation myth and not an historical record. Apart from the first chapter dealing with the creation itself, which scholars date to the 10th Century BC, it was written in the 8th Century BC by somebody identified by academics as 'J'. The modern shape of the Old Testament

---

[37] There have been five previous Extinctions. In 1969 Christopher Booker wrote *The Neophiliacs*, in which, well before our computer age, he argued that a craving for novelty and sensation was a 'psychic epidemic'. On the eve of the Sixth Great Extinction he wrote of "man's steady destruction of all forms of wild life, from the growing pollution of earth, air and water, and the destruction of forests, flowers, birds, beasts and butterflies, to the actual extinction of whole species." (p. 321).

began to form when *Genesis* was merged with the work of somebody referred to as Elohim and later added to and amended by the Deuteronomists, who insisted on the exclusive worship of Yahweh, as opposed to other gods appearing in the texts. Further additions to the Old Testament were later made by Ezekiel and his followers after the Jews were deported to Babylon in 597 BC. *Leviticus* was added to allow the individual to live with purity in exile. Further addition was made after the return of Ezra and his followers to Israel from Babylon, reflecting their displeasure at the way of life of those Jews who had not been exiled.[38] Each of these major alterations, and most of the minor ones too, reflected the agenda of those dominating Judaism at the time. The prevailing agenda underlying the evolution of these texts seems to have been a desire for a tribal God, who would, through fear, intimidate both Gentiles and insufficiently devout Jews alike, and who would, when fear proved insufficient, do a lot of smiting. Later non-Jewish Christians,

---

[38] For an excellent summary of the evolution of the Old Testament please see Karen Armstrong's *The Case for God*, chapter 2, or for even more detail, her *The Bible: A Biography*.

notably the ascetic Greek, Origen Adamantius,[39] contributed to adapting the Jewish texts into what is now the Old Testament.

Scripture is clearly not an historic record. The world is beyond doubt older than the six thousand and twenty-odd years calculated by Archbishop James Ussher using the Bible as the reference book for his ludicrous computation.[40] In fairness to those believing Ussher, they are in error by only a little over four and a half billion years. Creationism is patently absurd and yet sadly many cling on to it in the name of their Biblical God. Likewise, the arbitrary rules for living laid down by religions, which are over-reliant on their sacred writings, can make God look rather foolish. Like Jean-Paul Sartre (1905-1980), we may conclude that this personal God, portrayed by many religions, really appears to be a tyrant, leaving us no personal freedom or privacy. The obituary of Warren Mitchell recalled that, "His earliest acting ambitions were thwarted by the orthodoxy of his grandmother, who

---

[39] *Ὠριγένης Ἀδαμάντιος*, 185-254 AD. It was historically accepted that Origen was such a fundamentalist that he castrated himself to follow *Matthew* 19:12, "… there be eunuchs, which have made themselves eunuchs for the kingdom of heaven's sake." Scholars now doubt the report, because, unlike modern evangelists, Origen sensibly disagreed with reading scripture literally.

[40] Creation date: 23rd October, 4004 BC.

47

stopped him from appearing as Tiny Tim in a school production of *A Christmas Carol* because the Christmas pudding he would eat at the end of the play was not kosher. After a childhood punctuated by not being allowed to do things because of his faith, he became an avowed atheist in later life, opposing all religious dogma."[41] I should not want to fall into the same trap as St Paul by seeming to suggest that those who do not agree with my beliefs are in any way inferior. Many of those I love, or have loved, are/were religionists, or atheists. Despite their fundamental misapprehension and even in some cases because of it, many people of faith *and* of none are wonderful human beings. It is perhaps their very goodness that makes religionists vulnerable to the siren song of religion. On the other hand, some of the most dishonest, judgemental, disagreeable and untrustworthy people I have ever encountered have been ostentatiously religious, like the vain Pharisee in the Temple, whom Jesus condemned.

When we encounter vain people in positions of power, who demand to be flattered, grovelled to or even bribed, we tend to despise them. Julius Caesar and the Roman Emperor, Caligula, were both assassinated in part because they were

---

[41] *The Times*, 16th November, 2015.

48

seen to be trying to assume the role of gods. Why then is God represented by religions as an entity demanding worship, flattery, grovelling, bribes and sacrifices? In December, 2016, PIA, Pakistan's national airline, one of whose planes had crashed, ritually sacrificed a goat to God at Islamabad airport in exchange for better air safety. Earlier, in 2014, Malaysian Airlines suffered two great tragedies. The first was the loss of a passenger plane, when the pilots took the plane off course and lost it in the ocean, which is still a mystery. The second was the shooting down of an airliner over Ukraine, which was the direct or indirect responsibility of President Putin, who is *not* divine. However, as a result of fears that these disasters were in fact the consequence of divine displeasure with the airline for being insufficiently Islamic, a new more Islamic airline, Rayani Air, was established. It is mystifying how anyone could think that there was an all-powerful deity, who might decide: 'That Malaysian Airline is insufficiently Islamic so I shall smite those aeroplanes and everybody on board.' The concept that God intervenes in the world to kill innocent people is surely even harder to justify on a moral and spiritual basis than God's conspicuous failures to intervene to prevent natural and man-made horrors. Was the great tsunami of 2004 an Act of God, or did God merely elect not to prevent it? Either way, an interventionist deity does not come out of the question very well. My purpose is not to refute God, but rather to seek to show some distinction between God and the improbable image of a not very nice interventionist God painted by most major religions. Our instinctive sense that there is something more to life than chemical reaction and a selfish gene is a key part of humanity. However, that instinctive sense of wonder at the possibility of a mystical element in life should not be harnessed by religion for the purpose of exploiting or subjugating the vulnerable and credulous.

It is often said with much justification that religions give great consolation to believers, especially in times of distress. Imagine that you are in an aeroplane, which, due to an insufficiency of sacrificed goats, crashes in the jungle. The radio is capable of transmitting on one wavelength and a radio operator responds to your calls for help. Without having any evidence to support his belief, the operator assures you that a rescue party is on the way. Every day, till you and your fellow survivors die, he misguidedly promises that you will soon be saved. You would undoubtedly be greatly reassured and comforted by these confident promises of rescue and the social order in the surviving group might be better maintained. However, these benefits obviously do not justify the charade. In the absence of the radio operator's promises, the survivors would probably have planned a route to salvation for themselves. It might well be that help lay only a short distance off, but, in their reliance on the radio operator's representations, they did not begin their own search. There may have been opportunities for the survivors to save themselves, but, while they exclusively relied on somebody else's promise of salvation, these chances would never be explored.

We as individual human beings most urgently need each to awaken our own personal awareness of the spiritual element in life. The spirit is an element which can be found in most religions, though almost concealed and overlaid by man-made rules and concepts, some of which range from the absurd to the truly evil. Through the ages, religions have insisted on acting as an intermediary between the individual and the spiritual world, thereby taking control and blocking individual perception. Religions have declared, and do declare, that they have all the answers and that free thinking and disagreement are heresies. Religion and modern materialism[42] both tend to repress a free thinking use of conscience. Both disparage personal investigation of the Great Mystery of Life as mere superstition. It is at least as urgent to begin a spiritual quest now, as it was when Socrates regularly urged his audience to question whether the moral, spiritual and allegedly rational system we have chosen to follow in regulating our lives has a satisfactory foundation. It is only by each of us reawakening our own individual spiritual awareness that we humans can make this a better world. The late Colin Wilson describes our ability to make a personal link with the non-material spiritual world as "Faculty X". He is absolutely right that "... man's future lies in the cultivation of Faculty X."[43] With our continuing failure to rediscover this link comes a very bleak future, if any, for mankind.

---

[42] 'Materialism' has two meanings: either it is a reference to those, like Richard Dawkins, who believe that there is no spiritual element and that all is material, or it refers to excessive attachment to material wealth and comfort and the encouragement thereof by those seeking to profit from it. Here I mean the former, but elsewhere the latter is sometimes meant.

[43] *The Occult*, page 763.

Chapter Two

The New Testament

[References are to the King James Bible]

I was born a Christian. My family, my school and my society were structured on Christianity. Mrs Martin looks almost unimaginative compared with the promises made to me; apparently I had a divine Father, who knew my every thought and action and would either reward or smite me. This is where my spiritual life began and for nine years I energetically embraced my received faith. I thought that many of Jesus' ideas were wonderful and I still do. However, as I began to think more independently, much of what was said by those pontificating about the Bible and many passages in the Bible itself began to trouble me. Also, the history and practice of Christianity has been strikingly discordant with many of the teachings of its founder member. This is where my search for the evidence began.

The word 'bible' comes from the Greek word for 'papyrus' or 'scrolls.' The Bible did not suddenly appear as a fully formed book. The text of the Mormon Bible was allegedly presented on gold plates to the founder, but nobody suggests that the Christian Bible was so conveniently created. After the death of Jesus, Christians formed various groups and sects and were, to a greater or lesser degree, a persecuted minority for 300 years. Conspicuous amongst the splinter groups were the Donatists and Novatians, who had broken away following persecution by the Emperors Decius and Valerian, and the Paulianists, followers of Paul of Samosata, who had been condemned for heresy in 268 AD. Each group had its own creed and collection of scriptural writings. The gospels started life as oral stories about Jesus and were only later written down. The earliest known existing written canonical gospel is probably the 'Gospel of John,' more technically called P66, dated to circa 200AD. There were many gospels in circulation, including those quite recently discovered in libraries and archaeological finds, including the Gospels of the Hebrews, Judas, Mary, Nicodemus, Peter, Philip, the Ebionites, the Egyptians, the Nazoraeans, the Saviour and Truth. There are probably around forty distinct gospels still existing.[1]

In 313 AD the Roman Emperor Constantine purported

---

[1] Paul Foster, *The Apocryphal Gospels*, page 11.

to convert to Christianity. In 325-6 AD, having only recently had his son, Crispus, strangled, and his wife, Fausta, boiled in a bath, this Christian emperor called the First Council of Nicaea to select the doctrine, or creed, to be unanimously chosen from a wide choice of existing creeds and religions. Constantine, who wanted a united Christianity which would, in turn, support him militarily, asked Eusebius of Caesarea provisionally to propose the creed. A final version of the creed was at last agreed. This agreement was significantly aimed at resisting the 'heresy of Arius,' which in essence was that Jesus had not been God on earth, though this is a gross simplification of Arian theology. It was not at this First Council that the Bible was finally formed as a Canonical entity, but it was at about this time that collections of books, roughly approximating to what we would now recognize as a Bible, began to be assembled.

It is said that Constantine ordered Eusebius to 'Search these books, and retain whatever is good in them, but whatsoever is evil, that cast away. What is good in one book, unite with that which is good in another book. And whatsoever is thus brought together shall be called *The Book of Books*. And it shall be the doctrine of my people, which I will recommend unto all nations, that there shall be no more war for religion's sake."[2] As a matter of historical fact we know that in 331 AD Constantine ordered that fifty bibles should be provided for the churches in Constantinople. So, not later than five years after the First Council a recognizable form of the Bible did exist. The point is that the Bible was an assemblage of books/scrolls created by adopting some texts, altering some texts and rejecting many texts. So, for instance, the delightful story of Jesus' birth in the stable – stable is not actually specified in the biblical text – is clearly plagiarized from the earlier story of the birth of Mithras in a cave, just as, in the Old Testament, the myth of the Great Flood is a crib either from *The Epic of Gilgamesh*, or some earlier Babylonian story. A huge amount of written material relating to Jesus and Christianity was destroyed at this time, because it did not accord with the chosen version.

The Codex Sinaiticus, or Sinai Bible, is probably the oldest existing Bible and it is dated to about 350 AD. It shows hundreds of marked differences from the standard modern Bible. One very significant difference is that there is no mention of the virgin birth and the orthodox reference to Jesus as the Son of God – Mark 1:1 – is not included. The stories of the Resurrection are also absent from the Sinai Bible and all

---

[2] *God's Book of Eskra*, chapter xlviii, paragraph 31.

other ancient bibles, such as the Alexandrian Bible and the Vatican Bible.

At the request of Pope Damasus I, St Jerome – Eusebius Hieronymus, circa 342 to 420 AD, not to be confused with Constantine's Eusebius – devoted himself to producing his own translation of the Bible. Having laboured on the many Latin versions, he decided to return to Hebrew for the Old Testament and Greek for the New Testament. St Jerome excluded at least six books from his version of the Old Testament, including Ecclesiasticus and Judith, because he could not find the Hebrew texts. Although he excluded them as apocryphal, these books were later copied back into some Bibles using the highly inaccurate Latin translations. His version of the New Testament did not include the epistles of James and Peter I-II. St Jerome infamously tried to defend the concept of virgin birth by arguing that clear biblical references to the 'brothers' of Jesus should be construed as references to 'cousins,' not for linguistic reasons, but simply because this text was so inconvenient. However, Jerome faithfully translated the Lord's Prayer, which in Luke 11:4 reads "Lead us not into temptation." The original Greek verb, 'eisenenkês' means 'do not take inside' and was translated into Latin 'non inducere', which means 'do not bring us in.' Hence do not take us into/bring us into/lead us into temptation. Many Christians, including the Pope at the end of 2017, have now arbitrarily changed the words to something like 'do not let me fall into temptation,' not on the basis of the text, but purely because it is unthinkable that God might lead anyone into temptation.

After the death of St Jerome, the Bible was reproduced by copying. Naturally errors crept into the text and, as already mentioned, various parts were returned to the Bible using the very same imperfect Latin texts, the inaccuracy of which had prompted Pope Damasus to ask St Jerome to revise the Bible in the first place. Individual creeds and theological interpretations were allowed to influence copying so that, for instance, Luke 22:43f was omitted because it did not conform to the theology of the scribes.[3] Apart from vigorous editing, embroidering and bowdlerization of the Bible's text, there is the problem of translation. Clearly there is ample scope for error and difference of opinion in any translation. For instance, scholars suggest that the text about "a camel passing through the eye of a needle" was a mistranslation for a 'large rope' or 'hawser' passing through the eye of a needle. This duller translation does seem to make more sense. There are, of course, arguments about other sacred texts. For example the *hadith,* a group of traditional Islamic sayings – promises

---

[3] Williams' *Alterations to the Synoptic Gospels and Acts.*

seventy-two virgins to men entering paradise and this is often held out as an inducement for religious martyrdom while killing others. There has been a suggestion that the word, *hur* – white raisin – was confused in translation with *houri* – virgin. Although the majority of scholars now reject this idea, I find the thought of a suicide bomber receiving seventy-two raisins slightly consoling.

Even in the modern Bible the number of books to be found in the Old Testament will vary significantly depending upon whether it is a Protestant, Catholic, or Orthodox Bible. There are many varying versions of the Bible still extant, although the earlier texts, used by St Jerome, are not. There are individual Bibles such as: the Vercelli Codex – circa 350 AD, preserved as a relic of Saint Eusebius; the Sinai Bible; Alexandrian Bible; and Vatican Bible, and more generalized versions like: the Latin Bibles; the Vulgate Bible – also Latin; the Gutenberg Bible; the Peshitta – an early Bible in Syriac, much like the Aramaic spoken in Palestine at the time of Jesus; and numerous others, in most languages. If the Bible is to be strictly construed as the 'Word of God', as Baptists and other American evangelists demand, then it is necessary to know which Bible should be viewed as definitive and why. Many would vote for Robert Barker's *King James Bible* of 1631, which misprinted the seventh commandment: "Thou shalt commit adultery."

It is clear that our present New Testament is a compilation of ancient stories with many subsequent insertions and alterations. Religious writings should never be used as a literal guide to the word of God. However, in the New Testament, despite all that has been done to the Gospels, a clear and attractive message still stands out. In brief, that message, which should attract atheist, pagan and religionist alike, is one of love, peace, pacifism, individual conscience, forgiveness, rejection of materialism and, perhaps most amazing of all, a warning about the dangers of religion. In a world now ravaged by wars, religious terrorism[4] and greedy bankers, these precepts look particularly attractive.

Pacifism

In Exodus 21, following the Ten Commandments, God personally lays down a legal framework for Moses to impose. Verses 23-25 contain the famous passage:

"And if any mischief follow, then thou shalt give life for

---

[4] "Allied to weapons of mass destruction, extremist religious attitudes threaten the very security of life on earth." Rabbi Jonathan Sacks, *The Dignity of Difference*.

life,

Eye for eye, tooth for tooth, hand for hand, foot for foot,
Burning for burning, wound for wound, stripe for
stripe."

It is odd to note that 'life for a life' contradicts the sixth
commandment, "Thou shall not kill." This commandment has
in modern translations been given the more convenient and
arguably more accurate interpretation, "You shall not murder,"
thereby arguably permitting war, judicial killing and the like.
This is reminiscent of Orwell's *Animal Farm*, where Napoleon
Pig changes the animal commandment from "No animal shall
kill any other animal" to "No animal shall kill any other
animal without cause."

Seemingly, Jesus disagreed with *Exodus*. He is quoted
as saying, "Ye have heard that it hath been said, An eye for an
eye, and a tooth for a tooth: but whosoever shall smite thee on
thy right cheek, turn to him the other also ... Ye have heard
that it hath been said, Thou shalt love thy neighbour, and hate
thine enemy. But I say unto you, Love your enemies, bless
them that curse you, do good to them that hate you, and pray
for them which despitefully use you and persecute you ..."[5]

---

[5] *Matthew* 5:38-45.

This message of pacifism is incredibly brave and radical, though not original. For those Christians who proclaim the Bible to be the precise word of God we have here an example of Jesus expressly contradicting the Old Testament – *both* cannot be the word of God. Given this declaration by Jesus, it is impossible to understand how Christians over the last two thousand years could have for a moment contemplated the wars, crusades, inquisitions, burnings, massacres and all the other mayhem they have enjoyed in the name of religion.

These pacifist thoughts are not unique to Jesus. A passage from Babylonian wisdom literature written prior to 700 BC states:

"Unto your opponent do no evil
Your evildoer recompense with good."

Likewise, Socrates – born circa 470 BC – is quoted as saying, "If a man slaps my face, he does me no evil, only himself." In a similar vein, he is also reported as saying, "A just man is one who does good by his friends, certainly, but also does good to those who have harmed him, thereby seeking to convert an enemy into a friend" and "It is never right to do wrong, or to requite wrong with wrong, or when we suffer evil to defend ourselves by doing evil in return" *(Crito)*.

Libanius (*circa* 314-393 AD), a pagan, gave the funeral oration for Constantine's successor, the Roman Emperor Julian, who had tried in his short reign to reinstate paganism and tolerance in place of Christianity. Libanius was typical of fourth century philosophers in stressing the importance of loving one's fellow men and who regarded "forgiveness of one's enemies as a divine and typically Athenian virtue." [6]

You do not have to be religious to appreciate that dwelling overlong on grievances does great harm. We have all seen relatives, or friends, corroded by resentment. While it is not right to acquiesce in the wrongful behaviour of others, it is usually right and in our own best interests at a later stage to forgive, or to understand, or simply to let bitterness go. Whilst we should not allow ourselves freely to disregard our conscience and the consequences of doing so, we should be equally ready to understand and forgive ourselves. Regardless of who or what is to be forgiven, from a Buddhist perspective Thich Nhat Hanh puts it beautifully: "Healing has many avenues. When we feel anger, distress, or despair, we only need to breathe in and out consciously and recognize the feeling of anger, distress, or despair, and then we can leave the work of healing to our consciousness. But it is not only by

---

[6] A. H. M. Jones, *The Later Roman Empire*, vol. 2, page 970.

touching our pain that we can heal. In fact, if we are not ready to do that, touching it may only make it worse. We have to strengthen ourselves first, and the easiest way to do this is by touching joy and peace. There are many wonderful things, but because we have focused our attention on what is wrong, we have not been able to touch what is *not* wrong."[7]

Conscience

Conscience is a tool given to us as part of our free will. Whether this comes from a supreme creator, or some evolutionary directive, it is surely beyond doubt that most people have a conscience and that this is a key to living a good moral life and forming meaningful relationships with others. Those without what we should term a conscience are psychopaths/sociopaths and not only do these people do great injury to others, but they themselves are unable to form relationships and to find spiritual peace. They are doomed to be lonely, miserable and destructive. Horace (Q. Horatius

---

[7] *Touching Peace*, pp 26-27. Maya Angelou's wisdom was, "I would say to everybody, 'Do your best not to give harbour to bitterness.' To be angry is very good, I think. Anger is like fire, it burns things out and leaves nutrients in the soil. You should always be ready to be angered at injustice and cruelty, but not to be bitter."

Flaccus, 65 BC to 8 AD) summed up the happy person: "It is not the rich man you should rightly call happy, but he who knows how to use with wisdom the gifts of the gods, and to bear the annoyances of poverty with patience, *fearing a shameful deed worse than death ...*" [8]

I have often suspected that Christians, who declare that we are all sinners[9] and that no man should judge, are conveniently sidestepping the duty of every person to judge themselves. In the film *High Noon* the townsfolk follow the guidance of their priest and skulk in the church leaving the marshal to fight alone against evil. Every time we act and every time we fail to act, we should first question and judge whether we are behaving well. It is more comfortable to pose as generalized sinners wallowing in a bath of universal sin[10] than it is to scrutinize ourselves and to admit that in specific

---

[8] Od.iv.9, 45."What doth it profit a man, if he shall gain the whole world, and lose his own soul?" Jesus, *Mark* 8:36.

[9] See for instance, *The Litany*, in which the congregation are obliged repeatedly to intone, "O God the Father of heaven: have mercy upon us miserable sinners."

[10] "Our religion is made so as to wipe out vices; it covers them up, nourishes them, incites them." Michel Eyquem de Montaigne (1533-92): "Notre religion est faite pour extirper les vices; elle les couvre, les nourrit, les incite." *Essais* (1580), bk. 2, chapter 12.

personal matters we have been wrong, cruel, weak, or thoughtless.

Jesus is quoted at *Matthew* 7:1-2 as saying, "Judge not, that ye be not judged. For with what judgement ye judge, ye shall be judged." This is often taken as meaning that the uncomfortable task of judging can and should be avoided, but from verse 3 the guidance continues, "And why beholdest thou the mote that is in thy brother's eye, but considerest not the beam that is in thine own eye? ... Thou hypocrite, first cast out the beam out of thine own eye ..." The prime directive of Jesus then is that we should, first and foremost, judge ourselves – and yet religious people so often present as smug, self-satisfied and highly censorious of others. Jesus' suggestion that we should examine our own faults is a good one, whether or not we believe in God. This must to some extent involve judging others and particularly judging the value of any guidance they offer us. This means not rushing to judgment with moral superiority, but still facing up to the fact that some things are bad and must be opposed even at personal risk. As in *High Noon*, it is sometimes necessary to have the moral courage to ignore the disapproval of the priest and the majority, to think for ourselves, to leave the short-term safety of the church and to go to the marshal's aid.

Religion does not like free thinking. Pope Innocent III –

he of the Cathar genocide – said, 'Anyone who attempts to interpret a personal view of God, which conflicts with Church dogma, must be burned without pity.' There were prolonged Inquisitions. Smug religious fanatics were willing in the Middle Ages to murder and torture in the name of their purportedly Christian beliefs without any sensible self-examination, just as Muslim extremists today somehow feel justified in blowing up aeroplanes, or spraying the audience in a Paris theatre with bullets, or massacring children in a Pakistani school. Some atrocities are planned, like the twelve coordinated shooting and bombing attacks in Mumbai in 2008, and others are more random, like the attack on the Orlando gay club by a single religious nutcase in 2016.[11] These people substitute religious dogma, as interpreted by questionable dogmatists, for their own consciences. In many ways it is easier to relinquish free will and conscience in favour of mindlessly following the dictates of a religion as interpreted by others. Stephen Weinburg –American physicist, born

---

[11] Pastor Steven L. Anderson of a Baptist Church in Arizona, who reads the Bible literally, commented, 'The good news is that there's 50 less pedophiles in this world, because, you know, these homosexuals are a bunch of disgusting perverts and pedophiles, That's who was a victim here, are a bunch of just disgusting homosexuals at a gay bar, OK?' As kindly as he is grammatical!

1933 – wrote, "With or without religion, you would have good people doing good things and evil people doing evil things. But for good people to do evil things, that takes religion."[12] The religious dark side of Muhammad Ali, who has received much deserved praise since his death in 2016, exemplifies this. He was interviewed in 1975 by *Playboy* following his conversion to Islam. After an enthusiastic prediction that Allah was going to destroy America and recommending hanging for those involved in inter-racial sex, he was then asked, 'And what if a Muslim woman wants to go out with non-Muslim blacks – or white men, for that matter?' His chilling reply was, 'Then she dies. Kill her, too.' Religion can drive out conscience and good sense in the best of us.

Individual Conscience and Rejection of Religion

Like Socrates, Jesus' inclination was not to give direct answers to questions but to prompt the questioners to think for themselves. Again, like Socrates, he did not write down his ideas, but instead we must rely on the reports of others. Just as Plato in his writings about Socrates gradually yielded to the

---

[12] Lucretius said much the same thing: "So much wrong could religion induce." ("Tantum religio potuit suadere malorum.") *De Rerum Natura*, bk 1, 1:101.

temptation to mix his own thoughts with those of his former master, so those storytellers, who at least sixty years after the death of Jesus began to compile a history, could not have avoided distorting their accounts.

It is clear from the Gospels, even after so much tampering, that Jesus was not seeking to found a religion. Quite the reverse, because his message was that every person may have direct communication with God. Stephen also preached that God is not to be found in temples[13] and was stoned to death with the consent of Saul, who, after his Damascene conversion, became Saint Paul.

So Jesus condemns "hypocrites", who make charitable donations ostentatiously in the synagogues[14] and "hypocrites", who pray ostentatiously in the synagogues[15]. He advises, "But thou, when thou prayest, enter into thy closet, and when thou hast shut thy door, pray to thy Father which is in secret …"[16] This was part of the Cathar heresy, which drove the then dominant Catholic Church to genocide, namely the idea that the ordinary person could communicate with God without intervention of priest, Church, or ritualistic mumbo-jumbo.

---

[13] *Acts* 7:48

[14] *Matthew* 6:2

[15] *Matthew* 6:5

[16] *Matthew* 6:6

The importance of conscience rather than religious observance is made clear by Jesus in the story of the Pharisee and publican – probably a mistranslation for tax collector: "Two men went up into the temple to pray; the one a Pharisee, and the other a publican. The Pharisee stood and prayed thus with himself, God, I thank thee, that I am not as other men are, extortioners, unjust, adulterers, or even as this publican. I fast twice in the week, I give tithes of all that I possess. And the publican, standing afar off, would not lift up so much as his eyes unto heaven, but smote upon his breast, saying, God be merciful to me a sinner. I tell you, this man went down to his house justified rather than the other ..."[17] In those days Pharisees had enormously complex and onerous religious observances – including highly demanding regimes relating to prayer, cooking and sex – which are only briefly summarised in the biblical text. The point is that complex and rigorous religious observance is not the way to be a good person; rather it is important to examine one's own conduct by reviewing it using one's own conscience. It is only by consulting our own conscience that failings in conduct can be identified and through this sometimes painful process it is possible to become a better person. So religious observance, far from

---

[17] *Luke* 18:10-14.

70

helping, can blind devotees to what is actually right and wrong; compliance with a set of formulaic observances can replace open-minded consideration of what is in fact morally right. This happened explicitly in the days of Pardoners and 'Peter's Pennies', when a pardon could simply be purchased for past sins. Now the same thing happens, though less blatantly, in the minds of those comfortable in their obedience to religious ritual. By intoning that we are all sinners we may comfortably avoid confronting the specifics of our own personal sins.

Rejection of Materialism

When approached by the Rich Young Ruler, Jesus is said to have advised him, "If thou wilt be perfect, go and sell that thou hast, and give to the poor, and thou shalt have treasure in heaven: and come and follow me."[18] Materialism is important to empires and I doubt that Emperor Constantine would actually have wished either to give up his own earthly trappings, or to see his subjects selling up to pursue spiritual lives instead of being productive members of society. Again that is a radical message; a message in stark contrast to the

---

[18] *Matthew* 19:21.

great wealth amassed by the Christian Church and by most other religions too. The greed of those running the world banks brought down recession upon us, the ordinary people of the world. Since then, from 2010 to 2015, the wealth of the richest three hundred and eighty-eight people in the world rose by forty-four per cent, while the poorest were forty-one per cent poorer. The richest one per cent people in the world have more wealth than the rest of us put together. A movement of people individually rejecting materialism and greed is overdue.

Love, Forgiveness and Understanding

When dealing with 'an eye for an eye' Jesus is quoted as saying, "Love your enemy." When confronted with the Rich Young Ruler he significantly omitted the first four commandments relating to religious observances and added, "Thou shalt love thy neighbour as thyself."[19] The Hebrew Bible repeats the commandment 'to love the stranger' thirty-six times. At the Last Supper, Jesus gave his disciples a powerful new commandment for mankind: "That ye love one

---

[19] *Matthew* 19:19.

72

another."[20] Whether you are a religionist, a pagan, a humanist, or an atheist, this is really the only guideline needed for a good and spiritual life.

So when Jesus was condemned by Pharisees for allowing a prostitute to wash his feet, because he was, in that process, touched by a sinner, he forgave her.[21] Likewise, when confronted by a mob wanting to stone a woman taken in adultery in accordance with the law of Moses, he is recorded as saying, "He that is without sin among you, let him first cast a stone at her." Each man in turn was "convicted by their own conscience" and left, till all were gone and the woman was sent away with the injunction, "Sin no more."[22] And yet, historically, Christianity has been conspicuous in its merciless condemnation of sinners. Likewise, Muslims, who claim Jesus as a prophet, still stone those they perceive as sinners in Afghanistan and Pakistan. These 'sinners' include adulterers, though more often only alleged *female* adulterers. It should, however, be noted that Jesus never expressly disagreed with capital punishment for adultery or other breaches of Judaic law.

---

[20] *John* 13:34.

[21] *Luke* 7:36 et seq.

[22] *John* 8:3 et seq.

Worrying Characteristics of Jesus as Portrayed

Not everything reported about Jesus is entirely good. There is, of course, no reason to suppose that these troubling passages are any more reliable than the flattering ones.

In the apocryphal gospel, *The Infancy Gospel of Thomas*, the child Jesus is playing in a brook and collects a pool of clean water. Another boy, son of Annas the Scribe[23], uses a willow branch to disperse and muddy this collected water and "when Jesus saw what was done, he was wroth and said unto him: O evil, ungodly, and foolish one, what hurt did the pools and the waters do thee? behold, now also thou shalt be withered like a tree, and shalt not bear leaves, neither root, nor fruit. And straightway that lad withered up wholly ...".[24] In the next paragraph he strikes down a boy who runs into him and then blinds the dead boy's parents for complaining to Joseph. Joseph gives the child Jesus a well-deserved ear twisting as punishment.

It is an interesting question whether Jesus did behave that badly, whether he really did turn his school fellows into

---

[23] Annas appears in other apocryphal gospels.

[24] www.fumcrogers.org/ot101/2014-05-21.pdf:3:III:2-3.

goats, create birds from clay[25], or used super powers to lengthen a piece of wood in the family carpentry shop, as suggested in other apocryphal gospels. Indeed, I go further than 'the heresy of Arius', who saw Jesus as a divine distinct from and less than God. It seems clear that, despite the later insertions of passages relating to the virgin birth, Jesus was depicted as a man. Indeed, the 'Virgin' Mary had five sons and "some" daughters[26], and St Paul, for all his extensive hyperbole, fails to mention the divine conception.[27] The Jewish Christian sect led by James, who was, after all, the brother of Jesus, contested the virgin birth and for accepting this denial the Ebionites, as they became known, were declared heretical. Whether she was a virgin or not, Jesus was often quite rude to his mother, showing little empathy. For instance, when Joseph and Mary found him in the Temple

---

[25] *Ibid* and see also *Al-Tabari* (7:127)

[26] *Mark* 6:3.

[27] In *Romans* 1:3, he describes Jesus as "made of the seed of David according to the flesh." At *Galatians* 1:4 he uses this description: "made of a woman, made under the law", which has been seized upon by Christians as suggesting that Joseph was a supernumerary, but anybody familiar with St Paul would know that there would have been no ambiguity had he had just a sniff of divine birth.

after losing him in Jerusalem,[28] Jesus certainly lacked proper understanding of the terror his parents had experienced and also when Mary drew his attention to the lack of wine at the marriage in Cana he snapped, "Woman, what have I to do with thee?"[29] He is even more cross and surly in the Apocryphal Gospels. His general image was dubious. Jesus himself candidly admitted that his contemporaries saw him as "… a man gluttonous, and a winebibber, a friend of publicans and sinners."[30]

Jesus was probably an exceptionally wise and spiritually aware man, but even the Bible reports his bad temper. He did not like Mondays. On Monday he cursed a fig tree to death for not having any ripe figs and then stormed into the Temple to overturn the tables of the money changers.[31] He may well have been a psychic and healer. The genealogies in Matthew and Luke, although radically different in names and number, suggest that he was a man and not a God. Admittedly Jesus is sometimes quoted in the Gospels as indirectly referring to himself as the Son of God. There was clearly a lot of late tampering to try to portray Jesus as God, or part of the Trinity,

---

[28] *Luke* 2:48.

[29] *John* 2:4.

[30] *Matthew* 11:19.

[31] *Mark* 11:12-21.

though this later concept is expressly absent from John. The point surely is that he thought of his fellow man and woman – or more accurately his fellow Jews – as the children of God. The Lord's Prayer, after all, begins, "Our Father ..." According to Jewish theology of the time Jews regarded themselves as the 'children of God'. Much in the Gospels makes no sense if Jesus were a God, or part of God by way of the Trinity or otherwise. For instance, what purpose is there in the story of the Temptation[32] if Jesus were God? If Jesus was God, or part of God, then Satan was wasting his time in his efforts to tempt Jesus and the story is meaningless. It is surely an allegorical story seeking to illustrate that a human being can with spiritual strength resist temptation even in the most extreme circumstances. Jesus' question on the cross – "My God, my God, why hast thou forsaken me?"[33] – seems quite inappropriate if Jesus were God, or part of God. This cry of momentary despair does seem quite moving if these were the words of a man suffering an agonizing death for his beliefs.

Oddly, Jesus' reported references to himself as the "Son of man" should be much more worrying for those who wish to see him as a humble religious messenger. This self-description

---

[32] e.g. *Luke* 4.

[33] *Matthew* 27:46.

is a reference to the ultra-nationalist Book of Daniel: "I saw in the night visions, and, behold one like *the Son of man [my italics]* came ... and there was given to him dominion and glory, and a kingdom, that all people, nations, and languages, should serve him ..."[34] So when Jesus rode a donkey into Jerusalem, which is now wrongly regarded as a token of humility, most contemporaries would have known that this was to fulfil the prophecy of Zechariah[35] that 'the King' would arrive in such a way. *John* 12:14 onwards, when describing Jesus' arrival on the ass, confirms that "... as it is written ... thy King cometh," so Jesus, if mortal, must have had quite a big ego. When a woman poured a very valuable cosmetic onto his hair Jesus rebuked his disciples for suggesting that the proceeds might better have benefitted the poor on the basis that he was, as we should now say, 'worth it.'[36]

By modern standards Jesus was a racist, because he was generally hostile to non-Jews. At *Matthew* 10:5-6 it is

---

[34] *Daniel* 7:13-14. Also, "The Son of Man" is a heavenly apocalyptic figure in the Second Book of Enoch.

[35] Please see *Zechariah* 9:9-17 for the full power and greatness prophesied.

[36] *Mark* 14:7-8 "For ye have the poor with you always ... but me ye have not always."

recorded that, "These twelve [the disciples] Jesus sent forth, and commanded them, saying, Go not into the way of the Gentiles, and into any city of the Samaritans enter ye not: but go rather to the lost sheep of the house of Israel." Likewise, when confronted with the woman of Canaan asking that a devil be cast out of her daughter, Jesus' first reaction is to say, "I am not sent but unto the lost sheep of the house of Israel."[37] This is probably the same incident described at *Mark* 7:24-30, though this time relating to 'a Greek woman.' In both accounts Jesus likens Gentiles to "dogs", which was about as racist as you could be in those days. The Bible as a whole refers primarily to the laws, duties and rights of Jews. It was much later that St Paul saw the value of selling the Christian brand to Gentiles.

There also seems to be a limit to love and forgiveness in the Jesus of the canonical Gospels. For cities which are insufficiently attentive to the message of his disciples, Jesus predicts, "It shall be more tolerable for the land of Sodom and Gomorrah in the day of judgement, than for that city."[38] At *Matthew* 25:31 et seq. it is clearly specified that the sinners will be singled out to be "... cursed, into everlasting fire,

---

[37] *Matthew* 15:24.

[38] *Matthew* 10:15.

79

prepared for the devil and his angels ... And these shall go away into everlasting punishment ..." These and similar messages in the New Testament are so strongly discordant with the main theme of love and forgiveness and yet so typical of later Christianity that they are especially suspect. Threats of eternal damnation are an unattractive and almost universal feature of religions. The carrot enticing faith is the promise of heaven, salvation and eternal life, and the stick is a threat of infinite suffering. It is small wonder that religion can so effectively control the weak-minded and credulous. An infinite afterlife is, in any case, a somewhat gloomy prospect whether in Heaven, Hell, Hades – even if you are admitted to the Elysian Fields – Paradise or Valhalla. An eternal life of total ease might initially appear attractive, but I suspect that most of us would find it unbearable for just a few years, let alone for infinity. These detailed afterlives promised by religions jump to the eye as wishful thinking, calculated to induce the naïve to invest themselves and their wealth in the religion, just as a conman will convince a credulous investor that the worthless piece of land he is selling has gold hidden beneath it. An afterlife of eternal suffering for non-believers and the insufficiently devout is equally incredible. One of the main competing religions in the fourth century AD, when Christianity wanted to be the brand leader, was the older and better established one of Mithras, the sun-god, which carried the same commercially attractive features of everlasting bliss for believers and terrible suffering for non-believers and backsliders. Afterlives as promised and described so confidently by religion may be ludicrous, but we should not let the absurdity of religion close our minds to the possibility that death is not the end.

Whether or not Jesus himself really did threaten everlasting punishment, it does seem that he took a hard line on other moral issues. For instance, his reported view on divorce is incompatible with *Deuteronomy*[39] and modern ethics: "And I say unto you, Whosoever shall put away his wife, except it be for fornication, and shall marry another, committeth adultery: and whoso marrieth her which is put away doth commit adultery."[40] Not forgetting that the Biblical punishment for adultery was death, this strict injunction, which was probably more severe than the prevailing Jewish practice at the time, is so clearly part of a primitive society and so self-evidently discordant with the tolerance of today that only the harshest religionist would now maintain such dogma.

---

[39] *Deuteronomy* 24:1 expressly provides for divorce, although, of course, the specified method of presenting a wife with a "bill of divorcement" was a privilege reserved for men only.

[40] *Matthew* 19:9.

On this occasion at least, Jesus had indeed come to "fulfil" the law and the prophets,[41], but in the very same chapter Jesus sets out his new and contradictory directions.

Jesus' reported requirements for his disciples do not seem very attractive: "If any man come to me, and hate not his father, and mother, and wife, and children, and brethren, and sisters, yea, and his own life also, he cannot be my disciple."[42] We should be very worried about a person, who seems to reject loving and being loved and prefers people full of hate and self-loathing. It is, however, just such sad, maladjusted people who can become particularly zealous in a cause or religion. They are easy converts and victims, because they so desperately need something to fill their spiritual emptiness. The disciples' job description looks more like a psychological profile for the modern religious mass-killers and terrorists, who run amok shooting holidaymakers on a beach. Evildoers are so often loners and social misfits.

It is difficult to suggest that Jesus took any objection to slavery, which was commonplace at the time of his teachings. Slavery is now rightly accepted as morally abhorrent and yet at best Jesus remained silent and the New Testament, like the

---

[41] *Matthew* 5:17.

[42] *Luke* 14:26.

Old, expressly condones slavery. For instance: "Let as many servants as are under the yoke [slaves] count their own masters worthy of all honour, that the name of God and his doctrine be not blasphemed."[43]

The Radical Message

These problematical parts of the New Testament aside, the radical message of love, pacifism, individual spiritual development and anti-materialism is surely one with which most humanists and atheists would tend to agree. If humanity could even begin to follow these precepts what a wonderful world we would have. Established religions, on the other hand, tend in many ways to encourage joylessness, censoriousness, smugness, superiority, small-mindedness and greed. This is a particular puzzle when it comes to Christianity, because Jesus, even on the limited insight into him left in the four mangled Gospels, stood for a very different set of values from those exhibited by Christianity over the last two millennia. I am a 'derisive sceptic', but my scepticism goes only so far as to deride the idea that the Bible should be read as an accurate history possessing, in its literal form, divine force. I do not

---

[43] *First Timothy* 6:1.

deride scripture as being valueless, especially some of the key thoughts of Jesus. It is a tragedy that Christianity, in practice, did not follow any of the essentials of Jesus' radical message. There would seem to be two main reasons for the fact that Christianity has so tragically diverged from the path of love and tolerance.

The first reason is that those – starting with the appalling Paul – serving in positions of influence in the various branches of Christianity put the standing and power of the Church before all else.[44] They have, too often, been willing to cast stones at others while being deaf to the voice of their own conscience. Churches, cathedrals and the Vatican City have been built at great cost and filled with precious things, and it is not difficult to imagine that if Jesus visited one of these places today, or looked at the rich balance sheets of religions, he would assume that this accumulation of wealth must mean that there are no longer poor people in the world.

---

[44] George Bernard Shaw (1856-1950) writes that Paul was "always hopelessly in the toils of Sin, Death, and Logic, which had no power over Jesus. ... It was by introducing this bondage and terror of his into Christian doctrine that he adapted it to the Church and State systems which Jesus transcended, and made it practicable by destroying the specifically Jesuist side of it." *The Complete Prefaces*, volume II, page 226.

Religion has been used as an instrument of power to lay down rules and to control others. In Christianity these rules have reflected Paul's hatred of joy, which preference for gloominess was perpetuated even by Cardinal Newman.[45] The Puritans were once generally recognized as typifying sanctimonious intolerance of anything joyful. This is well satirized in the character of Zeal of the Land Busy in Jonson's *Bartholomew Fair*. This fanatical Puritan condemns others for any pleasure and, in particular, for gluttony and eating meat. He declares himself to be a hater of meat and he therefore justifies himself in eating two pigs, because he claims to be inflicting suffering upon himself. We are, of course, left in no doubt that he is, in fact, a gluttonous hypocrite, who prefers that only others should practise self-denial.

I remember, as a child of about eight, hearing a sermon at St James' Church, Gerrards Cross. The vicar told us of the conspicuous Christian virtue of a little girl, who particularly liked a type of chocolate, called a 'coffee cream.' She would, he said, offer the box of chocolates around to her parents' guests and while proffering them would say, 'The coffee

---

[45] "It would be a gain to the country were it vastly more superstitious, more bigoted, more gloomy, more fierce in its religion than at present it shows itself to be." *Apologia Pro Vita Sua* (1864) – *A defence of one's own life*.

85

creams are especially nice.' This, according to the vicar, was the essence of Christianity. After I had stopped marvelling at the opulence of a household that had guests and chocolates to offer to them, it struck me that the girl's conduct was an absurd act of self-denial. If she had put one coffee cream in a place of safety we could hardly have blamed her. If she had offered the chocolates around in the hope that a coffee cream would be left, she would have shown stoic generosity. However, actually to urge the guests to take the coffee creams was an act of poisonous self-flagellation. Indeed, it was even sillier, because many of the guests would have assumed that she was trying to discourage them from taking a different type of chocolate. The satisfaction of a moment's Pauline smugness is unlikely fully to have compensated the girl for missing out on the coffee creams.

Given that he is a conservative Baptist, Tony Campolo has a startlingly brave opinion about the divergence of Christianity from the path of love. He thinks that the problem arose in 313 AD, when the conversion of Emperor Constantine led to Christianity becoming the main religion in the Western world. The church became very powerful. Mr Campolo suggests, "… that the Church was not meant to wield power and that when it did, it betrayed its calling as the primary agent of God's love. As the Church increased in power, it decreased in authority. It came to be known more by the power its bishops wielded than the sacrifices made by its people."[46] Although I should put the emphasis on *love* rather than sacrifice, Mr Campolo is probably right.

The Acts of the Apostles, which in the Bible immediately follow the canonical Gospels, emphatically do not share the passion of Jesus for welcoming and forgiving sinners. They do, however, foreshadow the future path of the Christian Church in the account of poor Ananias and his wife, Sapphira, whose act of generosity to the new Christian Church went spectacularly wrong. Ananias and Sapphira sold some land and placed a portion of the sale price at the feet of St Peter, who was the founder of the Jewish Christian Church. For failing to pay over the *whole* sale price and possibly for not making full disclosure about it, the unfortunate couple were struck dead on the spot by God "And great fear came upon all the church, and upon as many as heard these things."[47] What a departure this is from the message of love, poverty and forgiveness preached by Jesus. Here is a return to the God of the Old Testament, who prefers fear to love. Here, on the face of its own instruction manual, is a clear portrait of

---

[46] *Choose Love Not Power*, page 94.

[47] *The Acts* 5:1-11.

a greedy Church grasping for money and power without any love or compassion for Ananias and his wife.

Whether the blame falls on St Paul, or St Peter, who fought like rats in a sack,[48] or on the later power granted to the Church by Constantine, it is clear that Christianity veered away from Jesus' idea of humble loving service and rushed towards the very opposite position of utilizing religion to amass power and wealth: "And why call ye me, Lord, Lord, and do not the things which I say?"[49]

The second main cause for the historic divergence of Christianity from the path of love is the extraordinary decision to attach the Old Testament to the Gospels. This is especially odd when the Apocryphal Gospels suggest even more strongly than the canonical ones that a significant part of the message of Jesus was a denunciation of the vindictive and small-minded God of the Old Testament. Of course, it might be more accurate to refer to the failure of Christians to uncouple key New Testament texts from the Old Testament, because the majority of the original contributors to the New Testament were themselves Jews.

---

[48] "But when Peter was come to Antioch, I withstood him to the face, because he was to be blamed." *Galatians* 2:11.

[49] Jesus, *Luke* 6:46.

88

Chapter Three

The Old Testament

[References to the *King James Bible*]

Some time before 350 AD, the New Testament was formally bolted onto the Old Testament to form an early version of the Bible. This would have appealed as much to St Paul as to St Peter. Paul was according to himself 'a Pharisee born of Pharisees'. Apart from the obvious Jewish connection, the purpose of adopting these ancient texts, including the story of creation, had the commercial advantage of giving the impression of well-established historical roots to what was then a young religion. It had other advantages. The rather anarchistic and exacting strictures of Jesus in the New Testament, although already much transformed by self-appointed spokesmen such as St Paul, could be more easily sidestepped if mixed and muddied by the addition of the more comfortable 'eye for an eye' morality of ancient Jewish texts. Also, the theological concept of the Trinity, so strongly supported by Athanasius of Alexandria, who was a bishop's secretary at the First Council, could be the better propounded. Both the antiquity of the Old Testament and the elevation of Jesus to being the Son of God and part of the Trinity, were calculated to make Christianity a more spectacular and saleable product. So two of the Gospels, albeit with different factual accounts, declare that the man universally known as 'Jesus of <u>Nazareth</u>' was in fact born in Bethlehem, because birth in Bethlehem is one of the essential prerequisites in the Old Testament for qualification as 'the Messiah'. Likewise, as noted in the last chapter, the story of the resurrection was possibly added later also to give greater lustre.[1] It must however be accepted that St Paul was very keen on the resurrection and in *First Corinthians* 15:3-8 claimed five hundred eye witnesses, though the Gospels 'overlook' these. Incidentally, although everything Paul predicted in his *First Letter to the Thessalonians* failed to come true, this conspicuous failure had no more impact on Paul's authority than did the more recently failed prediction of Mrs Martin on hers.

Christianity caused distinct problems for itself by adding these ancient texts to the Bible. The first problem is that Jesus, even in the accepted canonical Gospels expressly

---

[1] *The Sinai Bible* and others.

disagreed with parts of the Old Testament text and implicitly disagreed with most of it. Secondly, the best that can be said, if you are inclined to accept the contents of the Gospels as gospel, is that Jesus approved the law of Moses, the prophets and psalms and then only insofar as they concerned him.[2] In his book of 170 AD, attacking Christianity, Celsus pointed out how Jesus' teachings contradict the rules purportedly ordained by the Jewish God in the Old Testament. Had Celsus lived now, he would have been equally dumfounded by most Christians' sublime indifference to the fundamental contradictions between the Old and New Testaments. Thirdly, a God completely different from the God of love and forgiveness described by Jesus in the New Testament emerges from the pages of the Old Testament.

This last contradiction struck many early scholars and most notably Marcion of Sinope, who, in Rome towards the middle of the second century, propounded a dualist belief system based on there being two Biblical Gods with the less attractive Hebrew God being subordinate. This logical interpretation was received with horror and angrily rejected by the monotheist Christian church. Any recognition of the dichotomy between the deities of the two Testaments clearly

---

[2] *Luke* 24:44-45.

tends to breach the first commandment – "No other gods before me" – and Jesus' reported injunction, "No man can serve two masters."[3] Athanasius' absurd concept of the Trinity also faces similar objections. Poor Marcion's obvious conclusion that the Bible must describe contradictory concepts of God won him no friends.

Religions' refusal to face facts has attracted the contempt of atheists. One of the better points made by Richard Dawkins in *The God Delusion* [4] is that the Old Testament God is "arguably the most unpleasant character in all fiction: jealous and proud of it; a petty, unjust, unforgiving control-freak; a vindictive, bloodthirsty ethnic cleanser; a mysonogynistic, homophobic, racist, infanticidal, genocidal, filicidal, pestilential, megalomaniacal, sadomasochistic, capriciously malevolent bully."

The Old Testament is an easy target for commentators like Richard Dawkins and the estimable Christopher Hitchens. Some straw men, like Genesis and Creationism, are so feeble and tottery that they hardly require knocking down at all. To weld into the Bible a set of old Hebrew scriptures containing so much hatred and violence was not much less absurd than it

---

[3] *Matthew* 6:24.

[4] Page 51.

would have been if the religious beliefs and practices of the Aztecs had been adopted to accompany a teaching based on love and forgiveness. The Old Testament must surely be rejected by any objective mind, because it is primitive, immoral, irrational and expressly portrays a God of fear not love. The Old Testament God persistently intervenes in the world by smiting people with great floods and other destruction, but in more modern times this God has conspicuously failed to stop or prevent terrible suffering, or to appear at all. A particularly stark example of God's failure to intervene is the Aberfan disaster. In 1966 a huge heap of industrial coal waste slipped down a hill in Wales engulfing a school. As a result one hundred and sixteen young and innocent children lost their lives. What were they doing at the moment the slag heap began to slide? They were singing a hymn in praise of God. Yet God did nothing. The self-evident failures of any interventionist God to intervene, the character of the Old Testament God and the unloving way in which Christianity has been imposed over the last two millennia are all recruiting sergeants for atheism.

"There is no wickedness in denying the gods of the multitude; but there is wickedness in following the multitude's

93

beliefs about the gods."[5]

It does not follow that the concept of God should be denied, simply because the Old Testament God is so unpleasant. Rejection of the ethics of the Old Testament may be applauded, but the acceptability of a God depicted in a selected and bowdlerized set of ancient Hebrew texts is no more a 'litmus test' for the existence of God than would be consideration of the sacrificial practices of the Aztecs. Christopher Hitchens' engaging refrain is, "Religion poisons everything." It also poisons God. John McEnroe, in his wonderfully honest and insightful autobiography *Serious*, writes, "... I had decided for myself that organized religion is a sham, and that God, if He exists, must be deaf, dumb and blind ..." That is good logic. Religion is rejected. The 'Superman' God is rejected, but the possibility of the existence of God is preserved. It is as easy to ridicule primitive concepts of God as it is impossible to disprove the existence of God.

The OT God's Violence and Cruelty

Next time you are confronted by a fundamentalist

---

[5] "Non deos vulgi negare profanum; sed vulgi opiniones diis applicare profanum," Epicurus.

Christian with burning eyes declaring that 'the Good Book' is the absolute Word of God, please refer him or her to *II Kings* 2:23-24, which describes part of a tour by the Prophet Elisha around Israel. Little children met Elisha on the road and teased him about being bald and he called upon God and conjured up bears, which killed forty-two of them:

"And he went up from thence unto Beth-el: as he was going up by the way, there came forth little children out of the city, and mocked him, and said unto him, Go up, thou bald head. And he turned back, and looked on them, and cursed them in the name of the Lord. And there came forth two she bears out of the wood, and tare forty and two children of them."

How can such a deed be justified? How can any acceptable religion be based on a book which describes God assisting in the killing of 'little children' at the behest of a man whose petty vanity has been pricked? Although this egregious incident is not described in the Qur'an, Elisha himself is characterised as a 'good-doer'[6] and 'excellent'.[7]

---

[6] *Surat Al-'An`ām* (The Cattle) 6:86.

[7] *Surah Sad* 38:48.

The story of the Great Flood, plagiarism though it is, does not reflect well on God. Oddly, just prior to the Flood, "the sons of God" are reported to have interbred with the "daughters of man", so the Flood may have been a family tiff.[8] Whatever, the killing of everything on earth other than those creatures on the Ark[9], including the deaths of millions of children, is the ultimate act of genocide. An all-powerful God with a little love and imagination could have surely thought of a more constructive and merciful solution. According to the text, God's heart was "grieved" that he had made man in the first place, but it was not reportedly grieved by the worldwide destruction, nor is there any hint of love in this Biblical description of brutal extermination.

---

[8] *Genesis* 6:4: "There were giants in the earth in those days; and also after that, when the sons of God came in unto the daughters of men, and they bare children to them ..."

[9] That even a fraction of the world's fauna could have been saved in the Ark, even at 450-510 feet in length – well done, Noah – is clearly nonsensical and how Noah caught Australian kangaroos and South American armadillos is puzzling. How did the flood straddle the oceans to kill those on every continent? How was it that nobody else had a boat, with which to survive the flood, is also a mystery. With forty days of rain they had plenty of warning, but maybe they thought it was just an English summer.

Talking of brutality, Abraham is a key figure in all three great monotheistic religions: Judaism, Islam and Christianity.[10] Abraham was a most unattractive man from a moral perspective. When he went to Egypt to avoid the famine he told his beautiful wife, Sarai, to pretend to be his sister. In consequence, Pharaoh took Sarai as a concubine and showered Abraham with riches. Most unjustly, as Pharaoh had been deceived, God sent down great plagues not on Abraham, but on Pharaoh's house.[11] Despite God's disapproval, Abraham subsequently tried to do exactly the same thing again by deceiving King Abimelech of Gerar into believing that his then wife, Sarah, could be taken by that king as a concubine.[12]

The story of the Flood is followed by an account of Lot's escape from Sodom and Gomorrah – sadly, though, not of his wife, who was turned to a pillar of salt for looking back – and the destruction by God of these cities with "brimstone and fire," despite the probability that the dead included innocent children, babies and people not beyond

---

[10] "Jews, Christians and Muslims disagree on many things, but they also agree on some, not least tracing their descent, spiritual or biological, from Abraham." Rabbi Jonathan Sacks, *The Dignity of Difference*, page viii.

[11] *Genesis* 12:10-20.

[12] *Genesis* 20:1-16.

redemption. After this, Lot, who had been selected by God as the only person worthy of being saved, gets drunk and impregnates his daughters. After these tales of slaughter and debauchery, comes the story of Abraham and Isaac.[13] God 'tempts' Abraham by telling him to take his son, Isaac, to Moriah and there to sacrifice him as a burnt offering. Abraham, who had been willing to prostitute his wives due to fear for his own life, obeys without demur. When Isaac is lying on the wooden altar ready to be killed, an angel of the Lord orders, "Lay not thine hand upon the lad, neither do thou any thing unto him: for now I know that thou *fearest [my italics]* God ..." If God is omniscient then he must already have known that Abraham feared him. More importantly, what a wicked thing it would have been for Abraham to have stabbed and burned his son. Far from congratulating Abraham, surely God should have rebuked him for not consulting his own conscience and for being so ready to comply with such a wicked command. We have here Biblical authority for the iniquitous defence, 'I was only obeying orders.'

Sadly no such reprieve came for the young daughter of Jephthah the Gileadite. Jephthah promised God that he would sacrifice the first person to greet him on his return if granted a

---

[13] *Genesis* 22.

victory in an imminent battle. Accordingly God arranged "a very great slaughter" – par for the course – and upon his return Jephthah was greeted by his young daughter. Jephthah wailed, tore his clothes and prevaricated for two months, but God granted no stay of execution and the poor child was murdered.[14]

Nor does God emerge with credit from the book of *Exodus*. Every year Jews celebrate the 'Passover' but, while the escape of the Jews from Egypt to the Promised Land may be cause for celebration, the underlying morality of the method of their exodus is highly questionable. God tells Moses to ask Pharaoh to release the Jews, but it is a rigged game, because every time Moses makes a request God intervenes and 'hardens' Pharaoh's heart.[15] So Pharaoh, although each time inclined to mercy and generosity, has no free will as to whether to release the Jews or not. The purpose of hardening Pharaoh's heart is specified as being to enable God to demonstrate his powers. In consequence, Egypt suffered the great plagues, which must have killed many innocent people by starvation and illness, not to mention the deaths of all of the Egyptian firstborn, while God 'passed

---

[14] *Judges* 11:29-40.

[15] e.g. *Exodus* 5:21, 7:3, 10:10, 14:4

over' the Jews. Eventually the Jews are freed but, even then, God makes Pharaoh change his mind and pursue the Jews so that he, God, may further demonstrate his mightiness by drowning the Egyptian army without regard to the lives of the soldiers, or the feelings and future of their dependants. The whole story is a wicked charade, in which God shows off, when the Exodus could have been achieved by a deity without any suffering at all. Indeed, according to the text it could easily have been achieved for the asking, but for the intervention of God in hardening Pharaoh's heart. At least God's objective was achieved: "Israel saw that great work which the Lord did upon the Egyptians: and the people *feared* the Lord ..."[16] On the reported facts, the people had *every* reason for fear. Just as in the story of Abraham, God's objective in the Old Testament is specified as being to create "fear". It is not surprising that Christianity guided by the Old Testament has been historically instrumental in so much killing and suffering. What *is* surprising is that so many Christians still see the Bible as 'the Word of God', or any kind of moral guide at all. I recently came across a typical Victorian school, which had written above its door this quotation from *Proverbs* 9:10: "The fear of the Lord is the beginning of

---

[16] *Exodus* 14:31.

wisdom." This hateful advice must have poisoned the children's spiritual development and their perception of God.

By the time the reader of the Old Testament has reached *Exodus* 32, Moses has been up the mountain and received from God "the two tables of testimony" containing the Ten Commandments. When he returns he finds that the people have created and begun to worship the Golden Calf. He angrily throws down the tables which, oddly, as Christopher Hitchens points out, break despite having been made by God. Moses calls upon his adherents and gives them God's orders: "And all the sons of Levi gathered themselves together unto him. And he said unto them, Thus saith the Lord God of Israel, Put every man his sword by his side, and go in and out from the gate throughout the camp, and slay every man his brother, and every man his companion, and every man his neighbour. And the children of Levi did according to the word of Moses: and there fell of the people that day about three thousand men. For Moses had said, Consecrate yourselves to day to the Lord, even every man upon his son, and upon his brother; that he may bestow upon you a blessing this day." When I heard this story of the Golden Calf as a child I remember how this genocidal inclination of God disturbed me even then. "Any system of religion that has anything in it that shocks the mind of a child cannot be a true religion."[17]

In *Deuteronomy* 5 the narrative again comes to the Covenant and the Law of Moses. As part of the deal/covenant between God and the Children of Israel, the Jews are promised other races' cities and other peoples' wells, vineyards and olive trees.[18] "When the Lord thy God shall bring thee into the land whither thou goest to possess it, and hath cast out the many nations before thee, the Hittites, and the Girgashites, and the Amorites, and the Canaanites, and the Perizzites, and the Hivites, and the Jebusites … **thou** *shalt smite them, and utterly destroy them*, thou shalt make no covenant with them, *nor show mercy unto them [my italics]* …"[19]

More genocide.

Misogyny

If the 'Good Book' is to be followed, then men should mistrust women and treat them as inferior. From Eve through Jezebel to Delilah, women tempt men to sin. Even the wise King Solomon "did outlandish women cause to sin".[20] In the

---

[17] Thomas Paine (1737-1809), *The Age of Reason* part 1.

[18] *Deuteronomy* 6:10-12.

[19] *Deuteronomy* 7:1- 6.

[20] *Nehemiah* 13:26.

New Testament, poor Mary Magdalene who was, on the evidence, probably a Disciple and at least as important in the life of Jesus as the male Disciples, has been falsely demeaned as a reformed prostitute by the Western Christian Church.

Eve, who had already the scriptural demerit of being created from Adam's rib, is told by God that Adam "shall rule over thee".[21] I prefer the Greek allegory of man and woman having been created by cutting one being in half. That allegorically explains why man and woman are at once so similar and yet different. More importantly, as halves, man and woman are self-evidently equal.

Leviticus is a particularly absurd book in the Bible. If you read the prescription for treating leprosy by killing a bird over running water and sprinkling the sufferer with the blood[22] the primitive nature of this text is clear. However, this ancient nonsense has greatly influenced the way in which women have been viewed historically. At 27:1-9 it appears that the value to be apportioned to a woman is just two thirds that of a man. This misogyny of religion lingers on today in the form of unequal pay.

Although woman with all her biological functions was

---

[21] *Genesis* 3:16.

[22] *Leviticus* 14 et seq.

allegedly created by God, when a woman gives birth to a boy she is deemed to be 'unclean' for a week and for two weeks if she has had a girl.[23] It is further specified that during her monthly period – referred to down the ages as 'the curse of Eve' – she is unclean as is anybody coming into contact with her.[24] The Biblical punishment for lying with a woman at such a time is comparatively lenient in Biblical terms: merely exile for life for both parties.[25] Women in the Old Testament are effectively property. If a man rapes a virgin, who is unengaged to another, and pays her father fifty shekels of silver she is his.[26] This is holy writ and not even President Trump could explain it away as 'locker room talk.' Hopefully #MeToo marks the approach of dawn in the dark world of sexual abuse.

The manifest sexism of the Old Testament is echoed in the New. In *First Corinthians*, Paul says, "Let your women keep silence in the churches: for it is not permitted unto them to speak; but to be under obedience, as also saith the law. And if they will learn any thing, let them ask their husbands at home: for it is a shame for women to speak in the church."[27]

---

[23] *Leviticus* 12:2-5.

[24] *Leviticus* 15:19.

[25] *Leviticus* 20:18

[26] *Deuteronomy* 22:28-9

[27] *First Corinthians* 14:34-5.

Likewise *First Timothy*, in which Christians are instructed: "Let the woman learn in silence with all subjection. But I suffer not a woman to teach, nor to usurp authority over the man, but to be in silence."[28] St Peter ordains that "... ye wives, be in subjugation to your own husbands." [29] There is much more of the same.

Other religions tend to discriminate against women. For instance, just under four thousand years ago, a huge stone was erected in Mesopotamia recording the Code of Hammurabi, the king. The Code had conveniently been revealed to Hammurabi by the gods Anu, Enhlil and Marduk. According to this stone these gods first approved the king and his position as well as the existing class/caste system, including slavery. As far as women were concerned, they were divinely deemed inferior; for instance the fine for killing a common woman was exactly half the penalty for blinding a common man in one eye. Christianity is historically unexceptional in its misogyny. Even Confucius ignored women. The present-day plight of women in Muslim countries, such as Saudi Arabia, Afghanistan, Iran and Pakistan, is striking. At least women in Saudi Arabia may soon be allowed to drive. This relaxation of

---

[28] *First Timothy* 2:11-5.

[29] *First Peter* 3:1.

the law is not without risk, because several years ago conservative Saudi cleric, Sheikh Saleh al-Lohaidan, warned that women's reproductive systems are threatened by driving, which "affects the ovaries and pushes the pelvis upwards."

In theory at least, Judaism also contains rules tending against equality.[30]

Religions tend to oppress women. It seems strongly arguable that the Burqa is a part of this oppression. At least Christianity has only managed to impose such extreme covering on its nuns. Whilst perhaps we in the West could benefit from a little more decorum in our choice of beach-wear, the present fuss in France over the 'Burkini' is both troubling and farcical. With that inclination that religions have to side with each other against anything secular, the Catholic

---

[30] My great friend, Michael Beckman Q.C., was at an international symposium on human rights, when the speaker referred to the oppression of Muslim and Jewish women. Beckman rose and caused hilarity by demanding to be told when the speaker had last actually encountered an oppressed Jewish woman. It should, however, be noted that Rabbi Eliyahu Falk sent letters to five thousand Orthodox Jewish homes in north London reminding orthodox women that it is "loathsome" to wear skirts less than four inches below the knee, bright colours and fitted blouses (*The Times*, 22nd September, 2016)

Church supports a woman's 'right' to wear a Burkini. In May 2016, the Pope declared, "Everyone must have freedom to externalise his or her own faith. If a Muslim woman wishes to wear a veil, she must be able to do so."[31] Religionists and some feminists, who say a woman has the right to decide what to wear, miss, or choose not to ask, five key questions:

1. Is it probable that God would have created woman in a form requiring a repressive and uncomfortable cover-all?

2. The Qur'an does not require the Burqa so is there any justification for it?[32]

3. Does the Burqa, in fact, reflect and represent an unhealthy and subjugating view of women and their role in life?

---

[31] Interview in *Le Croix*. He spoke similarly to *Corriere Della Sera* in September, 2016, and Bishop Nunzio Galantino defended covering up and referred to nuns.

[32] The Qur'an does not require a Burqa, but is limited to the wise suggestion that *both* sexes dress modestly. For a helpful exposition please see for instance *The Burqa – Islamic or Cultural?* by Chris Moore on www.quran-islam.org

4. Was the woman, who wishes to wear a Burqa/Burkini, indoctrinated or otherwise compelled to that wish by religious instruction, or intolerance?

5. If a woman prefers *not* to wear a Burqa, or a Burkini, does she, in reality, have free choice?

Whilst the Burqa is championed by male Christian priests, they refuse to recognize that women played a very important part in early Christianity. For instance, frescos dating between 230 and 240 AD in the Catacombs of Priscilla – on Rome's Via Salaria – clearly depict women acting as priests, but this interpretation is disputed by the Vatican. Women lost the right to be priests for nearly two thousand years, just as Mary Magdalene was demoted from disciple to prostitute. After agonizing so long about female priests, the Church of England is now struggling with the issue of women bishops. The present Archbishop of Canterbury has a good joke: "How many Anglican priests does it take to change a light bulb?" Answer: "Change!?"

As recently as 1913 the valiant Gwyneth Bebb was denied the right to be an English solicitor, because she was a woman. Her legal challenge failed on the basis that in law a woman was not "a person" within the meaning of the

108

Solicitors Act.[33] It was only in 1918 that some women in Britain received the right to vote – full suffrage 1928. In 1920 women in the USA received suffrage, but women in France and Italy had to wait till 1945. Most of Switzerland allowed women a federal vote in 1971, but the canton of Appenzell Innerrhoden held out till 1991. As recently as the year 2000, former President and Mrs Carter left the Southern Baptist Convention, because women had been formally declared inferior and "subservient", due to the belief that Eve was created second and was responsible for 'original sin'. In consequence, women were to be excluded from being pastors at a time when other churches were becoming more enlightened.

Slavery

As already mentioned, the Bible sets out specific guidance for the keeping of slaves.[34]

If you buy a male Hebrew slave he must be freed after

---

[33] Women were deemed incapable of carrying out a public function under the common law. The judgment was upheld on appeal in 1914, but reversed by statute in 1919.

[34] *Leviticus* 25:43 et seq.

six years[35], but a female slave may be kept for life and may be slept with, there being only a duty to feed and clothe her.[36] If you kill your slave you will be punished, unless he/she lives for more than a day "for he is his money" [i.e. the murderer's property to dispose of].[37]

Nor, as noted in the previous chapter, is approval of slavery limited to the Old Testament. One of a number of examples in the New Testament is: "Servants, be obedient to them that are your masters ... Knowing that whatsoever good thing any man doeth, the same he receive of the Lord, whether he be bond or free."[38]

The many references to slavery in the Bible were used as a justification for the Slave Trade and later for the continuation of slavery in the American Civil War. Indeed, Christian churches sanctioned slavery and, even after this evil was finally recognized and slavery abolished, the churches – including the Mormon Church – perpetuated racial prejudice until much too recently. Nelson Mandela, who was always very cautious about expressing his own religious beliefs or

---

[35] *Exodus* 21:2

[36] *Exodus* 21:7-11

[37] *Exodus* 21: 20-21

[38] *Ephesians* 6:5-8

lack of them, said, "The [apartheid] policy was supported by the Dutch Reformed Church, which furnished apartheid with its religious underpinnings by suggesting that Afrikaners were God's chosen people and that blacks were a subservient species."

One early bishop was so enthused by Christianity that he suggested that slaves should run away to become converts. For this threat to property rights he was promptly excommunicated. In fairness, I should mention that in 1435 St Thomas Aquinas reasoned that slavery was sinful and that in 1537 Pope Paul III made formal pronouncements against slavery. Also, William Wilberforce (1759-1833), who took a leading part in the abolition of the African slave trade, was strongly motivated by his Christian faith, but he was clearly able to free his mind and conscience from the shackles of strict Biblical text.

The Qur'an also fails to condemn slavery. It makes references to slavery as a recognized and acceptable part of life. A believing slave girl is ranked higher than a free woman, who does not believe.[39] Those *men* not prosperous enough to marry free women are permitted to take and marry a slave girl,

---

[39] *Sūrah al-Baqarah* (The Cow) 220 et seq.

if a believer.[40] On the other hand,[41] more benevolently, slave owners are encouraged to free slaves, if there is good known in them, and slave owners are enjoined not to force their slaves into prostitution. Islamic nations habitually plundered the southern coasts of Europe for slaves for many centuries. Estimates of the numbers taken in the three hundred and fifty years up to 1850 in the Barbary slave trade alone range upwards from one million.

Homophobia

The Bible is very clear about homosexuality: "If a man also lie with mankind, as he lieth with a woman, both of them have committed an abomination: they shall surely be put to death; their blood shall be upon them".[42]

So in *Deuteronomy* it says – homosexuals are often referred to as 'dogs' in the Bible: "There shall be no whore of the daughters of Israel, nor any sodomite of the sons of Israel. Thou shalt not bring the hire of a whore, or the price of a dog, into the house of the Lord thy God for any vow: for even both

---

[40] *Surah An-Nisa* 4

[41] Light 30. (An-nur)

[42] *Leviticus* 20:13

of these are abomination unto the Lord thy God."[43] There are many more egregious examples of homophobia.[44] St Paul – a 'confirmed bachelor' – violently denounced homosexuals.[45] In 390 AD, under the influence of St Ambrose, an imperial decree against homosexuality was made, requiring death by burning. However, guilty parties were often 'let off' with castration, torture and flogging, till the Biblical hatred of homosexuality culminated in the even crueller laws of the Emperor Justinian in 538 and 544 AD.

Nigeria, an extremely religious country with extreme Christians in the south and extreme Muslims in the north, brought in new anti-homosexual laws, which were effective from 13th January, 2014. These new laws impose a prison sentence of up to fourteen years. This is, of course, quite merciful compared with the death sentence demanded both in the Bible and the Qur'an, the latter declaring that homosexuality is a 'transgression beyond bounds'. Hard-line believers will be comforted to know that homosexuals are still executed by the Taliban in Afghanistan and by ISIS in Syria.

---

[43] *Deuteronomy* 23:17 and 18.

[44] Please see also, for instance, *1 Samuel* 20:33 and *1 Kings* 14:24 and 22:46.

[45] For instance *Romans* 1:27-28. For his bachelor status, please see for instance *1 Corinthians* 7:7.

In Aceh, the Sharī'ah province of Indonesia, the going rate for homosexuality is a mere eighty-five lashes.

In ancient Greece, homosexuality was socially obligatory amongst the upper classes. However, modern Christian Greece required extreme pressure from the European Court of Justice finally to make same sex relationships legal in 2015. A year later, the Orthodox Church held a vigil in Thessaloniki ahead of a gay pride festival, which it regarded as a celebration "of abnormality and dishonour." Orthodox Christian spokesman, Father Stephanos, was quoted as saying that they could not accept "this class of people ... because their actions simply go against the preachings of the Bible and the New Testament."[46]

In 1950s Britain homosexuality was often punished with suspiciously extreme severity. Prison sentences of up to ten years' hard labour were not uncommon. Others were compelled to submit to organotherapy, a type of chemical castration. In 1952 an ungrateful nation sentenced Alan Turing, the famous code-breaker of Bletchley Park who singlehandedly contributed so much to the Allied victory in the Second World War, to organotherapy. This brutality

---

[46] *The Times*, 24th June, 2016. Nor will you find these 'preachings' in the Gospels, but rather you have to go to Paul's 'rantings' in *Romans* 1:26-32 and *1 Corinthians* 6:9-10.

almost certainly caused the suicide of this genius, who for better or worse was the father of computers. In 2013, sixty-one years too late, Turing was granted a posthumous pardon.

The Church of Jesus Christ of Latter-day Saints is still adamant that homosexuality is a sin. In 2017 it declared that it was withdrawing one hundred and eighty-five thousand Mormon teenagers from the Boy Scouts of America after the Scout movement relaxed restrictions on gay and transsexual members. The decision was, the Church claimed, unrelated to this change in scouting policy.

So in Britain, Tim Farron M.P., being both an evangelical Christian and the leader of the Liberal Democrats, appeared to find it impossible to declare that gay sex was not a sin. Eventually in the face of the 2017 General Election he conceded that it was not a sin 'for non-theological purposes', but sounded as if he was speaking through a mouthful of broken glass. The present Pope more elegantly sidestepped the question with his reply, "Who am I to judge?" After the election Farron resigned saying, "To be a political leader – especially of a progressive, liberal party in 2017 – and to live as a committed Christian, to hold faithfully to the Bible's teaching, has felt impossible for me." Surely any enlightened person, especially the leader of a progressive party, should realize that we need to think for ourselves, rather than reverencing bigotry contained in ancient scripture.

Religion can create, perpetuate and magnify prejudice and it has demonstrably done so in the area of same-sex relationships.

Miracles

The Old Testament is full of miracles, or rather dramatic interventions by God of a less welcome type. When God was so willing to manifest himself and his power over the period covered by the Old Testament why has he become so coy in modern times? The Holocaust would have been an obvious moment for God to act. When Pope John Paul II was shot in 1981, he attributed his survival to the intervention of Our Lady of Fatima in diverting the bullet to prevent it being fatal. After so many theatrical interventions in the Old Testament this would have been a spectacular moment for God, or Our Lady of Fatima, to have diverted the bullet in such a way as simultaneously to protect the Pope from all injury and to provide evidence of God's existence. If God truly was willing so regularly to manifest himself three thousand years ago, which is the blink of an eye in cosmic terms, there is no logical reason why he should have been so reticent more recently. Of course, evangelists, like Franklin Graham – son of

Billy – believe that God is still intervening. By way of example, he declares that the election of Donald Trump was through "God's hand." However, for the less credulous there is no modern evidence for an Old Testament type of God and believers are really left to base their faith on Biblical testimony and guidance.

Chapter Four

The Bible as the Word of God

The black walnut tree releases a poison which kills all plants beneath and near it. Religion, especially in its more fundamental forms, can be like a black walnut tree. Any tendrils of alternative thought emerging beneath it are remorselessly exterminated. This is, of course, completely logical, because if a religion is truly the revealed word of God and if God is truly an all-knowing and benevolent being, then anything tending to contradict that revealed truth must be wrong. The problem is, of course, that if a religion is not, in fact, based on the revealed and precise word of God then it may be poisoning what is good and true. Beware of all those claiming certainty in a realm where there can be no certainty.

Christianity has been particularly walnut-like. It has been violently intolerant of paganism and any person not sharing the correct form of faith. The Western world, which is still influenced by Christianity, is currently angrily censorious about the destruction of wonderful archaeological ruins in Syria by extreme Islamists. This criticism is never tempered by an acknowledgement that parts of those ruins themselves result from the systematic pillage and destruction by Christians of pagan temples, artworks and other artefacts in Syria. The destruction of the great 4th century Buddhas of Bamiyan in Afghanistan by the Taliban has rightly been condemned, but, at about the time that these statues were being constructed, Christians destroyed and stole the contents of the great Temple of Serapis in Alexandria, which was then generally considered to be the most magnificent building in the world. The vast repository of books containing ancient knowledge and wisdom in the Temple was also destroyed. Christianity systematically destroyed and despoiled all structures, artefacts and books inconsistent with its faith.[1] It has been estimated that ninety-nine per cent of pre-Christian Latin writings were destroyed, although happily somebody must have kept a copy of *The Golden Ass*, a delightful, if smutty, Latin novel, hidden in his wardrobe. As to buildings, St Martin won his sainthood for destroying temples in France and St Marcellus can attribute his elevation to having brought down the temple of Zeus at Apamea.

Monotheistic religion is historically unusual and very

---

[1] For a detailed survey of this exhaustive destruction of all symbols of other religions please see for instance Catherine Nixey's *The Darkening Age*.

often confrontational. Tolerance of many gods allows productive racial and religious coexistence. As early as 173 BC the Roman Senate, which theoretically worshipped the Greek gods with Roman names, decreed, "Idem ubique di immortalis" (*Everywhere the immortal gods are the same.*) The pre-Christian pagan world had been tolerant and in consequence had vibrated with philosophical, spiritual and scientific debate. In 388 AD, after the Christian walnut tree had begun to grow large, it became a crime for any person in the Empire publically to argue about, discuss, or even express an opinion about religion. Once Christianity got the upper hand there was little toleration. As early as 356 AD the death penalty had been introduced for worshipping images. Restrictions on paganism grew ever more brutal, and in 529 AD pagans were forbidden to teach, everybody had to choose between baptism and exile, and those who had been baptized and continued pagan worship were to be executed. In its historic intolerance of, and violence towards, dissent, and in its use of fear and not love, Christianity simply followed God's example in the Old Testament.

The Old Testament highlights a fundamental contradiction at the heart of most religions. The general theme is that God, having created man and woman, places them in the world and gives them free will, which includes the freedom to do things, which religions consider sinful. Having given humanity its freedom, God then sets out a strict list of guidelines recorded in holy writings, which control and direct every thought and action on pain of punishment of the utmost cruelty and duration. What is given with one hand is taken away with the other. If the scriptural writings, by which most religions seek to impose total control on their adherents, are to be regarded as the word of God then this whole process of giving free will and then effectively withdrawing it seems perverse. The reality is, of course, that the requirement strictly to follow scriptural writings as interpreted by those claiming authority is simply a way of gaining religious power, influence and wealth. Religious fundamentalists' belief in the sanctity and absolute truth of their ancient scripture is, as we are currently so painfully aware, very dangerous.

Jews and Orthodox Christians wisely tend to read their scriptures not as strict historical truth and the absolute word of God, but rather as texts requiring constant reinterpretation. This same view of the Bible was historically taken by many early Christians of the West. If scripture is seen more as allegorical, rather than literal and above reinterpretation, its contradictory and objectionable passages do not undermine it in the same way. There is potential benefit to be taken from scripture viewed as an allegory, just as there is potential danger in reading it literally. Karen Armstrong considers prehistoric peoples, who would for instance have a sacred rock around which they would gather for religious purposes. She rightly suggests that the rock was not itself the object of worship, but rather "the rock was simply a focus that directed their attention to the mysterious essence of life."[2] Once the reader of religious texts sheds the notion that scripture is absolute and to be venerated for its own sake and instead uses it as a tool to look beyond at spiritual matters then scripture can have real value, just as Richard Dawkins' arguments in *The God Delusion* can help to illuminate the spiritual quest of those confident enough to think for themselves.

However, today many Western Christians, especially evangelicals and other fundamentalists, believe that the Bible is the absolute and literal truth. So Timothy Keller writes, "Now, what happens if you eliminate anything from the Bible that offends your sensibility and crosses your will? If you pick and choose what you want to believe and reject the rest, how will you ever have a God who can contradict you? You won't. … So an authoritative Bible is not the enemy of a personal relationship with God. It is the precondition for it."[3]

---

[2] *The Case for God*, page 21.

[3] *The Reason for God*, page 114.

This assertion, which demands that you abdicate your spiritual free will to slavish obedience to the literal text of ancient scripture, raises many objections. For your comfort and convenience I have curbed my indignation and so managed to restrict my objections to just eight:

1. Which Bible and in which language is the 'authoritative' Bible? In any Bible there are passages, which are not supposed to be read literally. A striking example of a non-literal text is *Revelation*, which concludes modern Bibles. This was written about a hundred years after the death of Jesus. The late entry of this book into the Bible was expressly by permission of St Augustine. He was the leading proselytizer of the abominable concept of 'Original Sin' and a strong supporter of violence against non-believers, which he called "merciful savagery." Under the misapprehension that the author of this crazed text, predicting destruction and eternal suffering for non-believers, was John the Disciple, he formally consented to the inclusion of *Revelation* as part of the modern Bible in about 394 AD. St Augustine's decision was conditional upon this book being read symbolically and not literally. This edict is and has been overlooked by Christians like Mr Keller. President George W. Bush and his conservative Christian associates certainly read *Revelation* as

literal and authoritative. It has been speculated that its requirement for a 'great war in the Middle East'[4] as a precursor to the Second Coming fuelled evangelical enthusiasm for the disastrous Iraq War and yet, with just a little theological knowledge, evangelicals should have known that it was at best allegorical and at worst the product of a bad trip on magic mushrooms. Many conservative Christians impatiently await 'The Rapture', when they expect to be lifted to heaven to avoid the Apocalypse, which according to *Revelation* will engulf the rest of us. In 1910, leading fundamentalist Baptist pastor, Isaac M. Haldane, clearly impervious to Jesus' message of love and forgiveness, predicted that the Christ of *Revelation* "comes forth as one who no longer seeks either friendship or love. ... His garments are dipped in blood, the blood of others. He descends that he may shed the blood of men."[5] Religionists of Haldane's type have, of course, always favoured bloodletting and an imminent end of the world. There is a sadistic smugness in evangelists, who so obviously savour the prospect of abandoning the rest

---

[4] A current favourite Biblical reference for the location of this final war in *Revelation* is *Ezekiel* 38:1-6, referring to the war with Gog in the land of Magog, which is possibly Asia Minor/Asian Turkey, though was Iraq considered a possibility?

[5] *The Signs of the Times*.

of us to limitless torment. According to Thomas Aquinas in *Summa Theologica* the especial reward of saints in heaven was to be "allowed to see perfectly the sufferings of the damned."

2. How can any version of the Bible with its doubtful compilation and clear tampering be authoritative at all? Mr Keller chooses the straw dog of *The Da Vinci Code* to attack. I was so repulsed by the bad grammar in this book, which Mr Keller should note is a popular novel and not an academic text, that I only managed fifty pages. Mr Keller denounces the idea, which he finds in the novel, that the Emperor Constantine "determined the New Testament canon, casting aside the earlier and supposedly more authentic Gnostic Gospels." As explained above, the Bible was, as a matter of historical fact and without any need to refer to *The Da Vinci Code*, constructed in a completely haphazard way and quite possibly by order of Constantine. Passages from many texts were certainly patched together. As part of this process the many texts referring to Jesus, the existing remnants of which are referred to as the Apocryphal Gospels, were rejected. Clearly a poorly crafted novel is not the best source for determining the history of the very many different versions of the Bible available. Given the dubious way in which the Bible was compiled, the usual way in which Christians seek to maintain

the authority of the Bible is to assert that each mistranslation, copying error, random deletion and insertion was done by those guided by the Holy Spirit. Gadarene swine may fly!

3. Mr Keller asserts that the 'canonical Gospels' – Matthew, Mark, Luke and John – were "written at the very most forty to sixty years after Jesus' death", but this is not the generally held view, save perhaps for Mark. There are many Christian sources available from the second century –e.g. Barnabas, Hermas, Polycarp, Ignatius and Clement – and none of these refer to the 'canonical gospels' as surely they would have done if the works of Matthew, Mark, Luke and John had been written and were pre-eminent at the time. Clement of Alexandria, Origen and Didymus the Blind – ranging from the 2nd to 4th centuries– do mention the "Gospel according to the Hebrews", which is the earliest evidence of a Jewish-Christian gospel. The first mention of John's Gospel is by Theophilus of Antioch in about 170 AD. The first mention of the full set of what are now the canonical gospels is in about 180 AD by Bishop Irenaeus.[6] The canonical Gospels were first put into written form between 60 AD and 180 AD, but clearly they continued to evolve for several hundred years before being

---

[6] *Ad. Hear.*3.11.8.

recognized as 'canonical'.

4. Mr Keller thinks that "the literary form of the Gospels is too detailed to be legend."[7] If you have read the legends dealing with the Greek gods and Norse gods then you will know just how beautifully written and detailed they are. Thor's journey to Utgard is especially entertaining, but few modern readers are compelled by the detail and literary merit of these stories to give them credence as spiritual blueprints. They do contain food for thought and Thor's visit to the land of the giants contains warnings against vanity, aggression and too easily taking things at face value. Equally detailed and vivid are some of the non-canonical gospels, yet Mr Keller denies their validity and rather inaccurately calls them 'gnostic'. The very detail itself in the Canonical Gospels produces contradiction. For instance, Matthew and Luke disagree about the detail of Jesus' genealogy, birth and the reason for the journey to Bethlehem and Mark and Luke differ on major details of Jesus' death. Also, the detail contradicts known historical facts, such as:

- *Matthew* 2:1 records that Herod was King of Judea at

---

[7] Page 106.

the date of Jesus' birth, but Herod died four years too early in 4 BC;

• *Luke* 2:2 reports that Quirinius was Roman governor of Judea at the time, but Quirinius did not govern during the lifetime of Herod;

• the reason given for the highly doubtful trip to Bethlehem was a census. Passing over the highly improbable nature of a census which seeks information about people at their place of birth rather than where they actually live, there was no census at all – Roman records are quite detailed – till 6 AD and then not one of the eccentric type described. Also, it appears from John's Gospel that Jesus was neither from Bethlehem nor descended from King David.[8] Bethlehem, or not Bethlehem? Which is authoritative?

• a very interesting point arising from the contradictory texts of the four canonical Gospels, is raised about the Eucharist by A. N. Wilson in his wonderful and scholarly book, *Jesus*. The Eucharist is, of course, the sacrament of giving bread and wine. The first three Gospels claim that Jesus and his disciples were at the traditional Jewish Passover meal when the Eucharist was instituted. As Mr Wilson points out, if this were so then the Jewish authorities would have had to

---

[8] *John* 7:32 et seq., especially 7:42.

have broken their strict Passover observances to arrest, try and condemn Jesus. Historically and theologically this is impossible. John's Gospel, on the other hand, puts the Last Supper well before the Passover and does not mention the Eucharist.[9] Which Gospel is right about the date of the Last Supper and the Eucharist?

The Old Testament account of the poor man found gathering sticks on the Sabbath and stoned to death on this account by order of God himself is certainly detailed.[10] If this detailed story were true, then the punishment is so clearly wicked that even Mr Keller should face up to it: no argument about the mysteries of God being beyond our understanding can surely satisfy a reasonable mind that God's sentence of death by stoning was an appropriate punishment for collecting sticks on the Sabbath. A Sabbath, which Jesus later declared was 'made for man.'

Another evangelist wedded to the Old Testament, Steve Chalke, writes in all seriousness, "But God's anger is born of pure love, it is never fickle or malicious – it is measured and

---

[9] *Jesus*, pp 196 -197.

[10] *Numbers* 15:32-36.

shot through with mercy and compassion."[11] The Old Testament God's individual acts, like commanding the murder of the collector of sticks, to his genocide, as in the Great Flood and the Covenant, make it impossible not to splutter with indignation at Chalke's cheek. In the conquest of Jericho, a most *unloving* God appears to Joshua brandishing a sword before delivering up the city; "And they utterly destroyed all that was in the city, both man and woman, young and old, and ox, and sheep, and ass, with the edge of the sword."[12] "So the Lord was with Joshua."[13] Unlike sad Sodom, here there is not even the allegation of sinfulness to justify the slaughter. The poor people of Jericho were simply being ethnically cleansed as part of the Covenant. This is not a matter of interpretation; it is what the Bible itself expressly states. To suggest that the genocide in the Old Testament represents God's love is much like St Augustine's declaration that the Church in its mass murder and torture of dissenters "persecutes in the spirit of love."[14]

5. Does it never occur to religious fanatics that scripture

---

[11] *The Lost Message of Jesus*, page 62.

[12] *Joshua* 7:21.

[13] *Joshua* 7:27.

[14] Augustine, Ep. 185.2 ed. Schaff

was produced by human writers? These writers may have been quite unpleasant people with sexual or mental problems, or they may have had personal agendas. Jewish nationalism underlies much of the Old Testament and particularly Daniel. There is every reason to pick and choose what to accept, when reading any scripture. If it is wrong to do so, then presumably Mr Keller agrees with the Old Testament that death is the proper punishment for:

- homosexuality – some states in the USA once followed the Bible and themselves had the death penalty
- women, who upon marriage fail to bleed satisfactorily as a token of virginity[15]
- adultery[16]
- blaspheming[17]
- working – including collecting sticks – on the Sabbath[18]
- cursing your mother or father[19]

---

[15] *Deuteronomy* 22:20-21.

[16] *Deuteronomy* 22:22.

[17] *Leviticus* 24:14

[18] *Exodus* 31:14-15.

[19] *Leviticus* 20:9

- being a rebellious, gluttonous or alcoholic child[20]
- and an almost endless list of other capital offences

Indeed, scripture fanatics must be particularly careful to read each prohibitive passage for themselves, or they could easily deserve death by accident; for instance, God killed Onan, *not* for masturbation as is generally believed and preached,[21] but for practising birth control by *coitus interruptus*.

Happily, some Biblical punishments are comparatively benevolent, as in *Deuteronomy* 25:11: "When men strive together one with another, and the wife of one draweth near for to deliver her husband out of the hand of him, and putteth forth her hand, and taketh him by the secrets[22]: then thou shalt cut off her hand, thine eye shall not pity her." So wives must keep their hands well away from men's 'secrets' if Mr Keller or any other Bible fanatic is close by.

I assume that in compliance with Biblical instruction, Mr Keller:

---

[20] *Deuteronomy*:21:20-21

[21] *Genesis* 38:8-11

[22] Genitals.

- is circumcised[23] and maybe even castrated in deference to Jesus' words in *Matthew* 19:12

- makes regular animal sacrifices in compliance with, say, *Leviticus* 17:3 *et seq*

- does not cut his hair or beard on the sides[24] – now very much the fashion

- avoids black pudding and pink meat still containing blood[25]

- avoids mixing meat and dairy products (no cheeseburgers), eating pork,[26] fat[27] and prawns and all other aquatic creatures lacking fins and scales[28]

Mr Keller does not grapple with the contradictions in the Bible such as Jesus' express disagreement with parts of the Old Testament and the stark fact that Jesus' family tree given at the beginning of *Matthew* is wholly different both in names and numbers from the one set out by *Luke* 3:23-38, or that both family trees are contradicted by the later insertion of

---

[23] *Genesis* 17:10 and very many other passages.

[24] *Leviticus* 19:27.

[25] *Leviticus* 19:13-14.

[26] *Leviticus* 11:7-8.

[27] *Leviticus* 3:17

[28] *Deuteronomy* 14:9-10.

passages claiming the virgin birth. Also *John* 7:41 flatly contradicts Matthew and Luke's claim that Jesus descended from King David or was born in Bethlehem. These are both Biblical requirements for a Messiah, although not even Mr Keller claims that Jesus conquered the Assyrians, as the *true* Messiah is obliged to do. At least two of these three versions of Jesus' genealogy cannot be authoritative or true; the reader absolutely must pick and choose only one – or none – of them.

Of the many appalling practices approved by the Bible, Mr Keller sheepishly toys only with the question of slavery, which both the Old and New Testaments sanction. The Bible excuses the murder and rape of slaves. Mr Keller depicts slavery in the time of the Bible as almost benevolent. He suggests that it did not equate to the more recent African slave trade and that it was, in terms of the culture of the time, comparatively benign. According to him, slaves were generally indistinguishable from other workmen and had "the same wages." First, the principle of slavery – *owning* another human being – is itself abhorrent. Even if it were true that Biblical slaves were *comparatively* comfortable, this would not excuse any religion for approving it. Secondly, in Rome, where the slave laws *were* comparatively liberal, slaves were sold naked in the market and were regarded as sub-human

chattels. Those from overseas would have their ears bored.[29]
Masters had absolute power over their slaves and could make
them provide sexual services, scourge them and put them to
death at their pleasure.[30] For perceived misdeeds slaves were
often lashed, branded, made to carry a bulky piece of wood – a
furca – round their necks, locked away in dreadful conditions,
and even crucified, till Constantine prohibited this last form of
killing them, not out of humanity, but because it mimicked
The Crucifixion. If a slave owner were killed and no
perpetrator discovered then all his/her slaves would be
executed. Slaves were allowed a *menstruum*, which was a
monthly allowance of five pecks of grain and five denarii.[31] If
a slave were unlucky enough to be sent to the mines, or
chained in a galley, his life would be particularly brutal and
short. So I respectfully disagree with Mr Keller's historical
appraisal of the contemporary lives of slaves, as I do with his
very lame suggestion[32] that the Bible is somehow redeemed,
because it "unconditionally condemns kidnapping and
trafficking in slaves." It is true that *Deuteronomy* 24:7
condemns kidnapping and selling those slaves of the 'children

---

[29] *auribus perforates* Iuvenalis Saturae.i.104.

[30] Juv.Sat.vi.219.

[31] *Roman Antiques*, Alexander Adam, page 31.

[32] *The Reason for God*, page 111.

of Israel', but not those of other races. *1 Timothy* 1:10 condemns 'menstealers' – kidnappers – but neither of these passages in any way condemns slavery itself and, indeed, scripture clearly approves ownership of fellow humans. Like these passages, most of the Bible relates exclusively to the rights and protection of Jews and so it is the case here that even this Biblical rule against theft and kidnapping does not protect people or slaves of other races.

Many religionists tend to be quite myopic when it comes to issues like slavery in their scriptures. So Rabbi Jonathan Sacks writes, "The politics of ancient Israel begins with an act inconceivable to the cosmological mind, namely that God, creator of the universe, intervenes in history to *liberate slaves*."[33] [his italics] This liberation, which is identified as climaxing in *Exodus*, was, of course, the escape of the Children of Israel from Egypt, where they were seemingly living as a subservient race. Please note, Rabbi Sacks, that God did not liberate slaves generally, not even the slaves owned by the Children of Israel. Why did God allow

---

[33] *The Dignity of Difference*, page 133. There is little historical evidence for Exodus, but the Roman historian, Josephus, considered that the Jews had originally been the Hyksos, who ruled northern Egypt in about 1500 BC and were driven across the Sinai Desert – not the Red Sea – by the southern kingdom.

slavery in the first place? Why does God allow slavery now?

6. The assertion that the Bible is a precondition for a relationship with God is typical of the vanity of most religions, which claim that the only the way to God and spiritual salvation is by strictly and unquestioningly following the demands of their own scripture.

7. The assertion that "an authoritative Bible ... is the precondition" for a relationship with God carries with it the alternative proposition that if you find parts abhorrent, unacceptable, or contradictory, then you should also consider shunning any relationship with Mr Keller's God. Nobody should so far desert reason and conscience as slavishly to follow Mr Keller's demand that the Bible should be treated as having such absolute authority. When religious leaders demand that the texts of their religion should be venerated as authoritative and absolute, they are really saying that the opinions of those appointed, or self-appointed, as religious leaders should be held absolute.

8. Certainty, which is inherent both in fundamentalist religious faith and in materialist atheism, is inappropriate, when spiritual questions are raised. I consider that the

evidence available to us demonstrates that we have a soul, but I should need much more evidence to declare that what I think to be the case is certain beyond all reasonable doubt. It is of the essence of spiritual questions that there can be no comprehensive answer for the living. The whole purpose of the spiritual quest is to enquire and learn. The quest is an essential part of being alive and developing. Certainty, like that of Mr Keller and other religious fundamentalists, makes open-minded inquiry and discussion impossible. Acceptance of fundamentalist opinion ends any quest and effectively makes any quest a kind of blasphemy, because to question is to doubt religious certainty. Worse, as the bloody history of religion demonstrates, certainty is highly dangerous. In 1981 Sir Isaiah Berlin (1909-1997) wrote some rough notes on the danger of certainty:

"Few things have done more harm than the belief on the part of individuals and groups ... that he or she or they are in *sole* possession of the truth. ... It is a terrible and dangerous arrogance to believe that you alone are right: have a magical eye which sees *the* truth: and that others cannot be right if they disagree. This makes one certain that there is *one* goal and only one for one's nation or church or the whole of humanity, and that is worth any amount of suffering (particularly on the part of other people) if only the goal is attained – 'through the ocean of blood to the kingdom of love' (or something like this) said Robespierre: ... I daresay leaders in religious wars of Christian v. Muslim or Catholics v. Protestants sincerely believed this: the belief that there is one and only one true answer to the central questions which have agonized mankind and that one has it oneself ... was responsible for oceans of blood: but no Kingdom of Love sprang from it – or could ..."[34]

Apart from religious terrorism, we live in an age, when historic sexual abuse by priests has been revealed as widespread and systematically concealed. The heartless treatment of unmarried mothers and their children by religious institutions has become common knowledge, as depicted in the films like *Philomena.* More specifically, Tony Campolo, a committed conservative evangelist, unwittingly gives a typical example of the individual evil that can occur when the Bible is interpreted as authoritative:

"One young woman was engaged to be married to someone who was not a Christian. Her pastor advised her not

---

[34] *Berlin*, page 345.

to go through with the wedding because, as he interpreted Scripture, the Bible clearly teaches that Christians are not supposed to marry non-Christians. He read to her, 'Do not be yoked together with unbelievers. For what do righteousness and wickedness have in common? Or what fellowship can light have with darkness?'[35] *[St Paul again!]* Her pastor said that she should break off the relationship and trust the Lord to bring a Christian man into her life. He assured her that God had somebody else in store for her future. The young woman did as she was told and as she believed the Bible taught – but no Christian man came into her life."[36]

As I read this passage, I expected, as I suspect you will have done, that Mr Campolo would condemn this simplistic, arrogant and destructive interference in the poor woman's life. He does not. In fact, he simply muses that this religiously abused woman probably "resents God deeply." She has every reason to resent Paul's religion and the bigoted scriptural advice of her pastor. Sadly she probably has not even now reached the state of independent consciousness where she can throw off her years of religious servitude and think for herself.

---

[35] *2 Corinthians.* 6:14

[36] *Choose Love Not Power*, pp 165-166.

Where, Mr Campolo, was the love in this advice not to marry the non-Christian man she loved? I can clearly see the operation of power. Also, on what theological basis did the pontificating Paul have authority to give such instruction in the first place? He demonstrates a dangerous but typical attitude for a religionist by directing the Corinthians to regard any person who is not a Christian, as being for that reason alone 'a wicked creature of darkness'.[37] Paul's type of extreme intolerance and contempt for persons of different faiths can be found today in Muslim extremism and violence. There is great potential evil in treating ancient writings as 'authoritative'. There is great evil, as we are now bitterly aware, in treating those with different beliefs as 'wicked and dark.'

It is sad how religion can at times lead the faithful to inhumanity. Evangelist Steve Chalke, without even blinking at the harshness of his church, tells a story about a friend who was a trainee pastor. So devoted to his vocation was this young man that it led to the breakdown of his marriage and his wife and children moved away.[38] Because of his marriage breakdown the "church then asked him to resign his job. So this young man, who had set out with so many dreams of

---

[37] *2 Corinthians* 6:14, the text used to blight the Christian woman's life, above.

[38] *The Lost Message of Jesus*, pp. 64-65.

142

serving God, found himself alone and broken." Just how unforgiving is that? Sadly, Mr Chalke does not pause to consider. Mr Chalke's book is called *The Lost Message of Jesus* and this sad story shows just how grievously lost the message of love and forgiveness has been.

Rigid application of scripture has tended to create and sustain prejudice and to resist beneficial scientific advances. Yet the Christian handbook, the Bible, is still venerated, even though it contains so many contradictions and so much immoral and primitive guidance. In 2012 the then British Minister of Education, Michael Gove, despite severe financial cuts at the time, formulated a plan to send a Bible to each state school. During the 2016 election of Presidential Candidates in the USA, Ted Cruz sacked his communications director for circulating a doctored video of a devout Presidential rival, Marco Rubio. The altered video depicted Mr Rubio being accosted by a man with a Bible and suggested that Mr Rubio had said that the Bible contained "not many answers". In fact, Mr Rubio had said the Bible had "all the answers". How can anybody, who has actually read the Bible and scrutinized it through the prism of reason and conscience, think it contains "all the answers"? In a society where Reason should play an important role, the doctored video should have been the vote winner and the disclosure that any potential leader actually thought that the Bible had 'all the answers' should have instantly ended his chances of election. It is a strange and sad irony that in the United States, which was founded by people dedicated to secularism and tolerance, there is so much religiosity that it would probably be impossible for a professed atheist to win an election. There is some hope though, because for the first time ever a poll[39] in the USA has showed atheists as having been replaced by socialists as the least likely category of person to be elected.

Unlike religiosity, the myth of Father Christmas – Santa Claus, as opposed to St Nicholas – *is* comparatively benign. Suppose though that at the point when children begin questioning the reality of Santa they were told that to doubt his existence would involve eternal suffering and that all those not believing – possibly including some of their own friends and relatives – would suffer eternal damnation too. Please consider a world in which it were obligatory to attend services venerating Father Christmas, to eat a diet of mince pies and sherry in deference to the alleged wishes of Father Christmas and to make significant payments to support the Santa movement. We should say that such indoctrination of children was both wrong-headed and evil. Yet this is what happens

---

[39] *Gallup Poll*, 22.6.15.

with religion. If there were Father Christmas schools, which required purported belief in and worship of the 'Gift Bringer', all rational people would find such an arrangement unacceptable both for its absurdity and for creating social division between 'Christmasists' and non-believers. Yet religious schools are not just tolerated, but often encouraged. We are upset when our teenage children are drawn away by the Moonies and overt mind control techniques, but we are entirely comfortable that all around us children are being indoctrinated from birth in ancient religious superstition.

My argument about Father Christmas has already been made most elegantly by Bertrand Russell in relation to a teapot:[40]

"If I were to suggest that between the Earth and Mars there is a china teapot revolving about the sun in an elliptical orbit, nobody would be able to disprove my assertion provided I were careful to add that the teapot is too small to be revealed even by our most powerful telescopes. But if I were to go on to say that, since my assertion cannot be disproved, it is an intolerable presumption on the part of human reason to doubt

---

[40] Bertrand Russell, *Is There a God?*, https://www.goodreads.com/quotes/38828-if-i-were-to-suggest-that-between-the-earth-and

it, I should rightly be thought to be talking nonsense. If, however, the existence of such a teapot were affirmed in ancient books, taught as the sacred truth every Sunday, and instilled into the minds of children at school, hesitation to believe in its existence would become a mark of eccentricity and entitle the doubter to the attentions of the psychiatrist in an enlightened age or of the Inquisitor in an earlier time."

When persons come to maturity and doubt creeps into their consciousness it is often a difficult, or even a bitter, experience for those who would try to escape their early indoctrination. Islamic apostates can face death. Jehovah's Witnesses and Plymouth Brethren are most harsh in shutting out all those who lapse. Scientologists appear to be systematically vengeful against apostates.[41] The isolation for somebody whose whole previous social and spiritual life has centred on their religion can be agonizing. A modern example of this is the sad case of a husband and wife of the Charedi Jewish community in England. The husband opted to change his gender and was excluded from all contact with the five children. In considering this exclusion, Mr Justice Peter Jackson, who was bound to treat the interests of the children as

---

[41] Louis Theroux, *My Scientology Movie*.

paramount, reached "with real regret" the decision that the "likelihood of the children and their mother being marginalised or excluded by the ultra-Orthodox community is so real, and the consequences so great, that this one factor, despite its many disadvantages, must prevail over the many advantages of contact." I do not in any way criticize this judgement, but the inhuman intolerance demonstrated by the adherents of so many religions is truly distressing.

In George Eliot's *Silas Marner*, the eponymous hero is a respected member of a strict Calvinist sect. His supposed best friend, William Dane – "somewhat given to over-severity towards weaker brethren" – frames Marner with the theft of money. Lots are drawn in the chapel – like the religious tossing of a coin – to determine Marner's guilt. God's verdict, according to this game of chance, is that he is guilty. In consequence, Dane is able to keep the stolen money and to marry Marner's fiancée, who, following God's verdict, renounces Marner. Eliot notes, "To people accustomed to reason about the forms in which their religious feeling has incorporated itself, it is difficult to enter into that simple, untaught state of mind in which the form and the feeling have never been severed by *an act of reflection*. We are apt to think it inevitable that a man in Marner's position should have begun to question the validity of an appeal to the divine judgment by drawing lots: but to him this would have been *an effort of independent thought* such as he had never known … If there is an angel who records the sorrows of men as well as their sins, he knows *how many and deep are the sorrows that spring from false ideas* for which no man is culpable" *[my italics]*. We need to use our capacity for independent thought to question religion, politics, propaganda, rumour and, indeed, everything. The reason for so much evil is that, like the Martinites and Silas Marner, religious people do not generally incline to independent thought, however compelling the reason for doing so may be.

In 2015 the writer, Jonathan Meades, who is most definitely capable of independent thought, in a talk called *Composing the Past*, summed up his own feelings about religion, "The ascension, the feeding of the five thousand, the book of *Genesis*, the apple in the garden, that wretched snake, the freakish supernaturalism, the cannibalism of the Eucharist, the parting of the sea, the fifth horseman of the apocalypse, the one who developed osteo-inertia and couldn't be bothered to keep up so got written out of the preposterous tale – it's all balls. But then a religion without mumbo-jumbo is like a dominatrix without a whip. The practice of worshipping a hackneyed fantasy which has no existence save in the minds of people of faith – those who require no proof – is degrading, it diminishes humankind, it diminishes our achievements in science, in philosophy, in art – to understand and explain the world."

This same thought is put more temperately by A. N. Wilson:

"I began to see how it was possible that Paul might have invented the Christian religion – though this is too simple a way of putting it. It was a slow and, in my case, as it happens, a painful process, to discard a belief in Christianity; and when I did so, I did not feel it was honest to continue to call myself a Christian, to attend churches which addressed Jesus as if he was alive, to recite creeds which acknowledged Jesus as Lord and Judge of the world. I knew that many of my fellow Christians shared my doubts and have continued somehow or other to reconcile the practice of Christian faith with knowledge that it is founded on a fundamental untruth; but I could not do this."[42]

The book *Father and Son* is a powerful memoir by the poet, Edmund Gosse, who had the misfortune to be the son of a priest of the Plymouth Brethren. According to Gosse his

---

[42] *Jesus*, page xvi.

father hated and suspected anything pleasurable and ascribed all misfortunes to God's punishment of sin. This is the brilliant confidence trick underlying most religions: everything good that happens is thanks to the divine entity at their centre and everything bad is a result of the sins or failings of the believers. So a poor young wife, who broke her leg, was told that this was punishment for the 'sin' of loving her husband too much. The son, Edmund, struggles to believe and follow his father's loathsome credo till as a teenager he feels ready to call Jesus. When Jesus does not come he is shocked and in his "heart the artificial edifice of extravagant faith began to totter and crumble." In the Epilogue, Edmund finally concludes, "Let me speak plainly. After my long experience, after my patience and forbearance, I have surely the right to protest against the untruth (would that I could apply to it any other word!) that evangelical religion, or any religion in a violent form, is a wholesome or valuable or desirable adjunct to human life. It divides heart from heart. It sets up a vain, chimerical ideal, in the barren pursuit of which all the tender, indulgent affections, all the genial play of life, all the exquisite pleasures and soft resignations of the body, all that enlarges and calms the soul are exchanged for what is harsh and void and negative. It encourages a stern and ignorant spirit of condemnation; it throws altogether out of gear the healthy movement of the conscience; it invents virtues which are sterile and cruel; it invents sins which are no sins at all, but which darken the heaven of innocent joy with futile clouds of remorse. There is something horrible, if we will bring ourselves to face it, in the fanaticism that can do nothing with this pathetic and fugitive existence of ours but treat it as if it were the uncomfortable ante-chamber to a palace which no one has explored and the plan of which we know absolutely nothing." The book concludes happily with Edmund seizing "a human being's privilege to fashion his inner life for himself."

Leo Tolstoy (1828-1910) was determined to discover the meaning of life. At first he attempted to do this by piously following the Orthodox Faith. This way proved impossible: "It was then so necessary for me to believe in order to live, that I unconsciously concealed from myself the contradictions and obscurities of theology. But this reading of meaning into the [sacred] rights had its limits. Quite two thirds of all services either remained incomprehensible, or, when I forced an explanation into them, made me feel that I was lying, thereby quite destroying my relation to God and depriving me of all possibility of belief."[43] He was perplexed by the vicious conflict between religions and "horrified" by the violence

---

[43] *A Confession*, chapter: "Obstacles to Truth."

done in the name of Christianity. Eventually, he renounced Orthodoxy and found his own God of love and life.

Jumping forward to the present day, super-cool Google executive, Mo Gawdat, writes, "I was born a Muslim. As in most religions, Muslim scholars have focused for centuries on mechanical practices: do *this* and don't do *that*. They've ignored the core of Islam's spirituality, and they have even openly discouraged people from seeking their own answers. At sixteen, I rebelled and decided to revisit the hypothesis. I declared (if only to myself) that I was agnostic, and I went on a quest to seek my answer."[44]

When we are young our parents make the decisions about our lives. When we grow older our parents try to guide us. When we are adults we must think for ourselves and it would be quite unhealthy for us to be controlled by relatives however well meaning. It is the same with religion. There comes a time when we should think for ourselves, rather than finding comfort in received certainties. If a person has truly thought for himself and decided that he/she can consciously derive benefit from any religion I should have no quarrel with such a choice. However, we should all follow Gosse, Wilson, Meades, Tolstoy and Gawdat by thinking for ourselves so that

---

[44] *Solve for Happy*, pp 303-304.

we can fashion our inner lives for ourselves according to our own consciences. Our consciences may be informed by religion, or other spiritual and philosophical opinion, but we should never delegate to others the ultimate control of our spiritual lives.

Chapter Five

Religions and Tolerance

Religion, we are told, rests on faith. The Oxford Dictionary defines 'faith' as: "reliance or trust *in*; belief founded on authority ... belief in religious doctrines, esp. such as affects character and conduct, spiritual apprehension of divine truth apart from proof; ..." To believe in anything, let alone something so profoundly controlling as a religion, with absolutely no proof does seem slightly misguided. "Do not ask questions; just believe," is how the arch critic of Christianity, Celsus, summed up faith in 170 AD.[1] Martin Luther[2] famously declared, "Reason is a whore, the greatest enemy that faith has; it never comes to the aid of spiritual things, but more frequently than not struggles against the divine Word, treating

---

[1] Celsus' anti-Christian book was effectively eradicated by Christianity, but his views are reported in Origen's *Contra Celsum*.

[2] 1483-1546. Luther was, according to his biography, misogynist, anti-Semitic and egotistical, but one truth he reintroduced was that we may each have a direct relationship with God.

with contempt all that emanates from God." Apart from the 'whore' bit, this is self-evidently true, so why do people favour blind unevidenced faith, when they have reason, instinct and the evidence of their own senses? Questions born of reason cannot disprove God, but they can establish what God is not. Questioning can, as Luther feared, reveal absurdities in religion. Moses Mendelssohn[3] devoted his life to proving religion should be rational and not revelatory. The way forward is by rational consideration of evidence and not by accepting with unquestioning faith the second hand revelation of some ancient mystic.

If faith is based on the beliefs of others then it is a house built on sand. If the basis of faith is the Bible, or other ancient scripture, then it is a house also built on a massive fault-line. The flimsiness of faith without proof may in part account for the venomous way in which the faithful react to anything perceived as a challenge to their beliefs. Have you noticed that people react most violently when they are deceiving themselves or others? So I have come across cases of a taxi driver, who reacted violently when accused of taking an

---

[3] 1729-1786, German Jewish philosopher, whose philosophical mistrust of religion led to a generally held but false belief that he was an atheist. Towards the end of his life he wrote extensively about the nature of the soul; please see for instance *Phaedon*.

unnecessarily long route and a dentist, who went berserk, when asked if the treatment he recommended was really necessary. The taxi driver was indeed trying to cheat his passengers by taking a longer route and the dentist was carrying on the scam of recommending unnecessary treatment. If they had been honest they might still have been annoyed, but they would have answered rationally along the lines of, "There are road works in the high street", or "Why not get a second opinion?" When faith is challenged, the faithful tend to react by threatening the challenger with death, eternal damnation, or both.

The Old Testament God clearly lacked confidence. He dedicated his first four Commandments to the preservation of his own dignity. His reaction to the worship of the Golden Calf was to demand yet more genocide. For two thousand years Christianity has reflected this insecurity by the persecution of dissenters through the refined cruelty of the Crusades, the Inquisition, and numerous other massacres, as well as by more subtle means. Despite or because of religious violence, historically protection of religious sensitivity has been written into law.

In Britain as recently as 1697 a young student, James Aikenhead, was hanged for blasphemy. He was optimistic enough to believe that we all have an "insatiable inclination to truth and to seek for it as for hid treasure." Having a strong desire to strengthen his own faith he zealously studied the Bible, but to his increasing distress found it to be unconvincing. He unwisely communicated this opinion to his fellow students. For expressing his doubts he was arrested and tried. His indictment stipulated:

"That ... the prisoner had repeatedly maintained, in conversation, that theology was a rhapsody of ill-invented nonsense, patched up partly of the moral doctrines of philosophers, and partly of poetical fictions and extravagant chimeras: That he ridiculed the holy scriptures, calling the Old Testament Ezra's fables, in profane allusion to Esop's Fables; That he railed on Christ, saying, he had learned magick in Egypt, which enabled him to perform those pranks which were called miracles. ... That the Holy Scriptures were stuffed with such madness, nonsense, and contradictions, that he admired the stupidity of the world in being so long deluded by them: That he rejected the mystery of the Trinity as unworthy of refutation; and scoffed at the incarnation of Christ."

Sentencing Aikenhead to die for questioning a religion supposedly based on love, forgiveness and peace, the presiding judge with no perception of irony declared, "It is manifest that you are guilty of horrid blasphemy: railing against and cursing our saviour, Jesus Christ, and impugning and denying the truth of the Holy Scriptures and quarrelling and arguing against the being of God and ought to be punished by death."

Although poor Aikenhead was the last person to be judicially killed for blasphemy in Britain, prosecutions and punishments continued. More recently, one such was John William Gott. Several times between 1911 and 1921, Gott, a socialist campaigner, was imprisoned for blasphemy. He died in 1921, his health having been damaged by prison conditions, including 'hard labour.' Rejecting the dying Gott's appeal, the Lord Chief Justice stated, "It does not require a person of strong religious feelings to be outraged by a description of Jesus Christ entering Jerusalem 'like a circus clown on the back of two donkeys.'" Religious sensitivity was still so strong in 1964 that Peter Cook and Dudley Moore cancelled the release of *The Dead Sea Tapes*, because of fears that sketches mocking parts of the Bible would be prosecuted for blasphemy in the UK and USA.[4] As recently as 1977 the editor of *Gay News* was convicted of blasphemy in the UK and it was only

---

[4] It was quite mild stuff; e.g. 'How did Jesus like his clothes cut?' *Immaculate.*

in 2008 that the blasphemy laws were finally scrapped.

Religion still receives preferential treatment. In Britain the Queen, as head of state, is also head of the established Churches of England and Scotland. Historically people in Britain had to pay tithes to the Established Churches. Tithing meant payment of one tenth of all income and produce, usually to the Rector of their Parish, and it was a legal obligation, often harshly enforced. Although significantly changed in 1836, and pretty much abated in 1936, it was not till 1977 that the impact of tithes ended absolutely.[5]

The BBC, Britain's national public broadcaster, is obliged to provide large amounts of airtime for religious broadcasting. The BBC and the media generally take great pains not to offend religious groups. The BBC Editorial Guidelines make it almost impossible to criticize religion.[6]

We permit and even encourage religious schools. Catholic schools in Northern Ireland clearly perpetuate the

---

[5] For instance, the Tithe Act 1936 and the Finance Act 1977 (section 18)

[6] "12.3.1 Any content dealing with matters of religion and likely to cause offence to those with religious views and beliefs must be editorially justified as judged against generally accepted standards and must be referred to a senior editorial figure or, for independents, to the commissioning editor."

religious divide. In England, Church of England schools are commonplace and often a very popular choice. There is a legal obligation on all schools in Great Britain to ensure that pupils engage in "collective worship" daily in a distinct assembly.[7] There are Jewish and now Muslim schools, the latter being the subject of recent suspicion of promoting fundamentalism. Why does religion have any place in modern education? What is the reason for religions being given such extreme and preferential respect?

I heard a politician talking about embryo research. He commented on the main opposition coming from religions and went on to say "and, of course, we must very much respect their views." Why? Why are those sections of society, whose views are governed by ancient scripture rather than reason, especially to be singled out for respect? Socialists, communists, capitalists and fascists have no automatic entitlement to respect, or to supportive coverage on the BBC. Schools do not set aside time for daily appreciation of these political beliefs, nor could a school dedicated to a political belief system be established. This preferential treatment for religion extends to prisons. In Britain the state spends up to

[7] School Standards and Framework Act 1998, and previously the 1944 Education Act, where the law on compulsory collective worship began.

forty thousand pounds per annum per priest, funding prison chaplains of all faiths to minister to imprisoned religionists. In 2016, a government report was leaked suggesting that Muslim chaplains are routinely distributing 'hate literature'.[8] It found that of the two hundred full-time Muslim chaplains seventy per cent were of the Deobandi sect, which is highly conservative and anti-British.

In the USA, religious movements enjoy freedom from tax. Although, in America the Supreme Court[9] by reason of the constitutional right to free speech effectively put an end to blasphemy, it should be noted that the First Amendment right to freedom of religion itself severely curtails criticism of religion and challenges to religious absurdities and abuses. So in Nixon v. Northern Local School District of Education[10] the mother of young James Nixon (aged 12) bought a T-shirt at a church camp for her son. This T-shirt carried the following

---

[8] Six months later the government got round to confiscating this literature from Muslim prisoners and violently anti-Western, anti-Jewish, homophobic and misogynistic books were found, including the notorious jihadist *Milestones*. The imams, who had distributed this loathsome literature, allegedly claimed to have been too busy to know its content.

[9] Joseph Burstyn Inc v. Wilson 343 U.S. 495 (1952)

[10] 383 F.Supp.2d 965 (2005).

messages of Christian love:

INTOLERANT

Jesus said ... I am the way,
the truth and the life.
John 14

And on the back:

Homosexuality is a sin!
Islam is a lie!
Abortion is murder!
Some issues are just black and white!

The youth wore his T-shirt to school and the School Board was found to have infringed his First Amendment religious rights by directing him not to wear it. The now not-so-young Nixon would probably have been enraged when in 2016, under the same constitutional principle that he had invoked, two Muslim convicts were given settlements of forty-eight and a half thousand and thirty-two and a half thousand dollars respectively for being obliged to attend Baptist services at their prison in Cleveland, Ohio.

163

Religious intolerance and violence are often woven into the fabric of nation states. This religious oppression flatly contradicts the suggestion that religious excesses should be glossed over as exceptional acts by "defiantly unorthodox fundamentalists."

Pakistan has severe and obscurely generalized laws against anti-Islamic blasphemy and injury to the Qur'an and so young Nixon should take care not to visit Pakistan wearing his T-shirt. The punishment for these transgressions is death and those accused often suffer death by mob violence before there can be any judicial process. In June, 2017, a court in Pakistan made history by being the first tribunal ever to sentence somebody to death after using Facebook, when a young man called Shafiq Qureshi was found to have insulted the Prophet. However, Qureshi was marginally more fortunate that a student in the northern city of Mardan; Chaudry Nisar was dragged from his room and beaten to death by a mob incensed by false rumours that he had posted blasphemous material online. An accusation of blasphemy can be falsified to benefit the accuser. Infamously, in 2015 an Afghan woman, Farkhunda, was murdered by a mob after being falsely accused of burning the Qur'an by a Muslim cleric, whom she had bravely challenged for un-Islamically peddling charms. In Pakistan, it is usually non-Muslims who are accused of blasphemy. In the earlier history of Christianity such mob killings were also commonplace. Persons suspected of dissent or blasphemy, were often tortured, mutilated, or killed by Christian gangs acting with impunity. Acid-throwing, which is now again in vogue, became popular amongst violently pious Christians in the first millennium. Perhaps the most notorious example of a Christian mob killing is the murder of the great Alexandrian mathematician, Hypatia, in 415 AD. She was a pagan, who made the mistake of championing tolerance and peace. Perhaps, equally provocative to the mob was the fact that she was a woman of exceptional intelligence, learning and personality. She was snatched from her chariot, taken to a church and there stripped, blinded, tortured and killed. The leader of this Christian gang, Peter, was praised as a "perfect believer in Jesus." At least in modern Pakistan some more enlightened citizens are conscious of the abuse and impropriety in the use of blasphemy laws. One such was the Punjab governor, Salman Taseer, who in 2011 was murdered by his own bodyguard for expressing his concerns about blasphemy killings. Fundamentalists declared that the criticism of the blasphemy law was itself blasphemy, as was Taseer's concern that a Christian woman had been falsely accused. In 2016 Taseer's murderer was buried amidst crowds throwing flowers and allegedly shouting, "He lives! Qadri lives! From your blood, the revolution will come!" These demonstrators showed a sad lack of free will and conscience, because it would seem that they, just like their Christian predecessors, had not paused to consider whether their God was so insecure that he would want to see savage murder of blasphemers, let alone the murder of those falsely accused. The desire to treat dissenters with violence is man's not God's.

The tragic partition of the Indian subcontinent and the million or more deaths immediately following resulted from this same religious insanity. Mass expulsions, abductions, rapes and further violence followed and the consequent religious tension and violence has never ceased. Today in India itself Hindu nationalism is becoming ever more dominant and extreme. In 2017 the ruling Hindu party, the BJP, appointed a radical Hindu cleric, Yogi Adityanath, to be chief minister of Uttar Pradesh, the most populous state of India. Adityanath is reported as having encouraged his supporters to kill Muslims and to have told a rally in 2014, "If one Hindu girl marries a Muslim man, then we will take 100 Muslim girls in return." Adityanath has created 'morality squads' of vigilantes, ostensibly for the laudable purpose of protecting women from sexual harassment. Other party officials have made it clear that Muslims are the true target of these new squads. There are many recent examples of Hindu vigilantes using extreme violence when it comes to persons of other religions allegedly eating beef and killing sacred cows.[11] In 2017 Gauri Lankesh, a leading journalist, secularist and critic of Hindu nationalism was gunned down on her doorstep. Coincidentally, with the rise of Hindu fundamentalism in India, the numbers of reported rapes and of discriminatory abortions of female foetuses are increasing. If the Hindu caste system, with Brahmins at the top descending through thousands of gradations to 'untouchables' at the bottom, really *is* divinely ordained, then so be it. However, if the caste system is, in reality, devised by man then it is surely an abomination.

In Saudi Arabia the sanctity of Islam is guarded day-to-day by a type of police force, called the Commission for the Promotion of Virtue and the Prevention of Vice. This body, commonly known as *mutawa*, has long had a terrifying reputation based on arbitrary beatings and deaths. In 2002 the *mutawa* reportedly compelled fifteen schoolgirls to be burned to death, because they were not wearing correct Islamic dress

---

[11] Hindus regard all cows as sacred and in consequence cow urine is, in some places, officially accorded the all-round efficacy once claimed by snake oil salesmen: "10 to 20 ml a day will prevent fever, coughs and stomach related ailments", claims the superintendant of Ayurveda College and Hospital.

and it would have been a religious affront for them to flee the burning building improperly clad. In 2016 the *mutawa* again came to international prominence, when caught on video chasing and beating a young woman for allegedly having her face insufficiently covered. The Saudi Government, in response to the stark facts of the video and international reaction to it, announced that the *mutawa* would in future be made subordinate to the police. Of particular note here is that many Muslims expressed horror not at the savage beating of a young woman, but at the fact that during the beating her lower leg was momentarily exposed to the camera.

In Iran there are also savage anti-blasphemy laws and many alleged blasphemers either are sentenced to death or die in prison in suspicious circumstances – e.g. Iranian blogger Omid Mirsayafi. Here, the religious police are equally feared. In 2008 a young woman, Zahra Bani Yaghoub, was sitting on a park bench chatting to her fiancé when they were both arrested by the religious police. The fiancé was later released, but Ms Bani Yaghoub's dead body was delivered to her family two days later with no further questions asked. Ayatollah Yousef Tabatabai-Nejad has advocated whipping women for not being properly dressed. He has been accused of inciting acid attacks. He blamed the 2016 drought in Iraq on women not complying with Islamic dress code. When considering the

Facebook protest, where female Muslims pose without headscarves, his response was reportedly, "We'll find them. Strangle them."[12] At the beginning of 2018 Vida Movahed removed her veil while saying, "Many women in Iran consider the mandatory veil as continuous humiliation and a way of controlling their lives." This mother of a toddler 'disappeared' shortly afterwards.

The way in which ancient religious rules can turn humanity inside out is sadly clear in the United Arab Emirates, where rape victims unwise enough to complain to the police are routinely arrested and tried, because, on their own admission, they have had sex outside marriage. What a distorted mindset religion can produce.

In Bangladesh murder of both secular people and those of other religions is commonplace. Even more draconian laws on blasphemy may soon be introduced.

Turkey, which was founded as a modern religiously tolerant and essentially secular state by Mustafa Kemal Ataturk, is now lurching towards extreme Islam. The ban on headscarves in state high schools has been removed. President Recep Tayyip Erdoğan, who quotes the Qur'an extensively in his speeches, has severely restricted free speech and dissenting

---

[12] *The Times*, 14th June, 2016.

media. Religion and authoritarianism go together like smoking and cancer. Erdoğan told a women's group in Istanbul that "You cannot put women and men on an equal footing. It is against nature." In May 2016, he stated that "a woman is above all else a mother" and continued, "We will multiply our descendants. They talk about population planning, birth control. No Muslim family can have such an approach. Nobody can interfere in God's work. The first duty here belongs to mothers." In Turkey violence against women, including domestic murder, has risen steeply in parallel with this upsurge of fundamentalism.

In Egypt there is widespread religious intolerance. When President Morsi was overthrown in 2013, forty-seven Christian churches were set on fire. In the next three years over four hundred sectarian incidents were recorded, including kidnapping of Christians for ransom. In May 2016, suspicion spread that a young Coptic man had fallen in love with a young Muslim woman. This was not celebrated as a coming together of religions through love. The reaction of the devout was, of course, to form an armed group to loot and burn Coptic homes, with the police remaining inactive. The mother of the man alleged to be involved was stripped and paraded around her home town and injured. These performances of 'religious duty' brought earthly gains through ransoms, loot and probably a sexual frisson.

There are even religious enforcers in the west. The Ahmadiyya community are Muslims, who believe that there was a second and more recent Prophet. As such they are looked on as heretics by mainstream Islam. In the 1970s, the then dictator of Pakistan, Zia ul-Haq, criminalized this faith under pressure from Muslim hardliners. Many Ahmadis fled to Britain and these émigrés have been subjected to violence ranging from the 2010 demonstrations in London calling for death for all Ahmadis to, in 2016, the murder of an Ahmadi in Scotland, following which *The Independent* observed, "People who demand respect for their beliefs but can't afford tolerance to others don't deserve either." In the 11th century the Islamic world was quite tolerant of free thinking and dissenters. Even philosophers, who warned of the dangers of mass religion, were tolerated. Now Islamic extremists wish to purge Islam of all changes and to move their religion back to what they perceive it to have been shortly after its creation. In Berlin, the liberal Ibn Rushd Goethe Mosque was founded in June, 2017. This mosque, which emphasises sexual equality, welcomes believers of all Islamic sects, Islamic homosexuals and even non-believers. As a result of the violent reaction to this haven of tolerance, one of the founders, Seyran Ates, had to be given constant police protection.

Apart from extremism and punitive laws protecting religion, we are conventionally obliged to show extraordinary deference to religionists' beliefs and sensitivities. Following publication of *The Satanic Verses* – Rushdie was not describing the Qur'an as Satanic, but merely referring to those verses which mainstream Muslim theologians themselves refer to as 'Satanic' – Ayatolla Khomeini issued his famous *fatwa* calling on all Muslims to 'kill the author Salman Rushdie.' As a result of this brutal proclamation against a writer in a distant country, Mr Rushdie and his wife had to go into police protection in Britain and much violence followed, including murders and attempted murders of those involved in the book; the Japanese translator was stabbed to death, the Italian translator barely survived being stabbed and the Norwegian publisher was shot. The main reaction of other religionists was not to denounce the barbaric incitement of violence and murder, but to denounce the affront to religious sensitivity. Christopher Hitchens, in *God is Not Great* wrote:

"One might have thought that such arrogant state-sponsored homicide, directed at a lonely peaceful individual who pursued a life devoted to language, would have called forth a general condemnation. But such was not the case. In considered terms, the Vatican, the Archbishop of Canterbury and the Chief Sephardic Rabbi of Israel all took a stand in sympathy with – the Ayatollah. So did the Cardinal Archbishop of New York and many lesser religious figures. While they usually managed a few words in which to deplore the resort to violence, all these men stated that the main problem raised by the publication of *The Satanic Verses* was not murder by mercenaries, but blasphemy."

So, in the aftermath of the 2015 slaughter at the *Charlie Hebdo* office in Paris, there were many religionists who argued that the satirical magazine had taken 'offensiveness too far' by printing a cartoon of the Prophet on its front page. Mr Robert Wishart responded to this loss of perspective by writing to *The Times*, "Of course it is meant to ridicule. That is a valuable service and requires no apology. ... I fail to see why those who profess belief in the supernatural should be excluded. Many find the concept of god(s) ridiculous and therefore fair game. If 'believers' were to quietly practise their religions without foisting them on the wider public, or demanding unearned respect for their notions, the offence defence would have some merit. And the world would be a gentler place."

If you are, for instance, a socialist, you have a strong belief system. Quite rightly, there is no restriction on the

vigour of the verbal attacks and insults which may be made –
and, in the British media, are often made – on socialism and
specific socialists. No anti-socialist material, however
offensive, would ever be considered sufficient to justify
murdering the staff of a satirical magazine, or even attacking
the offices of the *Daily Mail*. If disgruntled socialists were to
attack the editor, nobody would think it right to justify the
violence by censuring the newspaper for its depiction of
socialism. However, we are obliged by traditional societal
pressure and often by the law to show incredible deference to
religions and their devotees. Religion has done great harm to
people throughout the ages and the basis for religious belief is
often hazy if not crazy and yet religionists react
disproportionately to criticism while at the same time
demanding a tender tolerance for themselves; a tolerance,
which historically they have so conspicuously failed to offer to
others. "No idea is sacred. Nothing should be sacred.
Everything should be open to question and ridicule and
scepticism."[13]

In 2004 the Birmingham Repertory Theatre put on a
play called *Behzti* [Dishonour]. It depicted sexual abuse in a

---

[13] Lawrence Krauss, leading atheist and cosmologist, *The Life
Scientific*, BBC Radio 4, 31.5.16.

Sikh Temple. Sikhs reacted with violence and, amongst other acts, smashed in the front of the theatre during a demonstration. Sadly, in a land giving lip-service to free speech, the play was taken off by reason of the violence and threats. Mohan Singh, representing an organisation of Sikh temples, was quoted as saying, "Free speech can go so far. Maybe 5,000 people would have seen this play over the run. Are you going to upset 600,000 Sikhs in Britain and maybe 20 million outside the UK for that? ... Religion is a very sensitive issue and you should be extremely careful."[14] In other words, free speech is subordinate to religious sensitivity and violence. According to believers, some things are just too sacred to be questioned. What ever happened to 'When in Rome, do as the

---

[14] *The Guardian*, 20th December, 2004.

Romans do'?[15] Sadly we do need to take these threats seriously and to 'be extremely careful' when it comes to offending religionists, both because they can be violently intolerant and because that intolerance is itself too often tolerated. Is this sad reality a reason for greater deference, or is it another compelling reason to question the "delusions and animosities of our ignorant ancestors"?[16] Religion can be so potent that adherents believe that they may, or even must, violently challenge objectionable aspects of a host nation.

Driven by insecurity, **Christians were most anxious for the imprimatur of Albert Einstein (1879-1955) for a Biblical God, but, despite some efforts to distort his sayings, it is no**

---

[15] In July, 2016, a Muslim man, who had moved from Morocco to France, felt impelled by his religion to stab two girls and their mother in an Alpine holiday resort for wearing shorts and T-shirts in the garden of their holiday home. Apart from a religion that could allow any adherent to believe his God would actually *want* young girls murdered for wearing T-shirts, there is the point that a guest in a foreign country should feel entitled to impose his religious standards in such a brutal way. Later the same month a group of Muslim men visited a naturist beach at the German resort of Straband Xantener Südsee to abuse the female bathers, while reportedly informing them that they should be wiped out.

[16] Sam Harris, *Waking Up*, page 202.

more true that he expressed belief in an interventionist God of the Christian model than is the fiction that Darwin recanted Natural Selection on his deathbed and became a devout Christian. Why do religions feel it necessary to distort the truth?[17] In 2006, the Danish newspaper *Jyllands-Posten*

---

[17] Many examples of religious distortion can be found. For instance http://rationalwiki.org/ reviews alleged misquotes and its first example is from *The Watchtower*: Sir David Attenborough is quoted as saying, "Rich food sources are available at both polar regions, so one scientist raises the question: 'How did they ever discover that such sources existed so far apart?' Evolution has no answer." An astounding revelation from a famous naturalist, but according to the site he in fact said, "The energy spent by such migrants in their vast journeys is gigantic, but the advantages are clear. At each end of their routes they can tap a rich food supply that exists for only half the year. But how did they ever discover that such sources existed so far apart? The answer seems to be that their journeys were not always so long. It was the warming of the world at the end of the Ice Age eleven thousand years ago that began to stretch them. [...] So each year, birds were able to find food by flying farther and farther until their annual journeys involved travelling thousands of miles."

Why do religions cling to primitive creation myths?

bravely published twelve cartoons relating to Islam. The one depicting suicide bombers approaching Paradise and being turned back with the words, "Stop, stop, we are out of virgins," does seem quite funny and does not in any way mock the religion itself, but rather it derides the wickedness done in its name. The publication of these cartoons represented Western freedom of speech. Copies were then circulated by Muslim extremists, but with false claims that *Jyllands-Posten* was a state-controlled newspaper and the dishonest addition of three more unrelated cartoons/pictures better calculated to enrage the devout. Riots and deaths, including the burning of people alive, ensued in the name of religion. A year earlier, Muslims, especially in Africa, were inflamed by a cartoon by the great African cartoonist Gado – Godfrey Mwampembwa – which depicted a woman suicide bomber asking, "I'm also going to get the 72 virgins ... right?" Yet this cartoon did not infringe any religious rule, such a forbidden portrayal of the Prophet, but only contained two reasonable messages: Islam is in danger of being associated with violence and Muslim women are accorded fewer rights.

Presently circulating is the astounding *How Fossils Refute Darwinism* by Adnam Oktar (Harun Yahya), an Islamic Creationist, whose other works are said by the Internet to include, *Soykırım Yalanı* (*The Holocaust Deception* or *The Holocaust Lie*).

The sensitivity of religions probably reflects their awareness that they have built houses of cards. Preachers turn the Biblical text upside down in creating their own wishful version. Just after I had completed my first draft of this book, I was dining with a dear friend, who is a committed Christian. I tactfully skated over many of my more controversial views; "Tread softly because you tread on my dreams."[18] I did mention, however, that Christianity had clearly diverged from the apparent message of Jesus. With this idea in mind he kindly gave me a copy of *The Lost Message of Jesus*, which I have already quoted and which comes with the questionable endorsement of the Bishop of Durham for being "rooted in

---

[18] *The Cloths of Heaven*, W.B. Yeats.

good scholarship."[19] I began reading this book with an enthusiastic expectation that the author, Mr Steve Chalke, would highlight the way in which Jesus' message of love and forgiveness had not just been reversed in later Christianity. I thought that Mr Chalke might identify the problems presented by the Old Testament God and the malign influence of St Paul and other Christian theologians. My hopes rose as I read his acknowledgement that the Old Testament God was a "tribal God," but my confidence in his Biblical reading plummeted

---

[19] This endorsement is questionable. For instance, at page 71 Mr Chalke asserts that the Roman Emperor Augustus "had single-handedly turned what had become a rocky republic into the greatest and most famous empire of them all." Augustus' uncle, Julius Caesar, effectively destroyed the Republic and then assisted Augustus by naming him his heir. Thereafter Augustus was aided by many of Caesar's former supporters, also for a crucial time by Cicero, then by an alliance with Anthony and Lepidus against the assassins who wanted to restore the Republic, by his great general, Agrippa, in defeating Anthony and Cleopatra and, above all, by his wife, Livia. Likewise, at page 67 Mr Chalke writes, "So from the seeds of Augustine's thinking, the doctrine of original sin was born." St Augustine did indeed popularize this abominable doctrine, but St Paul's theology touched upon original sin and the earliest known historical claimant to the fully formed idea was Irenaeus, Bishop of Lugdunum – now Lyon – (130-202 AD).

when he claimed that Jesus made it "abundantly clear" that "his version of the Kingdom was that it wasn't just for Israel but for the whole world."[20] Even in the Gospels, which by the time a form of Bible had come into being, had been embroidered to reflect:

• St Paul's sales pitch to Gentiles;

• the view that Jews should be persecuted for 'killing Jesus,' while skating over the fact that Jesus was a Jew;

• the reality, especially after Constantine's 'conversion', that it was diplomatic to keep on the right side of the Romans.

It is still expressly stated by Jesus that he is exclusively addressing his fellow Jews. That Jesus was addressing the Children of Israel is equally clear in the Qur'an.[21] Mr Chalke relies on the parable of the Good Samaritan to support his astonishing claim but, of course, the audience for this parable was not Gentile, but Jewish. A Samaritan was chosen as the hero and contrasted with the Priest and the Levite for the purpose of emphasising what was to be expected from a Jew,

---

[20] *The Lost Message of Jesus*, page 28.

[21] Please see, for instance, The Table 75.

if even a despised Samaritan with his five Gods[22] could act so well. Sadly Mr Chalke then turns to the Old Testament and things go from bad to worse. He refers to a Gary Larson cartoon depicting God with a video game and a button labelled 'smite' and concludes that in "the popular mind" God is "a sadistic monster, a powerful and spiteful punisher of people who are having a tough time on earth as it is."[23] No sensible person could think otherwise about the Old Testament God if they have truly read the Old Testament, but Mr Chalke disagrees. He seems to have read a different version of the Old Testament, because, after suggesting that "God's involvement in vengeance, violence and excessive acts of war" were somehow explained and excused by "his determination to be involved with the world," he then goes on to assert that, "From the very beginning, Yahweh's dealings with Israel were motivated by his desire to demonstrate his love." The only direct quote by God himself about love I can find is the passage in *Hosea* 11:1: "When Israel was a child, then I loved him ..." Some modern versions of the Bible have changed

---

[22] The conversation between Jesus and the Samaritan woman at the well in *John* is clearly allegorical with the five 'husbands' being the five gods.

[23] *The Lost Message of Jesus*, page 47.

"great kindness" to "love" in Joel.[24] There are, however, many examples of an unloving brutality and God's primary aim is expressly identified as being 'fear' and *not* love.[25] Mr Chalke is remorseless in his extraordinary claim about love in the Old Testament: e.g. "The Bible never defines God as anger, power or judgement – in fact it never defines him as anything other than love."[26] With his 'good scholarship' I should have liked him to cite some evidence for this wishful claim. Again he is wrong, because the Bible purports to quote God's own definition of himself: "for thou shalt worship no other god[27];

---

[24] *Joel* 2:13 and likewise 'love' now appears in place of 'kindness' in *Isaiah* 54:10. The earlier translation is to be preferred to the later self-serving one, because the word in question is well established to mean 'loyal and supportive.'

[25] Please see Chapter 3 and, for example, "but I will put my fear in their hearts" *Jeremiah* 32:40.

[26] *The Lost Message of Jesus*, page 63.

[27] It is extraordinary that the Old Testament recognizes the existence of other gods; please see for instance *Exodus* 18:11, "Now I know that the Lord is greater than all gods." Solomon worships "other gods" (*I Kings* 11:7-11). Of the many other gods in the polytheistic Old Testament to name just a few: Anamellech (*II Kings* 17:31); Ashtoreth (*I Kings* 11:5); Baal (*I Kings* 18:19); Bel (*Isaiah* 46:1); Molech (*I Kings* 11:7); and Tammuz (*Ezekiel* 8:14).

for the Lord, whose name is Jealous, is a jealous God."[28] Other evangelists with less fertile imaginations try to sidle round God's brutal behaviour in the Old Testament by trying to claim that God was only reacting so violently because of his great love, but this is a deluded refusal to face the actual contents of their own service manual. 'The things that you're liable to read *about* the Bible ain't necessarily so.' Mr Chalke then cautions us that, "We should never speak of any other attribute of God outside of the context of his love. To do so is to risk terrible misrepresentation of his character, which in turn leads to a distortion of the gospel."[29] I am sorry, Mr Chalke, but your claims about the Old Testament God are so breathtakingly contrary to the text that it is not surprising that Christianity is so sensitive to challenge. Your warning that we must never mention the reality of the OT (maybe *OTT*) God's unattractive character is reminiscent of dictatorships, where the leader must only be praised.

Communist and totalitarian regimes do not encourage free thought and free spiritual development either. During the reign of Emperor Kangxi (1654-1722), the longest-reigning

---

Ēl was the supreme Canaanite God and it appears that Abraham received Ēl's blessing (*Genesis* 14:18-20).

[28] *Exodus* 34:14.

[29] *The Lost Message of Jesus*, page 63.

emperor in the history of China, Islam in China preached first and foremost that the position of the Emperor should be respected and thereby obtained state tolerance. One of the first things that Napoleon did after crushing the French Revolution and becoming dictator of France was to restore the Catholic Church. The Catholic Church struck a mutually beneficial deal with the Nazis in 1933 by the Reichskonkordat treaty. A 'Te Deum' was sung by direction of the Cardinal Archbishop of Munich following a failed assassination attempt on Hitler in November, 1939. Hitler, Franco and Mussolini all used the Catholic Church as a strong supporter and ally. President Putin is very close to the leader of the Russian Orthodox Church – worse luck for *Pussy Riot*. The Patriarch has declared that Russia's alleged stability since Putin took control is "A miracle of God". More recently, the US Attorney General cited Paul's declaration that all governments are ordained by God and should be obeyed to justify separating immigrant children from their parents.[30] The late Benazir Bhutto – Prime Minister of Pakistan 1988-1990 and 1993-1996 – observed that, "Every dictator uses religion as a prop to keep himself in

---

[30] *Romans* 13.1-2: "… the powers that be are ordained by God. Whoever therefore resisteth the power, resisteth the ordinance of God …"

power."[31]

Capitalism encourages people to maximise their production and consumption. Spiritual development has the potential to impair the efficiency of the system and religion has the potential to restrain spiritual enquiry and development. Belief in an all-powerful God can indeed be the 'opium of the people,'[32] because it encourages unthinking quiescence by:

• encouraging believers to leave everything to God

• discouraging individual action, because matters are in the hands of God

• disapproving individual action to change or challenge the status quo, because this is, in effect, to challenge the order of things as ordained by God:

"O let us love our occupations,
Bless the squire and his relations,
Live upon our daily rations,

---

[31] Interview on *60 Minutes* CBS-TV, 8th August, 1986.

[32] Marx's famous observation is not as hostile as generally appears: "Religion is the sigh of the oppressed creature, the heart of a heartless world, and the soul of soulless conditions. It is the opium of the people" (*A Contribution to the Critique of Hegel's Philosophy of Right* 1843)

And always know our proper stations."[33]

Generally the main promises made by religions cannot be proved false. This is due to the need to be dead before we can authoritatively complain of being misled. There are some indicators though. Despite assiduous religiosity and human sacrifice on a grand scale, the Mayan Empire collapsed about a thousand years ago due to overpopulation. During the Second World War, the Japanese city of Hiroshima was hardly bombed at all. This good fortune was confidently attributed by devout followers of Shinto to the city's proximity to the Gokoku Shrine, but sadly this faith was most emphatically refuted. On a smaller scale is the recent tragedy at the First Baptist Church, Sutherland Springs, Texas. Having begun by singing *Happiness is the Lord*, the congregation were about thirty minutes into their worship, when a crazed gunman entered and killed and injured over fifty of them. Such examples of the promises of religion being so dramatically refuted should cause doubt in the minds of the faithful, but, as they would say, it is not for us to question the ways of the Lord. If not us, then who is to question?

---

[33] Dickens, *The Chimes: Second Quarter* 1844.

What would we say about a conman, who began by promising investors a great profit, but, who, upon the failure of his scheme, declared, "Well, despite the fact that common sense suggested that the money would be lost, I truly had <u>faith</u> that the venture would make a fortune," or "I based my forecast on my interpretation of ancient documents, which I regard as sacred"? One of the main selling points of religion is the offer of salvation after death in exchange for devotion and financial commitment during life. Christianity suggests that God in "his infinite mercy" will forgive penitent sinners after death, but God's mercy for those suffering before death seems sadly limited. The promise offered by religion is much more important than a mere get-rich-quick puff from a financial conman and the commitment by the convert, going as it does to the essential fabric of life, is far more profound than risking mere money. It is difficult to see on what basis promises of heaven and salvation can be so confidently made by proselytizers of any religion. If, of course, the promises made by religions to the devout are given without sufficient evidential support then this is worse than a confidence trick. Nor is religion free of more obvious scams. The sale of pardons and indulgences – promises of a reduction of time to be spent in purgatory for a price – was commonplace in medieval times. Time off purgatory was offered to crusaders,

188

who were willing to join in the slaughter. In 1517 sale of indulgences became especially scandalous. Under the authority of his principal, Cardinal Albert of Brandenburg, Johann Tetzel was appointed by Pope Leo X to sell indulgences. This he did with great zeal and the proceeds defrayed the cost of reconstructing St Peter's Basilica and the price of Albert's cardinal's hat. It is widely accepted that Tetzel sold indulgences for sins yet to be committed; a priceless spiritual 'get out of jail free' card. Despite the angry reaction of Martin Luther to purchased forgiveness generally and to Tetzel in particular, indulgences have not ended completely. Even in 2013 the Vatican was reported as offering an indulgence to those following the Pope's Twitter account.[34] The report continued, "Indulgences these days are granted to those who carry out certain tasks – such as climbing the Sacred Steps, in Rome (reportedly brought from Pontius Pilate's house after Jesus scaled them before his crucifixion), a feat that earns believers seven years off purgatory. But attendance at events such as the Catholic World Youth Day, in Rio de Janeiro … can also win an indulgence."

Whilst indulgence after sin was approved by the Church, religions tend to view indulgence itself as a sin.

---

[34] *The Guardian*, 16th July, 2013.

Sexual indulgence is especially disapproved. This inclination still does practical harm as exemplified by the Catholic view of condoms. Condoms can reduce the hazards of sexual activity. There is nothing inherently immoral about condoms. Condoms help in slowing population growth, empowering women, reducing the numbers of starving children, preventing unwanted pregnancies, avoiding the tragedy of abortion[35] and limiting sexually transmitted diseases. Yet, at the beginning of 2017, the Pope forced the resignation of the Grand Master of the Knights of Malta, because of disputed allegations that this previously independent branch of Catholic Order had allowed its humanitarian and medical missions to distribute condoms.

In South Africa, where the spread of Aids/HIV would seem to cry out for condoms, serious concern has arisen about the boom in religious exploitation. As a result, the CRL Rights Commission was asked to report on "Commercialisation of Religion and Abuse of People's Belief Systems." In its Preliminary Report, the Commission reported on the way religion had become a 'commodity … to enrich a few." It cited cases of advertisements promising miraculous results to be got

---

[35] So strong is the abhorrence of abortion in Catholic countries such as El Salvador that sentences of between thirty and forty years are often imposed on the women concerned, including some victims of a miscarriage (of justice).

from joining various sects and high prices demanded and paid in exchange for miracles. Pastors were abusing their flocks by ordering them to eat grass, or drink petrol to drive out evil spirits. One 'overarching theme' was said to be: "**Deliberate exploitation of the poor and vulnerable people because of the commercialisation of religious practices, through assumption of divine/missionary right to directly or indirectly solicit and receive gifts/offerings/tithes in cash or in kind from their members (e.g. earnings, pension payouts, movable property, immovable property, etc.) without commitment to responsible financial management and accounting.**" Surely with most religions it was ever thus.

For the greater part of its history, the Christian Church ran a lucrative market in holy relics. Holy places waxed rich by claiming particularly amazing curative powers for an alleged portion of the anatomy of some saint; from prophet to profit. The importance placed on relics was as primitive as it was lucrative. Primitive though it is, this macabre practice has not ceased. There is still a vast repository of venerated religious relics and a powerful religious folklore of miracles, such as weeping statues.[36] In May, 2016, a bone allegedly from the elbow of St Thomas Becket – set in a gold and bejewelled reliquary – was brought from Hungary to be placed on the altar of Westminster Cathedral as the subject of a Mass to be celebrated by the Cardinal Archbishops of Westminster and Esztergom. In 2017 part of the brain of St John Bosco – canonized in 1934 – which was worshipped in a church in Castelnuovo, Italy, was stolen. In 1983 an even more important relic was taken from a church in Rome. It was the alleged foreskin of Jesus himself, which foreskin had been preserved by somebody exercising astounding foresight. If a remote tribe were to be discovered, which cut bits off corpses and venerated them as having great curative and spiritual importance, it is not difficult to imagine the pitying contempt with which they would be viewed.

Although no particular cures are being expressly promised in respect of Becket's elbow, big business is still done by Christianity at Lourdes. The pilgrims are probably wasting their time and money. Carl Sagan analysed the alleged recovery from cancer at Lourdes and found no reason to be

---

[36] The statue of Our Lady of Akita, Japan, which allegedly weeps blood, was declared as worthy of belief by the Holy Office in 1988

impressed: "The spontaneous remission rate of all cancers, lumped together, is estimated to be something between one in ten thousand and one in a hundred thousand. If no more than five per cent of those who come to Lourdes were there to treat their cancers, there should have been something between fifty and five hundred 'miraculous' cures of cancer alone. Since only three of the attested sixty-five cures [accepted by the RC Church as *miraculous* cures] are cancer, the rate of spontaneous remission at Lourdes seems to be lower than if the victims had just stayed at home."[37] It is difficult to believe that a commercial non-religious enterprise offering miraculous cures in this way could possibly escape prosecution.

If God fails to intervene to prevent great disasters, it is difficult to see the reason why God would intervene to cure an individual, who has merely approached or touched the bone of a saint. Yet the faithful tend to attribute anything good to the credit of their God. The obvious fact that, despite modest credits claimed for them, the Gods of religion do not seem satisfactorily to intervene to prevent great evil makes many religionists over-sensitive to criticism and teasing. The concept of a God in the form of a force, or spirit, which does not directly intervene in world events, overcomes two

---

[37] *The Demon-Haunted World*, page 221.

problems: first it avoids the primitive trap of creating a God in our own image and, secondly, it answers the question of why God does not intervene to prevent disasters, or to offer miraculous cures. A religion devoted to such a passive God, though, would not have proved such good business. On the plus side, belief in an essentially passive God, leaving individuals to follow their consciences, would not have inspired so much violence and intolerance.

Tolerance has rightly been seen as a key part of modern society since the Enlightenment. Tolerance and freedom of religion are held to be essential ingredients of this enlightened thinking. We seem to ignore the contradiction inherent in this tolerance of intolerance. To some extent, battle has now been joined by the modern materialists, but they are equally intolerant in their own way. Happily, though, their weapon of choice is scornful rationalist superiority and not driving trucks into innocent pedestrians.

In Britain there is some cause for hope. The *British Social Attitudes Survey* published in 2017 suggested that fifty-three per cent of British people have no religion. This follows the earlier National Census, which revealed that about half of people in the UK declared no religion, but did not identify themselves as atheists. These surveys demonstrate that most people perceive a spiritual component in life despite being unsatisfied by religion. The Anglican Bishop of Liverpool, who responded to the Survey, was reported to have responded to these results: "Saying no religion is not the same thing as a considered atheism. People's minds and hearts remain open." His first assertion is obviously true. It is to be hoped that his faith in open minds and hearts is equally justified. One group of people with minds arguably closed to the existence of a spiritual element in life are atheists. More scornful still are the materialists, who declare us to be automata with no consciousness, free will, or spirit. Materialism describes us to be deluded puppets pulled by strings of chemical reactions. Are materialists correct in this utterly depressing conclusion? If they are correct then how did they themselves find the consciousness, free will and spirit to reach, formulate and communicate these conclusions?

Chapter Six

Atheism is Glib and Dispiriting

Many religionists are closed minded and hostile when challenged. The same can be said of many atheists too. The only difference being that religious fundamentalists have favoured massacres, inquisitions and more recently terrorism, while atheists prefer to use intellectual scorn to brand those not sharing their disbelief as irrational and superstitious. The Enlightenment introduced a new 'scientific-rationalist' way of thinking, of which Richard Dawkins is a current devotee. Freedom of thought was a key part of the Enlightenment and yet it sneeringly denies freedom to think intuitively, to use instinctive perception, or even to consider the mystical.

Materialists are zealous followers of Darwin and his theory of evolution. Darwin's most effective supporter, biologist Thomas Henry Huxley PC PRS FLS (1825-1895) was known as 'Darwin's Bulldog'. His guiding rule should inform all thought: "Sit down before fact as a little child, be prepared to give up every preconceived notion, follow humbly wherever and to whatever abysses nature leads, or you shall learn nothing. I have only begun to learn content and peace of mind since I have resolved at all risks to do this."[1]

Both religionists and materialists are often too sure of their position to be able to follow Huxley's advice. Both extremes seem to suffer from cognitive dissonance; "Convictions are more dangerous to truth than lies."[2] Questions relating to the existence of God and the spiritual world should not and cannot be answered with absolute certainty. This point is well made by Professor Kwame Anthony Appiah, who, in his Reith Lecture declared, "I draw on a philosophical tradition, in which one of the central thoughts is recognition of human fallibility. And I think that one of the ways in which we are fallible is that we seek for certainty in places where it is not to be found and where the correct attitude is not one of disbelief, not of certainty in the opposite direction, but of relatively relaxed convictions, which we leave open for challenge and revision, if new

---

[1] *Life and Letters of Thomas Henry Huxley*, volume one.

[2] Friedrich Wilhelm Nietzsche (1844-1900) *Truth and Illusion* 483 and Fyodor Mikhailovich Dostoyevsky (1821-1881) *Notes from Underground*: "But man has such a predilection for systems and abstract deductions that he is ready to distort the truth intentionally, he is ready to deny the evidence of his senses in order to justify his logic."

ideas ... come in. There is a problem when people are so certain of things that in the nature of the case seem to be exactly the sort of things that ... you should not be certain about. ... Everybody in the world agrees that most people in the world have incorrect religious beliefs."[3]

This last idea is expressed more bluntly by fictional atheist, Jack Reacher, who, when he is condemned by a fundamentalist Christian for his non-belief, replies, "We're all atheists. You don't believe in Zeus or Thor or Neptune or Augustus Caesar or Mars or Venus or Sun Ra. You reject a thousand gods. Why should it bother you if someone else rejects a thousand and one?"[4] Human history holds thousands of examples of once-mighty gods, who have been forgotten.

One real-life atheist, who realized how religions in India perpetuated the caste system, discrimination, injustice and the subjugation of women, was the great Indian activist, Thantai Periyar – E. V. Ramasamy Naicker (1879-1973). He began public meetings of his Self-Respect movement with this mantra:

---

[3] *Mistaken Identities*, The Reith Lecture 2016.

[4] Lee Child, *Nothing to Lose*, page 426.

"There is no God;

There is no God;

There is no God at all;

He who invented God is a fool;

He who proselytizes God is a scoundrel;

He who worships God is primitive."

Once, the most influential atheist was Ernst Haeckel (1834-1919), who, in *The Riddle of the Universe*, deployed the latest science to pooh-pooh life after death, free will and the concept of a personal God. His crown has now passed to Richard Dawkins, who is 'almost certain' that there is no God. Being an atheist is intellectually a somewhat thankless position, because by definition atheists will after death have no opportunity to know that they were right, or to say, 'I told you so.' I do not say this so as to urge acceptance of Pascal's unattractive suggestion that you should believe in God as an insurance policy, so that if there is a God you are saved and if there is no God nothing has been lost. I suggest that any God worth bothering with would embrace Richard Dawkins, Christopher Hitchens and Thantai Periyar as essentially good people regardless of and even because of their spiritual scepticism. Religions contend that salvation depends on joining the right belief system, but surely a worthwhile God would be more impressed by those who follow their conscience and live good and loving lives? Most religions preach that belief is rewarded and disbelief punished. We can choose to obey a law. We can deliberately opt to drive within the speed limit, or to avoid stealing. 'Belief' is not a matter of choice. You cannot 'believe,' or have 'faith,' to order. 'Belief' and 'faith' are not conscious choices. Why then would the God of religions threaten such dire punishment for those who fail to believe, when faith is not something we can make ourselves have? It is, of course, possible to simulate faith, but an all-knowing God would surely not be fooled. It is unjust and morally illogical for religions to declare that our salvation depends not on our actions, but on matters outside our control. The purpose of spiritual enlightenment should be to empower ourselves and not to seek power over others.

If we have faith in anything at all it should be faith in our own ability to examine for ourselves the evidence of our senses. As noted above, the one certain thing about God is that there can be no certainty. The great Greek philosopher, Protagoras, contemporary of and disputer with Socrates, wrote one of the millions of now 'lost' pagan books called *On the Gods*. His opinion was, "As for the gods, I have no means of knowing whether they exist or not. Or what they are like in form. Many things prevent us from knowing about them, including the sheer difficulty of the subject and the brevity of human life." A plague in Athens was attributed to the atheistic inclinations of Protagoras and his fellow philosophers. In 1750 London suffered two noticeable earthquakes and these were blamed by Christians on the publication of the bawdy novel, *Tom Jones*. In 1984 lightning struck York Minster and caused serious damage by fire. This looks a bit like an own goal by God, but the lightning strike was attributed by some believers to the consecration two days earlier of a Bishop of Durham, who had questioned the truth of the virgin birth. For my part, while I generally mistrust certainty, I do most certainly reject a God who is an angry old man destroying towns and nations in the Old Testament, permitting the torment of poor Job for a bet with Satan and, in more modern times, sending tsunamis, earthquakes and lightning to signal displeasure.

Religious fanatics and atheists alike tend to be unthinkingly dismissive of anything inconsistent with their beliefs. In *Harry Potter*, which seven books seem better to capture the true nature of spirituality than many religious texts, the Dursley family are modern and materialistic. "They were," according to the opening of the first book, "the last people you'd expect to be involved in anything strange or mysterious, *because they just didn't hold with such nonsense [my italics].*"[5] Materialists highlight the nonsensical aspects of religion and, as part of the rejection of this 'nonsense,' they also reject God and the possibility of a spiritual element in life. To them religion, God and spirituality are all part of the same 'nonsense'. This rejection is too glib a reaction. "It is true, that a little philosophy inclineth man's mind to atheism ..."[6] When deriding religion it is a seductively neat reaction intellectually to assert that there is nothing beyond the material world, which is solely made up of varied collections of atoms, chemical reactions and selfish genes. The 'strange and mysterious' are to be derided and through derision quickly dismissed. Richard

---

[5] Members of most religions have attacked J. K. Rowling's *Harry Potter* series. Conservative Christians and Conservative Catholics have been particularly vociferous, which is strange considering that it is a morality tale showing good overcoming evil through love; e.g. the late Father Gabriele Amorth, the leading Catholic exorcist, was quoted as saying, "Behind Harry Potter hides the signature of the king of the darkness, the devil." (*The Sydney Morning Herald*, 1st September, 2006)

[6] Francis Bacon (1561-1626), *Essays, Civil and Moral*, XVI "Of Atheism". Deeper philosophy and consideration of the evidence in the form of 'the chain of causes', he suggested, leads to "Providence and Deity."

Dawkins boasts, "I decry supernaturalism in all its forms ..."[7] He quotes with high approval the observation of the Chicago geneticist Jerry Coyne: "To scientists like Dawkins and Wilson the real war is between rationalism and superstition."[8] In these passages can be perceived a Dursley-like unwillingness to consider even the possibility that there may be something undreamt of in materialist philosophy. Anything spiritual, or mystical, is contemptuously rejected as 'superstition'. Materialists can be just as blinkered and prejudiced as religionists and I object as much to them arrogantly arrogating to themselves an exclusive claim to 'rationalism' as I do to their labelling of all those as 'superstitious', who consider there is, *or may be*, some spiritual content in our existence.

"Emancipate yourselves from mental slavery None but ourselves can free our minds"[9]

---

[7] *The God Delusion*, page 57.

[8] *The God Delusion*, page 92.

[9] Bob Marley (1945-1981), *Redemption Song*.

Consciousness

Are you conscious? I suggest that you are and that you can think for yourself and exercise free will. You can, at this moment, decide whether to continue to read this book. You can think about, analyse and have your own original thoughts about the ideas being discussed. You can also sense your feelings in reaction to what you read; strong feelings of agreement and pleasure I hope. Descartes famously said, "I think therefore I am."[10] It is our consciousness which shows us that we are not merely brains mechanistically reacting to stimulation, but rather that we each have a distinct controlling mind.

One important commentator on the failure in modern scientific-rationalist thought is Dr Rupert Sheldrake.[11] He considers that modern science holds false core beliefs based in materialism – rejection of the spiritual – which are harming progress:

"Contemporary science is based on the claim that all

---

[10] René Descartes, "Je pense, donc je suis"/"Cogito ergo sum", *Discourse on Method* 1637.

[11] Author of *Science Set Free*, retitled in the UK *The Science Delusion* to signal a riposte to Dawkins.

reality is material or physical. There is no reality but material reality. Consciousness is a by-product of the physical activity of the brain. Matter is unconscious. Evolution is purposeless. God exists only as an idea in human minds, and hence in human heads. These beliefs are powerful not because most scientists think about them critically, but because they do not."[12]

These core beliefs, according to Dr Sheldrake, include unthinking acceptance of the materialist theory that living things are mechanical with brains like genetically programmed computers, that human consciousness is an illusion produced by brain activities and that "Unexplained phenomena like telepathy are illusory."

Dr Sheldrake knew the great Francis Crick, who created the genetic code. He recalls how Crick, a devout atheist, applied himself to proving that consciousness was explained by physics and chemistry. His greatest aim was to refute 'vitalism,' which is the theory that living things are truly alive, rather than being a mere set of reactions explicable by science. Crick failed in his endeavour and finally conceded that dualism, which is the concept that we are made of

---

[12] "Setting Science Free from Materialism," *Explore* 2013; 9:211.

mind/brain/body *and* soul/spirit, "might become plausible."[13] Dr Sheldrake himself appears to incline to the third way, namely panpsychism, which conceives that there is a degree of consciousness in all matter.[14] It is possible.

Daniel Dennett is presently the most famous proponent of the theory that we humans, far from having souls, are, as Dawkins puts it, "lumbering robots."[15] In his book, *Consciousness Explained*, Dennett attempts to refute the existence of consciousness and dualism. There is, of course, a fundamental contradiction between, on the one hand, a thinker formulating a theory and communicating it to others and, on the other hand, the presupposition that neither thinker nor reader has consciousness. This was well put by J. R. Searle:

---

[13] Dr Sheldrake, "Setting Science Free from Materialism," *Explore* 2013; 9:214.

[14] Please see for instance, Thomas Nagel's *Mind and Cosmos: Why the Materialist Neo-Darwinian Conception of Nature is Almost Certainly False*. The author, Philip Pullman, also appears to favour consciousness in matter.

[15] Cosmologist, Professor Stephen Hawking (1942-2018), took an equally bleak view, not surprisingly seeing death as a form of Black Hole: "There is no heaven or afterlife for broken-down computers; that is a fairy story for people afraid of the dark." I hope that he now has cause to be more optimistic.

"To put it as clearly as I can: in his book, *Consciousness Explained*, Dennett denies the existence of consciousness. He continues to use the word, but he means something different by it. For him, it refers only to third-person phenomena, not to the first-person conscious feelings and experiences we all have. For Dennett there is no difference between us humans and complex zombies who lack any inner feelings, because we are all just complex zombies. ... I regard his view as self-refuting because it denies the existence of the data which a theory of consciousness is supposed to explain ... Here is the paradox of this exchange: I am a conscious reviewer consciously answering the objections of an author who gives every indication of being consciously and puzzlingly angry. I do this for a readership that I assume is conscious. How then can I take seriously his claim that consciousness does not really exist?"[16]

This same point was made more shortly by Dr

---

[16] *'The Mystery of Consciousness': An Exchange*, John R. Searle, www.nybooks.com, 21st December, 1995. Please see also J. R. Searle's *The Mystery of Consciousness* (1997).

Sheldrake himself.[17] Dr Sheldrake finds the strongest argument against dualism to be the inability to explain how the immaterial mind interacts with the brain. Undoubtedly it would end the argument if the link between mind and brain could be fully proved and explained in scientific terms. However, I do not find it troubling that there is no present explanation for what self-evidently exists. In the past we could not explain the way sight functioned, but we could certainly see and were conscious of doing so. "To say that consciousness is an illusion", Dr Sheldrake notes, "does not explain consciousness – it presupposes it. Illusion is a mode of consciousness."[18] Science cannot yet adequately explain dark matter, but it knows that dark matter exists. You know that you exist as an entity governed by a conscious mind. Even neuroscientist Dr Sam Harris, who famously challenges the existence of both free will and God, concludes, "Consciousness is the one thing in this universe that cannot be

---

[17] "… Dennett himself, although putting forward arguments he hopes will be persuasive, he seems to make an exception for himself and for those who read his book." "Setting Science Free from Materialism", *Explore* 2013; 9:213.

[18] "Setting Science Free from Materialism", *Explore* 2013; 9:214.

an illusion."[19]

Sir Roger Penrose, leading mathematician and collaborator in the concept of 'The Big Bang', is particularly impressed by consciousness. He believes that "something is going on in human consciousness that is not to do with computation." He has formed an institute to study consciousness.[20] Can Richard Dawkins and other scientific materialists prove to you that you lack consciousness? What actual evidence do they produce? If they cannot prove their automaton theory then you can surely trust your own perception that you have a free mind separate from your chemical brain functions; "... no testimony can be admitted which is contrary to reason; *reason is founded on the evidence of our own senses [my italics]*."[21] You have a conscious mind and you are more than a materialist organism responding to random events in a scientifically predictable way. Your own

---

[19] *Waking Up*, page 54. He adds an amusing footnote: "The state of being completely confused about the nature of consciousness is itself a demonstration of consciousness." (pp. 213-4)

[20] Institute for the Study of Consciousness, Creativity and the Physics of the Universe, University of California San Diego.

[21] Percy Bysshe Shelley, *The Necessity of Atheism*, in argument against an interventionist God, but equally applicable to the intellectual scorn of materialists.

senses tell you this.[22] You are a free-spirited dualist.

Body and Soul (Dualism)

The issue of whether we have a soul, by which I mean a spiritual element infusing but divisible from our material bodily function, is really much more important than whether there is a God. The spirit is not just "a pilot" sitting inside the body using it as a vehicle, but is an integral part of every living thing.[23]

The proposition that all living things are merely bundles of atoms and selfish genes making a brief one time only appearance seems truly bleak. It may be that it is an unwillingness to face the truth of such an empty prospect that tempts us to think otherwise, but most of us do sense, not through faith, scripture, or fear of the alternative, but through a tangible something established within ourselves, that there is a spiritual element beyond moving from birth to death as a mere organism. Are we just deluded organisms with brains no more

---

[22] Spinoza:"We feel and know by experience that we are eternal"

[23] René Descartes, "I am not present in my body merely as a pilot is present in a ship, I am tightly bound to it, and as it were mixed up with it, so that I and it form a unit." (*Meditations on First Philosophy* (1642))

211

than "the manifestation of matter" – Dawkins – or are living things made of a body together with an infusing but distinct life force, conventionally called the 'spirit' or 'soul'.[24] The belief, so instinctively shared by so many of us, that we are both body and spirit is, according to Dawkins, a delusion caused by a misfiring of brain modules.[25] We have yet to receive any rational scientific evidence of this alleged misfiring. Nor is it rational to equate religions, which may be challenged intellectually and found wanting, with the basic instinct that we are body and spirit and not just a monist organism. It is asserted in *The God Delusion*, without evidence but with obvious intent to demean belief in the soul, that children have a natural tendency towards dualism. If that is so, and again this seems more like speculative prejudice than a rationally evidenced fact, this would not necessarily debunk dualist thinking, but instead could demonstrate that children are more spiritually aware, more open-minded, less corrupted by the beliefs of others, more in touch with the spiritual nature

---

[24] In Hinduism the individual soul ("the Ātman") must be fused with the world soul ("the Brahman") to achieve enlightenment. Some mystics differentiate 'spirit', 'soul' and 'astral body', or 'spirit', 'soul' and 'nerve aura', but I need not investigate here, because my point is that we are not just a material lump.

[25] *The God Delusion*, page 209.

212

of their recent entry into life, or yet to have their left brain trained almost to exclude the right. Dawkins quickly redoubles his abuse: "Dualists readily interpret mental illness as 'possession by devils' ... Dualists personify inanimate objects at the slightest opportunity, seeing spirits and demons even in waterfalls and clouds."

Socrates was a dualist and he was not inclined to such primitive views and, indeed, it might reasonably be asserted that Socrates has the more powerful claim than Dawkins to supremacy in 'rationalism.' He said, "What is it that, when present in a body, makes it living? – a soul."[26] He saw the soul as immortal. Other stars of classical rationalism, including Plato, Aristotle and Epicurus, all believed with some variation that life forms were animated by an immortal soul. For this reason it is quite probable that some mental illnesses are linked to spiritual distress, but as a dualist I have never mistaken mental illness for possession.[27] Debunking

---

[26] *Phaedo*, 105C. Plato himself came to his own view of soul and body when he later wrote *Philebus*.

[27] Clinical psychiatrist, Dr Wilson Van Dusen, who practised at Mendocino State Hospital, California, sets out accounts of patients appearing to be possessed by spirits in *The Presence of Other Worlds*. Please see also psychotherapist, Dr Adam Crabtree's book, *Multiple Man*.

established religions is easy. In logic, this debunking has absolutely nothing to do with the entirely distinct allegation that we are spiritless organisms with misfiring brains. It is a materialist trick to conflate the rational weaknesses in religions with the clearly separate question of whether we have a body and a divisible spirit/life energy/'immortal spark', which infuses and vitalizes our living bodies. Our inclination to think that we are body and soul, or matter and life-force, may be a result of misfiring brain modules, but it is odd that Natural Selection so beloved by materialists has not eliminated those with misfiring brains. Surely those with a belief that death is not the end will be marginally less fearful of death and so less efficient in maintaining their lives? Surely nature would not favour the predominance of those with an inbuilt mental fault? The presumption must surely be against misfiring and in favour of proper brain function until proved otherwise, because efficient function must be the default position for living things honed by Natural Selection. I contend that the reason why we incline to a dualist view of ourselves is simply because we are body made alive by a vital energy, which does not simply disappear with death. With the advantage of being ourselves and observing others born, living and dying, we are well placed to use our own senses to judge our composition and our judgement is probably true for that

214

reason alone. Identical twins can differ in their character. It seems very significant that cloned animals, which are, by definition, physically identical in the cellular structure of their bodies and brains, often demonstrate very different personalities both from the original and from each other, when their environment is also the same.[28] What is the factor causing this difference in materially identical creatures living in the same environment? It seems that the only answer can be that each has its own distinct spirit. There are other points of evidence for consideration, especially for a truly open-minded rationalist. This evidence is ridiculed and rejected as 'superstition' by those finding it contradictory to their preconceptions, but the rational point is that if just one of these many instances of the paranormal is true then materialist certainty that there is no spiritual element in life is untenable. There would, of course, still be a lively debate on just what that spiritual element is and what it means. 'Paranormal' is an adjective describing normal things, which are not yet understood.

Materialism contends that the material is all and that any spiritual element is a delusion. There is a striking symmetry, because for thousands of years many spiritual

---

[28] BBC Radio 4, *PM*, 26.7.16.

adepts have regarded the material world to be the illusion, or *Maya*.[29] 'Maya,' the Great Illusion, is said to make us lose memory of our souls. 'Maya' is above my spiritual pay grade, but there is clearly an important difference between materialism, which denies the existence of any spiritual element in life, and atheism, which is limited to disbelieving the existence of God. By no means all atheists are materialists. For instance, leading French atheist, André Comte-Sponville, advances a strong argument for the existence of the soul and for the crucial importance of a spiritual element in life. He concludes, "Not believing in God does not prevent me from having a spirit, nor does it exempt me from having to use it."[30]

Materialists draw close to science like people huddled round a campfire for fear of the great expanse of unknown darkness behind them. They scornfully dismiss memories of previous lives, out of body experiences, spiritualism and ghosts as mere illusory figments of that darkness. Like them, science is itself too prone to cling to its own delusions and

---

[29] Please see for instance H. P. Blavatsky, *The Secret Doctrine*, vol. 1, page 39.

[30] Please page 134 onwards of *The Book of Atheist Spirituality* for a philosophically based argument for existence of the soul. Also, the real evidence of transcendental experiences is reviewed. Please see chapter 10 of this book for further consideration of this.

false certainties. There are, according to Dr Sheldrake, ten false core beliefs undermining scientific progress.[31] In 1847 Dr. Ignaz Semmelweis, an obstetrician in Vienna, reached the astonishing conclusion that, by washing their hands, doctors could reduce infection amongst patients. By putting his idea into practice he radically reduced women's deaths from puerperal fever, but his observation was so contrary to the established medical faith that he and his findings were generally derided. Thousands of patients continued to die of unnecessary infection throughout the world until hand-washing became the norm well after Semmelweis's death in obscurity. A more modern instance of scientific cognitive dissonance occurred in the early 1980s when two Australian doctors, Dr J. Robin Warren and Dr Barry J. Marshall, discovered that stomach ulcers were caused by bacterial infection. This again was so opposed to existing scientific dogma – though not, it should be noted, in veterinary science – that they were persecuted and vilified for many years by their peers. It took a long time for truth to prevail against the implacable certainty of scientific prejudice till eventually in 2005 Warren and Marshall were rightly awarded the Nobel

---

[31] Please see above and "*Setting Science Free from Materialism*", *Explore* 2013; 9:211.

Prize. Not so fortunate was Jimmy Keller, who upset the medical establishment in the United States by daring successfully to treat, by unconventional means, cancer patients who had been discarded as beyond hope by providers of conventional treatment. He was obliged to move from the USA to Mexico and there he continued to embarrass the establishment by his continuing success. Rather than wondering at the success of his treatment, the authorities kidnapped him back to the States and imprisoned him.[32] At the centre of physics there is an impossible contradiction between the certainties of quantum theory, which well describes the behaviour of small things, and of the theory of general relativity, which deals well with big things. Even Einstein, who finally demolished the once absolute certainty of Newtonian physics, was seemingly capable of error. So, when it appeared that the universe was in a steady state he added a 'cosmological constant' to his famous equations. In 1931, when the previous scientific certainty of steady state was disproved by Hubble, Einstein declared that adding the constant had been "the biggest blunder of his life." Now with new evidence that the universe is not only expanding, but that the expansion is accelerating, there is again a need to add a

---

[32] *Forbidden Medicine* by Ellen Brown.

constant to the equations. In 2015 the mighty NASA, after using billions of dollars and the finest brains to investigate Mars, announced that it had "convincing and unambiguous" evidence of water on Mars. Two years later NASA conceded that its announcement did not hold water. As recently as the 1950s and 1960s, and right up to 1980, lobotomy – a barbaric character destroying procedure of cutting into the prefrontal lobe of the brain – was conventionally viewed as appropriate treatment for schizophrenia in the UK, the USA and several other countries. It is not just religionists who have faith in the ridiculous and cling like blind limpets to false beliefs. Many books could be filled with examples of conventional scientific faith being quite absurd and yet being bitterly defended by the faithful.

Science can easily be seen as providing the answer to 'life, the universe and everything.' It can assume too great an authority. "Formerly, when religion was strong and science weak, men mistook magic for medicine: now, when science is strong and religion is weak, men mistake medicine for magic."[33] So, unfortunately, in criminal trials juries tend to be too easily impressed by scientific evidence. The tension

---

[33] Thomas Szasz, *The Second Sin* (1973) "Science and Scientism."

between scientific rationalists, like Richard Dawkins, and spirituality is summed up by physicist, Dr Fritjof Capra:

"Science does not need mysticism and mysticism does not need science; but men and women need both. Mystical experience is necessary to understand the deepest nature of things, and science is essential for modern life. What we need, therefore, is not a synthesis but a dynamic interplay between mystic intuition and scientific analysis."[34]

There is a vast body of evidence relating to mystic experiences. Only a minute part of this evidence is considered here, but even this small sample suggests that it is absurd for materialists so irrationally to dismiss the spirit within us, while so confidently claiming a monopoly of rationality.

There is a great difference between a living body and a dead one. What Lucretius referred to as "the vital spirit" has departed. It is well established by science that energy is never lost, or destroyed, but rather it simply changes its form into another type of energy. So potential energy may become kinetic energy and movement can generate heat. With something as significant as our life force it is logical to assume

_____

[34] *The Tao of Physics*, page 339.

that it is or behaves like other energy. Our vital spirit does not simply end, or dissipate to nothingness, but rather it continues in some other form. If the life force is not energy, but rather is immaterial then again it may exist after the body has ceased to function.[35] Is the soul immortal, or does it, as many belief systems suggest, finally merge back with something greater,[36] or is it transmuted into some other form? Whatever the true answer, the important point is that the evidence tends to suggest that we are more than biological machines controlled by evolutionary programming, which terminate totally when switched off by death.

Only because it is apposite, but without any particular enthusiasm, I begin by making brief mention of Dr Duncan MacDougall's 1901 experiment on six dying people, which purportedly showed an average twenty-one gram loss of

---

[35] Dr Rupert Sheldrake, "Setting Science Free from Materialism", *Explore* 2013; 9:213: "If the human soul is immaterial, it may exist after bodily death."

[36] For instance Jainism, which according to the 24th prophet ("Conqueror"), Mahavira, requires rigorous self-denial and penance to be liberated from the infinite cycle of rebirth. According to the Jainish sect, the Digambaras, this liberation is only available to those reborn as men. Mandaeism believes the soul moves through various realms from the material world to the world of light.

weight upon dying. He was, however, unable to detect any weight loss in dying dogs. He concluded that the weight loss in humans was due to the departure of the soul and that dogs had no appreciable soul. Humans share about eighty-four per cent of their DNA with dogs and even more with chimpanzees and pigs. Our inflated self-view causes us to believe ourselves to be set apart from other animals, to create gods in our own image and to call ourselves *Homo sapiens*, when we are so very far from being wise. Animals have a far better spiritual awareness than we do.[37] It is not least by reason of the result for dogs that I am sceptical about Dr MacDougall's research.

In the 1980s I had the pleasure of meeting the late Dr Douglas Baker and attending two of his meetings. Dr Baker, who looked like Captain Mainwaring from *Dad's Army* and wore a fisherman's jersey rather than a flowing robe, talked in the most matter-of-fact way of his regular forays into the spirit world and of his first-hand knowledge of reincarnation and other occult matters. It was clear from his brusque and dismissive answers to questions from the audience that he had

---

[37] Dr Karl Novotny reportedly recounted his death through a medium and recalled that, while his friends were unaware of his spirit, his dog was "unable to decide to which me he should go, for he saw me in two places at once, standing up and lying down on the ground." (Robert Crookall, *What Happens When You Die*, page 63)

not the slightest interest in converting his listeners or any concern about what they thought about him. Was he insane and deluded, or was he a reliable informant? I thought him to be a reliable informant, despite the amazing nature of much he said and has written. Whether or not the spirit undergoes reincarnation, as stated so convincingly by Dr Baker, it does seem probable that the life force does not simply dissipate into nothingness, but transmutes. Atheists tend to elide God and continuation of life after death as one concept, or at least interdependent concepts. They declare that after death total oblivion follows. Logically after death there could be some continuation of life force without a God and *vice versa*. However, I consciously adopt the atheists' logical error in reverse and suggest that as there is some form of continued existence after death then this is linked with and points to the existence of the force, which I, for the want of a better term, call God.

Many of our greatest thinkers have shared this view of the soul without necessity of formal religion. Socrates was convinced that we are made of body and soul and that death is marked by the departure of the soul from the body.[38]

Likewise Ovid – P. Ovidius Naso, 43 BC to 18 AD –

---

[38] e.g. *Phaedo*, 69e – 84b

wrote:[39]

"All things are subject to change, but nothing dies. The disembodied spirit wanders at large, here and there, lodging in any body, from beast passing into man, from man to beast, never perishing."[40]

Cicero – M. Tullius Cicero 106 to 43 BC – believed in an 'immortal soul' and a 'soul not annihilated by death.'[41] More recently Carl Jung (1875-1961), psychiatrist and associate of Freud, was inclined to believe in the spirit. Sir Laurens van der Post in his book, *Jung and the Story of Our Time*, recollects that Jung conceded "... that there was occasional evidence of a continuation of individual reality after death that could be better explained by some hypothesis of spirits than by the qualities and peculiarities of the subconscious." I have to accept that Jung was not a pure dualist in that he believed that the choice was not between good and evil, nor between dualism and monism, but that

---

[39] Met. XV. 165.

[40] "Omnia mutantur: nihil interit. Errat, et illinc huc venit, hinc illuc, et quoslibet occupant artus spiritus eque feris humania in corpora transit, inque feras noster, nec tempore deperit ullo."

[41] e.g. *Senect* 22 and 23 and *Amicit* 3.

these opposites should merge to create a whole. However, Richard Dawkins should please note that all these great dualists reached adulthood and, with the possible exception of Jung, they most emphatically did not believe that there were demons in waterfalls.

Reincarnation

There is a vast body of evidence for reincarnation, or at least for the existence of a soul distinct from the body. For example, there are many recorded cases of young children remembering provable details of past lives. If you are interested, you can find abundant details on the Internet. So, for instance, 'collective-evolution.com' has a 2015 feature about a boy called Luke, who remembered being a black woman, who had jumped from a tall building in Chicago to escape a fire. It turned out that there had been such a woman and Luke was able to pick out a picture of her in a televised test. He knew other facts about her and shared some of her tastes for a limited time. He is reported as saying to his mother, "I died and I went up to heaven, I saw God and eventually God pushed me back down and when I woke up I was a baby and you called me Luke."

Richard Dawkins ridicules the idea that the 'personality'

survives death, but neither reported cases of remembered lives nor the Buddhist and Hindu concepts of reincarnation suggest that the 'personality' survives. Quite the reverse, reported cases show distinct personality changes and central to most concepts of reincarnation is the idea that the personality *must* change, for the very purpose of refining and developing the spirit with each life. Again Dawkins creates his own straw man to trample.[42]

In 2008, University of Virginia psychiatrist, Jim Tucker, published a review of cases suggestive of reincarnation in the Journal *Explore*.[43] One reported case involved a boy who claimed to have been his own grandfather and was able to recount details of his grandfather's life, which, of course, the family could verify. Another case related to a boy called Ryan, who remembered being a little known Hollywood extra and agent, called Marty Martyn. He remembered fifty-five

---

[42] In fairness it must be allowed that Dawkins may have been thinking of Frederick Myers' great work, *Human Personality and Its Survival of Bodily Death*, which dreadful title does no justice to the comprehensive work within the book itself. Colin Wilson wrote, "If anything survives death, it is this basic substratum of the personality." (*Afterlife*, page 275)

[43] Also a book called *Return to Life: Extraordinary Cases of Children Who Remember Past Lives*.

verifiable facts about Martyn, including Martyn's address and that he had had two sisters, a fact previously unknown even by Martyn's own daughter.

Despite dubious cases, such as the notorious story exposed in *The Search for Bridey Murphy*, there is an overwhelming body of evidence of recollection of previous lives. Dr Ian Stevenson's *Twenty Cases Suggestive of Reincarnation* is drawn from over two hundred investigated instances.[44] One case relates to Maria de Oliveiro in Brazil who, before dying, told her friend, Ida Lorenz, that she would return as her daughter. About ten months later Mrs Lorenz gave birth to a daughter, who, as soon as she could speak, described details of her previous life as Maria and recognized former acquaintances unprompted. Generally these memories fade as the subject becomes older. The review contains another case relating to a boy, who had seemingly died of smallpox in India. When he came back to life, he was very different. To the acute discomfiture of his family, who were of the Jatt caste, he claimed to be of the superior Brahmin caste and from a comparatively distant village – about twenty miles away – and declined on that account to eat home-cooked food. He displayed such detailed knowledge of his former relatives,

---

[44] *Proceedings of the American S. P. R.* (vol. 26).

the places known to them and their family history that his previous Brahmin family actually accepted him back as a family member. This would seem to be a case of transmigration of souls, rather than reincarnation, but it still suggests that the soul/spirit/life force does not merely dissipate upon death.[45] There is much material available both in printed form[46] as well as on the Net. I remember being impressed by reports of one case, where the child with retained memories was able to identify the hiding place of wealth concealed by his previous self, which hiding place had escaped the systematic searches of the deceased's avaricious relatives.

Case histories suggestive of reincarnation could fill this book many times over. My purpose is briefly to point to possible horizons and not to encompass them. My point is that the atheists must refute every instance, whereas if only one of the thousands of relevant cases is true then it is established that some part of living things does survive death. To try to refute all these cases would require the supposition that there is a

---

[45] Many belief systems distinguish between 'soul' and 'spirit' and treat them as distinct entities, or concepts.

[46] e.g. Arnall Bloxham's *Who was Ann Ockenden?*, Dr Brian L.Weiss's *Many Lives, Many Masters* and Arthur Guirdham's *The Cathars and Reincarnation*, which involves memory of a life during which the great 1244 Catholic massacre of Cathars occurred.

series of grotesque frauds. To fall back on a theory of delusion cannot meet the case, because, the memories, if delusory, could not include verifiable facts or fit together so neatly, or indeed, at all.

Out-of-Body Experiences

Dr Douglas Baker claimed the power of astral projection – projecting the soul out of the body – and it is apparently within the power of most of us to learn to do this ourselves. Daniel Dunglas Home (born 1833) was an adept at astral projection as well as a famous medium and psychic furniture mover. He was able to perform paranormal feats, while sitting in plain sight, in bright light and even when tied up. The late Colin Wilson sets out powerful detail of Home's supernatural capabilities in *The Occult*. Others project their spirits accidentally. So, in one particularly celebrated case shortly before Easter 1905, **Major Sir Frederick Carne Rasch, a Unionist Member of the UK Parliament**, was at home suffering from influenza. He had particularly wanted to attend a debate in the House of Commons and was seen independently by at least three distinguished members sitting in the Chamber despite in fact being at home in bed. This incident was widely reported at the time. I personally know

229

somebody who, like Paul Roland the author of *Ghosts*, in her youth, used to experience this type of detachment of spirit accidentally. There is a well-documented case of a French schoolteacher, Emilee Sagee, whose spirit was often seen to move from her body causing her on occasions to be in two places at once, due to a split between her material body and her 'astral body'. Even though these occurrences were without her intent or knowledge, she so often frightened the girls by manifesting a doppelganger about the school that she was dismissed.[47] Again there are many other instances right up to the present. There are books recording details of out-of-body experiences, including G. N. M. Tyrrell's *The Personality of Man*, which contains a number of examples, including the story of Sir Alexander Ogston, who was in hospital during the Boer War. While delirious he experienced his 'mental self' leaving his body. During this experience he witnessed "a poor RAMC surgeon" dying in another part of the hospital and his detailed description was verified. For more modern books there are Dr Celia Green's *Out-of-the-Body Experiences* and those written by Robert A. Monroe.[48]

Apart from powerful anecdotal evidence, there has been

---

[47] *Ghosts*, Paul Roland, pages 113-116.

[48] See for instance his *Journeys Out of the Body*.

scientific research into out-of-body cases. In one experiment a subject was able to read a random five-digit number placed on a shelf above a point where lying prostrate she could not possibly see or read it.[49] There is also research on near-death experiences. A near-death experience happens at a point near possible death when people undergo a partial separation of body and spirit, so that they can recall events from a perspective distinctly separate from the position of their physical bodies. The most common form is a consciousness of looking down on their body from above, and sometimes from far above. I once defended a rather distinguished man from a foreign embassy. He was charged with shoplifting and his account was that at the time he found himself unexpectedly floating above himself. He was unknowingly describing an out-of-body experience, but Brighton Magistrates were not sufficiently enlightened and convicted him. There are many anecdotal accounts of this available, but there are also scientific studies. In December, 2014, a paper dealing with one hundred and forty near-death experiences was published in the journal, *Resuscitation*, and concluded: "The themes relating to the experience of death appear far broader than what has been

---

[49] *Journal of the American Society for Psychical Research*, 1968, vol. 62, pp. 3-27.

understood so far, or what has been described as so-called near-death experiences. In some cases of cardiac arrest, memories of visual awareness compatible with so-called out-of-body experiences may correspond with actual events."[50]

Near-death evidence dates back thousands of years, at least to the Egyptian *Book of the Dead*,[51] based on experiments suffocating a person in a sarcophagus and then, with luck, reviving them. The fortunate survivors would then recount their experiences. In the sixth century, Pope Gregory the Great compiled records of near-death experiences in a book called *Dialogues*. More modern evidence can be found carefully compiled by researchers such as Dr. Carol Zaleski and Dr Michael Newton.[52] Although Dr Newton started as a sceptic,

---

[50] Parnia et al., *Awareness during Resuscitation – a Prospective Study*, December, 2014, volume 85, issue 12, pp 1799-1805.

[51] Please see likewise the Aztec "*Song of the Dead*," the Tibetan "*Book of the Dead*" (c. 800 BC), and the Indian *Katha Upanishad* (c. 600 BC).

[52] Zaleski, *Otherworld Journeys: Accounts of Near-Death Experiences in Medieval and Modern Times* and Newton, *Journey of Souls*. In *Proof of Heaven; a Neurosurgeon's Journey into the Afterlife*, Dr Eben Alexander applies his expertise to his own near-death experience. He notes the evidence suggests the impersonal nature of God.

he was capable of responding to the evidence he found. Both Pope Gregory and Dr Zaleski suggested that this evidence supports Christianity. It certainly supports the probability that some part of us survives death. This extensive historic and scientific evidence should not be so glibly dismissed by materialists. If they are rationally seeking truth, rather than blindly defending their own materialist faith, their minds would be open.

There are, for instance, many reported cases of people being seen by loved ones at the time of their death some distance away. Charles Dickens, who had been sceptical about the supernatural, was shocked to discover that a story he had written about just such an event turned out to be true right down to the specific date he had chosen. So in a non-fictional case of death manifestation, a family in London – mother, son and younger daughter – all clearly saw the oldest daughter, Ellen, who had just thrown herself into the sea and drowned in Brighton fifty miles away.[53] Given that Jesus was a man of strong spirit it is quite possible that the resurrection was simply an example of these manifestations at or about the time of death.

What do you make of all this? It should not be forgotten

---

[53] *Ghosts*, Paul Roland, pages 77-80.

that Mr and Mrs Dursley in *Harry Potter* were more vehement in denying the paranormal, because they had been faced with hard evidence they did not like. Those of a Dursley-like disposition will already have stopped reading – if they ever started – but if you are inclined to join me in wondering at these things, I am not inviting you to join a religion, although both Hindus and Buddhists believe in reincarnation. Rather, I am inviting you to ponder whether the materialists are right to declare with quite such certainty that death is the end and that we are a single/monist entity. The evidence of our senses joins with extensive anecdotal evidence, scientific research and our intuition to suggest that part of us transcends the material and in consequence survives death.

Chapter Seven

The Paranormal

This subject may be a step too far for some readers. There is much prejudice about ghosts and such 'superstitious stuff.' It is certainly true that the modern world goes out of its way to deride and contemptuously to dismiss the supernatural as unworthy of consideration. Serious consideration of the paranormal is made more difficult by past frauds and by the way it attracts the attention of odd-balls, sensationalist horror films and television shows. Despite all this baggage there is a vast body of evidence for a phenomenon, which is generally categorized as ghost manifestation. For the open-minded seeker of truth it is at least worth thinking about. If there are even a few true examples of ghosts then this would be strong evidence that something within us survives death.

Although ghosts are generally dismissed as non-existent, most of us are afraid of them. Some people simply reject the idea of ghosts, as if by shutting our eyes we can make disturbing things go away. I met a man recently, who scorned the idea of ghosts. When drawn into discussion, he disclosed that he had twice when a child seen a spectral form, while feeling a drop in temperature and all the usual trimmings. Despite there being overwhelming evidence of ghosts, whatever they may be, many will continue to put a pillow over their heads and ridicule any evidence, as if every instance can be put down to mistake, delusion, mass hysteria, or dishonesty. There must be millions of ghost experiences. Are all these cases really complete nonsense? Is there an alternative material explanation in every case? Why are some people so excessively vehement in denying ghosts? Please for just a short time ignore materialist sneering and accompany me in briefly considering the possibility of ghosts and what these manifestations might mean.

The Christian Church has historically persecuted those involved in occult studies and practices, because the paranormal was declared to be the work of the devil. The Christian Church is still uncomfortably ambivalent in its attitude to ghosts. The Church has tended to be scornful about ghosts and yet there is a service of exorcism together with designated priests with responsibility for dealing with haunting. In the Bible, King Saul visited the Witch of Endor, who, at his request, raised the spirit of Samuel,[1] though the news he received from the ghost was somewhat depressing, as he was told that God would deliver the host of Israel to the Philistines.

Recently the BBC broadcast a programme featuring Canon Paul Greenwell, who has responsibility for dealing with ghosts in the Church of England.[2] Following a career of dealing with the paranormal, this sensible-sounding churchman, who began life as a scientist, said that he believed in ghosts and that his extensive experiences 'reassured him that there was life after death.'

In 1971 I had the pleasure of meeting and hearing a lecture by the then leading Christian ghost hunter, the Reverend Dom Robert Petitpierre.[3]

He placed ghosts into three categories:

1. Imprints

---

[1] *Samuel* 1:28:7-25. Islam recognizes ghostlike spirits about us called Jinn (الجن, al-jinn), but these are said to be created by fire, unlike humans, and the concept of ghosts contradicts Islamic teaching that the soul departs until the Day of Judgement.

[2] *One to One*, BBC Radio 4, 31.10.16.

[3] Editor of *Exorcism*, a commission report first published in 1972.

2. Poltergeists

3. Spirits in Limbo

One imprint example he referred to was the image of a fox, which was often seen in the snooker room of a pub and which always followed the same route. These manifestations he described as being like a film, which regularly replays. This phenomenon has also been referred to as "an echo across time."[4] These images are not ghosts, but merely imprints/echoes of some past event. It is impossible to interrelate with them. One of the best examples of this sort of imprint is the troop of Roman soldiers made famous by having been seen by Harry Martindale in the cellars of the Treasurer's House near the Minster in York. He was doing plumbing work in the cellar in 1953 when a number of weary Roman soldiers passed by him causing him to fall off his ladder in shock. There had been other sightings and so, when the terrified Martindale came up out of the cellars, the Curator reportedly said, "By the look of you, you've seen the Roman soldiers." The images were striking in two particular ways: first, the soldiers were only visible above their knees, when it was later

---

[4] Paul Roland, *Ghosts*, page 106.

established that the original Roman road was sixteen inches below the level of the cellar floor. Secondly, whilst Mr Martindale survived some very close questioning by experts – for instance as to the side the *gladius* hung – the descriptions of the uniforms given by Mr Martindale and others was strikingly different from what might have been conventionally expected. Much later, it was established that the local auxiliary troops of that area did indeed present in the way described. Sadly no legions appeared during the time I spent in these cellars, although, if they had, this type of 'echo' manifestation would not significantly have advanced my case for life after death.

Poltergeists were, according to Dom Petitpierre, manifestations of the disturbed mind/psyche of a living person. Colin Wilson, in his book about the well-documented case of 'The Black Monk of Pontefract,' takes a slightly different view, which is that poltergeists are "some mischievous entity of the elemental type, which draws some of its energy from human beings, and some from the site itself."[5] The most witnessed – including a solicitor and a hardened newspaper photographer – and evidenced case is probably The Enfield Poltergeist. This occurred in 1977 and 1978 and the entity

---

[5] *Poltergeist*, page 332.

claimed to be Bill Wilkins, who had gone blind and then died of a haemorrhage in a chair downstairs. These facts were later confirmed to be true by Mr Wilkins' son. Whatever the specifics of poltergeists, they do not necessarily advance my thesis apart from demonstrating the existence of something well beyond our ken. Roger Clarke suggests that, "the 1930s found the poltergeist."[6] If this means that the categorization became popular from that time on, I agree. If it implies a new invention, I should respectfully disagree. There are many recorded incidents prior to 1930, which are strongly suggestive of poltergeist action. In my own field, some medical experts sneered at Post-Traumatic Stress Disorder (PTSD), suggesting that this is no more than a modern invention. They pointed to the First World War, which was a prodigiously traumatic event, and asserted that there were no instances of PTSD then. Well, of course there were. I remember as a boy witnessing shambling old veterans in the street clearly suffering from PTSD. The simple explanation is that the specific condition had not been identified and named, although, of course, it was caught under the umbrella terminology of 'shell shock'.

True ghosts are the important category for the purpose of considering the possibility of life after death. Dom

---

[6] *A Natural History of Ghosts*, page 24.

Petitpierre, being a priest, naturally believed that ghosts were souls in limbo by reason of a sinful life. This 'limbo' is much like the Buddhist 'realm of hungry ghosts'. I should add four other categories of ghosts:

1. those who have become too attached to a particular thing or place;

2. those who have a particular grievance, or compelling unfinished business – e.g. having been murdered, or whose relatives fail to observe testamentary intentions due to the true will being mislaid;

3. those who simply are too timorous to move on;

4. (Dr Douglas Baker added this further category) people, who die sudden unexpected deaths and in consequence are unaware that they have died and so remain close by in spirit.[7] It was fortunate that I had attended Dr Baker's lectures, because a few years later I found myself involved in an example of this. I yearn to set out the detailed story, because it is fascinating, but sadly it is also confidential. In brief then, a

---

[7] A state also experienced by Canon Greenwell, above.

person had died suddenly in an accident and continued to manifest him/herself in ordinary life by, for instance, snatching back particularly prized belongings from other people. A good number of people had separately experienced this. The person, to whom I owe a duty of confidentiality, confided in me, having come to the end of their tether and I realized that this was the very problem described by Dr Baker. I passed on his advice, which was to go quietly into the area where the spirit was most active and to explain what had happened, that the person was dead and that the spirit should move on. It worked perfectly, because after this advice was most lovingly followed no further paranormal event occurred.

In 2016 the BBC's Radio 4 broadcast a programme, called *Ghosts of the Tsunami*, which described how people in Japan have been experiencing ghosts following the 2011 tsunami. One case involved a 'sad faced man', who hailed a taxi in Sendai and asked to go to the address of a house largely destroyed by the inundation. During the journey the man disappeared from the rear of the taxi, but the driver still proceeded to the address and opened the door.

Just as with the recent mass deaths in Japan, the First World War produced a great number of ghost sightings. One of the most celebrated sightings was by the great poet and writer, Robert Graves, who recalled the experience in his war memoir, *Goodbye to All That*:

"I saw a ghost at Béthune. He was a man called Private Challoner who had been at Lancaster with me and again in 'F' Company at Wrexham. When he went out with a draft to join the First Battalion he shook my hand and said: 'I'll meet you again in France, sir.' He had been killed at Festubert in May and in June he passed by our 'C' Company billet where we were just having a special dinner to celebrate our safe return from Cuinchy. There was fish, new potatoes, green peas, asparagus, mutton chops, strawberries and cream, and three bottles of Pommard. Challoner looked in at the window, saluted and passed on. There was no mistaking him or the cap-badge he was wearing. There was no Royal Welsh Battalion billeted within miles of Béthune at the time. I jumped up and looked out of the window, but saw nothing except a fag-end smoking on the pavement. Ghosts were numerous in France at the time."

Robert Graves was a single most impressive observer, but many ghosts were seen by large numbers of men. So on 1st November, 1916, a spectral officer was seen by an entire company of British soldiers over a prolonged period. This spectre appeared to turn back a German attack. The following day the same spectral officer returned and was witnessed by replacement troops. The spectre pointed to a spot in the floor of a dugout, which after excavation turned out to be above a mass of German explosives timed to go off thirteen hours later.[8]

In the case of ghosts you do not have to rely on books and the Internet. You probably have a personal experience, but, if not, somebody you know will have experienced a ghost. Apart from professionals, like Dom Petitpierre and Dr Baker, I know two people, who can see ghosts all the time and who say that there are a lot of them about. One of these is what the world would describe as 'a bit odd' and yet I can see no reason to doubt her. The second is a respected medical practitioner and her account would be quite credible to any open-minded person.

I have a friend, who went walking with his mother. Both my friend and his mother are very down-to-earth farming folk. They were walking along a cliff path above the sea and my friend was, as youths do, lagging behind. Suddenly his mother

---

[8] *Ghosts*, Paul Roland, pages 90-93.

turned round red with anger and shouted, "That was a very stupid thing to do!" She then stopped and stared at him as he was about fifteen yards away. She had felt something try to push her over the edge and had assumed that it was a silly joke by her son. They stopped for a restorative at the next village and were told that a number of people had fallen from the cliff at that point.

Two distinguished solicitors – father and son – told me that in the family home there was what they called a 'water ghost', which turned on taps at odd times. It is very easy in our busy and sceptical lives to ignore these instances, or to try to rationalize them. Some, of course, do have a rational explanation, but these analytically minded and naturally sceptical solicitors had realized that the instances were beyond a prosaic dismissal. I have experienced things switching themselves on in my house. I have found things like a rechargeable razor and a torch switched on. Because these items have batteries of only limited life it would not have been possible for me to have mistakenly left them on, when I had last touched them days before. Another friend told me that she has twice seen a ghost of a young lady, who threw herself to her death in Arundel after having been jilted. Later she discovered that this ghost is regularly seen by others.

Have you never experienced an object seemingly

jumping off a solid surface – we say to ourselves that we had somehow left it precariously balanced on the edge – or a well-fixed picture falling down, or a piece of furniture toppling? The other day I was walking through a car park, when, for no discernable reason, a parked car leapt forward with such force that it dented the barrier in front of it. Is the world as one dimensional as we are given to believe by those claiming to be rationalists? I know a typical farmer, who reared cattle with his father. Shortly after his father had died he needed a large green spray-can of antiseptic for a wound on a steer's heel. He hunted in all the cupboards and in the outhouses all the time regretting that he could not ask his father. When he returned to the cattle shed there in the middle of the walkway, which he had used several times in his search, was the green can. This type of intervention may sometimes be quite mischievous. So on one occasion my car keys disappeared inexplicably from my jacket pocket at Victoria station. I found them in the Gladstone bag I was carrying. That, in itself, would have been almost impossible to explain, but they were also in a thrice-folded foil-lined bag of cookies. Usually we simply see these incidents as odd and rationalize them away. It is only when it is beyond rational explanation that we sometimes recognize them and then only half-heartedly.

So ghosts, like other paranormal activity, can easily pass

unnoticed, not only because we are disinclined to believe in them, but also because they generally appear like normal people and not headless cavaliers. Many can look so normal that they are treated as living people. "Most ghosts are seen once and never again. Most instances of sightings are never written down or recorded."[9] When I was four I was playing on the window seat at the front of our small bungalow. I was surprised to see a sad-looking man of about fifty in a slightly shabby suit walk past the window and turn round the corner to the side gate, because any caller would have stopped to knock at the front door. I ran to tell my mother, who was in the kitchen by the side door that the man would be approaching. We rushed outside and there was no sign of him. I could probably still pick the man out in an identity parade. Was he a ghost? I have little doubt, though he looked quite normal. But for the fact that he had disappeared in a very limited area, I would have thought no more about it. I was as dogged and thorough in my search as Professor Dawkins could have wished and first checked the empty road outside and then all areas of concealment in our small enclosed back garden. In 1979 I heard and saw in the half-light a woman walk past my bed and out of the bedroom. I was not concerned, because I

---

[9] Roger Clarke, *A Natural History of Ghosts*.

thought it was my wife. My shock came moments later, when my wife moved in bed next to me.

These are some of my own experiences. The point is that if you speak to your own friends and relatives you will find that they probably have evidence of the paranormal to provide. You can also prove the matter for yourself.

Dom Petitpierre recounted many distressing experiences of people playing with Ouija boards, table turning etc.. He found, due he suggested to the spirits most easily reached being the most wicked, that it was common for those – usually young people – attempting to communicate with spirits in this way to be given some amazing proofs in the form of modest predictions as to the future. The predictions having come true, the participants would become increasingly enthusiastic and convinced. As soon as they were believers the messages would become destructive and untrustworthy. He had come across some tragic outcomes. A quick search of the Internet will disclose much evidence of psychic investigation, including spirit games turning very dark. Emanual Swedenborg – scientist, theologian and mystic, (1688-1772) – viewed the most common spirits as those who, on account of wickedness in life, had lost personal memory on death. He regarded speaking to spirits as "dangerous."[10]

A famous example of this was given by American researcher, Allan Vaughan. He and a friend dabbled with Ouija and got very impressive results. In particular, while dabbling they heard a radio announcement that a journalist called Dorothy Kilgallen had died from a heart attack. They received a message through the Ouija board that really she had been poisoned. They were impressed, when ten days later it was confirmed that she had been poisoned. It is supposed that the still-unknown murderer struck because of her knowledge of John F. Kennedy's assassination. The price for Vaughan was that he felt troubled by spirits and had prolonged and unpleasant time freeing himself.[11] Shakespeare puts this same idea of spirits luring us with prophecy into the mouth of Banquo, after Macbeth is given a series of predictions by the three witches. The first prediction, that Macbeth will become Thane of Cawdor, proves true, setting him of a path of destruction:

"But 'tis strange:
And oftentimes to win us to our harm,

---

[10] *Journal of Dreams*.

[11] Alan Vaughan, *Patterns of Prophecy*.

The instruments of darkness tell us truths:

Win us with honest trifles, to betray's

In deepest consequence."

Colin Wilson gives an interesting example of a Cornish couple convinced that they were receiving detailed spirit information about the active serial murderer then known as 'The Black Panther'. The information turned out to be as false as it was convincingly detailed. Colin Wilson had no doubt that the couple were genuine, but his own conclusion was that "the spirit had simply been a circumstantial and convincing liar."[12] On the other hand, in December, 2015, a medium, Alison Austin, was led to the stabbed body of Mrs Mika Cudworth in woodland after Mrs Cudworth had been missing for a fortnight, so not all spirits are liars.

In *The God Delusion* Richard Dawkins dismisses ghosts in less than a page on two main grounds. First, when he was a child he heard a ghost murmuring, but upon investigation discovered it was the wind blowing through his keyhole.[13] Secondly, as he rightly points out, the brain when interpreting input from the eyes can often distort true perception. I was

---

[12] *Poltergeist*, page 319.

[13] *The God Delusion*, page 115.

amazed to discover that if you hang upside down watching television the brain within seconds turns the picture up the other way to suit itself. I have no doubt that many ghost stories are the result of over-active imaginations, downright falsehood, genuine mistakes of perception, mental illness, or a failure to exercise the curiosity of a young Dawkins. However, the evidence for ghosts is so extensive that we really have to refute, or at least have some grounds to doubt, *every* single reported case to discount them entirely. How many more ghost sightings would there be reported, but for the derision and scepticism that can follow a report. How many manifestations are missed by reason of our own inclination to rationalize away and dismiss such experiences, or by reason of our failure to notice them in the first place?

Roger Clarke sums up this rigid anti-ghost scepticism:

"Children are now taught from a very early age not to see ghosts, since believing in ghosts violates natural law, and there are no sterner guardians of this law than the middle-class scientist ... Ghosts are no longer to be feared, but belief in them surely is. Still, the sightings and hauntings continue."[14]

---

[14] *A Natural History of Ghosts*, page 302.

A child Auberon Waugh 'imagined' that he saw the ghost of the cowman, who had previously used his bedroom: "As I lay in the dark one night the door opened suddenly. Light flooded in from the corridor outside, and a small man in trousers walked in and shut the door purposefully behind him, leaving me once again in the dark. When I turned my bedside light on, nobody was there."[15]

One of the few certain facts in the uncertain world of the paranormal is that most materialists have closed minds. Batting for the atheists, Comte-Sponville outdoes Dawkins by dismissing ghosts in just seven lines.[16] He comments derisively that "Some people claim to have seen ghosts or communicated with the dead by table-turning" and then he dismisses the whole matter as down to "credulity" and "self-suggestion." First, it is not just "some people", but millions of people over millennia. Secondly, have these atheists reviewed the wide body of evidence with an open mind? Possibly not. Are all witnesses of ghosts, table-turning, and séances merely the victims of credulity and self-deception? Very probably not. Witnesses really have to be dismissed *en bloc* as credulous or deluded, because otherwise atheists would have the almost

---

[15] *Will This Do?* page 47.

[16] A. Comte-Sonville, *The Book of Atheist Spirituality*, page 100.

impossible challenge of grappling with the evidence on a case-by-case basis. I approach the paranormal by asking, 'Here is evidence, so how strong is it and what would it suggest if it were true?' Many atheists and religionists say, 'This is what we believe to be true and any evidence contradicting our certainty must for that reason be superstitious nonsense.' Undoubtedly some reports do involve both fraud and self-deception, but there are hundreds of books and thousands of reports on the Internet dealing with ghosts, some involving very impressive witnesses and some involving multiple witnesses, who either saw the same event, or the same manifestation on different occasions. More significantly, either you or those close to you will have had direct experience of ghosts, so you do not have to make a leap of faith based on strangers' accounts.

Other less closed-minded commentators have suggested that ghosts are not manifestations of spirit at all. One psychic investigator of the 19th century, Frederick Myers, who investigated séances, believed that ghosts occupied a different dimension. This, however, would not prevent spirit manifestation being evidence for some continuation of life-force. One famous ghost-hunter of the last century was a humanist called Andrew Green. He believed that ghosts were generated by electrical fields in our brains, or that they were themselves electrical fields. Poltergeists do seem to be very much associated with electrical brain fields, but if ghosts are wholly or largely composed of electric fields this does not necessarily refute their evidential force in suggesting continuation of the spirit. For my part, I doubt that the phenomenon I have defined as ghost manifestation is produced by the brain, because there are so many accounts where the same ghost is seen by different witnesses on different occasions, or where the ghost imparts true knowledge completely unknown to the witnesses.

So Pliny the Younger[17] recorded the account of the philosopher, Athenodorus, who took lodgings, which were cheap due to regular haunting. Sure enough, a manacled ghost appeared to him and led him to a spot where the inquisitive philosopher directed men to dig the next day. He discovered the body of a murdered man in chains resembling those worn by the ghost. Once the remains had been moved and interred with due ceremony, the haunting ceased.[18] Nearly two thousand years later in North Carolina one James Chaffin was visited by his dead father in a dream and correctly informed

---

[17] Who recommended to the Emperor Trajan that he should suppress the Christians: Pliny: *Letters* X: 96-7.

[18] *Letters* VII.27, circa 100 AD.

that his father's will was in the family Bible.[19] There are many other instances, such as the thoroughly investigated case of the ghost of Michael Conley, who in 1885 told his daughter that he had money that nobody knew, or suspected he had, sewn in to his old work shirt in a piece of her old red dress[20] and the instance of the spectral officer – above – who pointed to the spot where, unsuspected by all present, the German explosives were concealed in a tunnel.

Mediums and Psychics

Stories of fraudulent mediums are commonplace. From the fictional Princess Popoffski in *Lucia Rising* and Madam Arcati in *Blithe Spirit* to the flesh and blood Davenport Brothers, who were mobbed by angry Liverpudlians after failing to produce a spiritualist performance due to being unable to escape the bindings, which had been too effectively applied by members of the audience, Spiritualism has certainly taken many knocks to its credibility.

However, there are many examples of highly credible mediums, like Daniel Dunglas Home, whose amazing record

---

[19] *Ghosts*, pages 80-83.

[20] *Ghosts*, page 80 and *Afterlife*, page 163.

is well worth examination.[21] Of more modern vintage there is the well-known Betty Shine (1929-2002), who was featured in *The Independent* of 14th January, 1993. The writer was struck by how down-to-earth she was and concluded, "Those who encounter Betty Shine's supernatural powers find it hard to remain sceptical." The article gives an interesting example of her telepathy with a young boy in a coma: Mrs Shine was able to describe to his parents true details of an incident, when the boy had mistakenly returned his goldfish to their tank killing them, because the tank was being cleansed with boiling water. Miss Shine wrote a number of books herself and accounts of her work can easily be found. American readers may be familiar with television psychic, John Edward, who has also written prolifically on the subject.

A less-celebrated medium was Mrs Ena Twigg of Acton, London. She played a key part in the story of American Bishop James Pike, which is told in his book, *The Other Side*. In 1966 Bishop Pike's son committed suicide after trying psychedelic drugs and began haunting Bishop Pike's American apartment. On a trip to England Bishop Pike visited Mrs Twigg. At the séance Bishop Pike received clearly

---

[21] See for instance Colin Wilson, *The Occult*, pages 606-630. Other leading psychics of the past are for instance Eusapia Palladino, Gerard Croiset and Robert Cracknell.

genuine messages both from his dead son and from a dead friend. There is an interesting postscript to the story. In 1969 Bishop Pike and his new wife got lost walking in the wilderness in Israel. By agreement Mrs Pike left the bishop in shelter and went on by herself to get help. Sadly, the rescuers could not locate him. Mrs Twigg, who was still in Acton, then received a psychic message from the bishop giving details of his location, which she was able pass on to assist the search team in locating his body.[22]

In 1930 the British airship, the R101, crashed in flames killing its crew. Under very formal conditions a medium, Mrs Eileen Garrett, acted as a channel for the dead airship commander, Flight-Lieutenant Irwin, who gave an account of the defects causing the accident. This account was officially noted and led to key improvements to the design of airships.[23]

The point is that, unless all psychics and mediums are either crooked or unconsciously able to make lucky guesses, there is indeed a spirit world. By dabbling with Ouija and similar basic methods you can very quickly attune yourself to the spirit world and prove the point for yourself, though I

---

[22] *Psychic News*, 7th November, 1970 and Colin Wilson, *The Occult*, pages 630-632.

[23] *Leaves From a Psychist's Case-Book*, Harry Price, www.harrypricewebsite.co.uk

should not recommend it. "However you view it, the Ouija board spells danger."[24] Many years ago, while a student, a friend of mine began taking a serious, but amateur, interest in this type of spiritualism and was convinced and excited by the clear results he was getting. He then had two unsettling experiences. The first was when he hitched a lift and the driver, who was a complete stranger, out of the blue told him that his contacts with the spirit world were dangerous for him. The second was when he was telephoned by a lecturer at his college, who said that he had been at a séance and the medium had described my friend precisely and warned that he was likely to suffer great harm from his dabbling. He heeded these warnings.

A fascinating footnote to the topic of spiritualism is the death of Houdini. In his youth, Houdini had operated a magic show, which pretty much amounted to fake spiritualism. Mr and Mrs Houdini later devoted much effort to unmasking fake mediums. Though always sceptical they remained open-minded enough to agree a secret message compiled in their special stage code. The purpose of this message was that the one who died first could divulge the secret message and prove once and for all the truth of life after death. Houdini died in

---

[24] Paul Roland, *Ghosts*, page 213.

1926 after the hapless J. Gordon Whitehead unexpectedly punched him in the stomach rupturing his appendix. In 1929 an American medium called Arthur Ford contacted Mrs Houdini with the secret message. That should have been conclusive, but then matters started to cloud. It was pointed out that the stage code had been published in a book about Houdini. Others responded by pointing out that the code itself was not the same thing as the message in the code. It was then alleged by the press that this was a dishonest stunt to publicise a new venture by Mrs Houdini, though in fact there was no such venture and she was in very poor health. It was then rumoured that Mrs Houdini had accidentally leaked the message to a journalist some years before. Sadly, Mrs Houdini was so distressed that she was unable to clarify the position before her own death. The general presumption is that this was all a hoax. Clearly no conclusion can be taken from this debacle, but if it were a hoax it would have required both the medium and the alleged journalist to have been party to quite unpleasant dishonesty. Even more to the point, it is really almost incredible that Mrs Houdini would ever have disclosed the secret message to anybody, whether accidentally or not, and least of all to a reporter. The thwarting of Houdini's last message seems to be part of what Colin Wilson saw as 'a deliberate ambiguity' maintained by the spirit world.

Metaphysical Conclusion

In summary we have the following evidence:

- All of us have manifest consciousness;

- Many people remember verifiable previous lives at least when young or under hypnosis;

- Many people experience separation of body and spirit, sometimes generally and sometimes as a near-death event;

- Many people claim to be able to project their spirit/astral body, there is some scientific support for this and, if you want, you can learn to do it yourself;[25]

- There are reported cases of people seeing the spirits of others, when there is a separation, sometimes at time of death, or near-death, but sometimes in more commonplace circumstances;

- There are probably many millions of cases of people seeing ghosts, possibly including many sightings by people you know personally;

- There are innumerable cases of people who appear to be able to contact spirits, or are, or have been, contacted by spirits;

---

[25] Please see for instance, Paul Roland, *Ghosts*, pp 138-141.

• There is the fact that you can get quite significant results yourself, if you choose to dabble in these matters.

All this evidence points to one conclusion, which is that we have a spirit, or soul, which is part of us and yet divisible. For me, my experience as a human being tells me that I do have a soul and that I am not just a bundle of chemical reactions stumbling through a universe empty of any spiritual dimension. The practical evidence presented by such diverse investigators as Dr Douglas Baker, Dom Petitpierre, Colin Wilson and many others, including personal friends, simply strengthens this conclusion. However, for materialists rationally and successfully to maintain their assertion that upon death our life-force abruptly terminates, they must face and refute the paranormal with more than mere dismissive scorn. Materialists are as determined to ignore the questions posed by ghosts and spiritualism, as St Jerome was to deny clear Biblical authority that Jesus had brothers and sisters. The redoubtable Jonathan Meades, who rejects religion and refers to God, Allah and Yahweh as "nightmarish psychopaths," is a typical materialist in that he declares, "There is no such thing as spirit, save in the minds of the deluded."[26] There is a vast and varied body of evidence to the contrary and many of those so rudely dismissed are witnesses of a quite sceptical and reliable disposition. Cognitive dissonance is not limited to the followers of Mrs Martin. I agree with Clifford, a 'poster boy' for atheists, that it is "sinful" to hold a belief unsupported by evidence.[27] Applying this principle he attacked mythology, religion and, in particular the "wicked" concept of eternal damnation, which not before time now appears to be doubted by the Pope himself.[28] Clifford is generally regarded as a champion of atheism, but he is really a powerful opponent of cognitive dissonance. It is equally sinful to dismiss all evidence of a spiritual element in life as mere superstition without conclusive evidence justifying that dismissal. Unwillingness at least to keep an open mind on this mass of evidence is suggestive of just that type of closed-mindedness

---

[26] *Ben Building; Mussolini, Monuments and Modernism*, BBC 4, 1st June, 2016.

[27] William Kingdom Clifford (1845-79), *Ethics of Belief*.

[28] The present Pope, if correctly quoted in *La Repubblica* (29.3.18), believes, "Hell does not exist, the disappearance of the souls of the sinners exists." The formal Christian line in the Catechism still "affirms the teaching of hell and its eternity," including "eternal fire."

that atheists so hate in their religious antagonists. Hugely fond though I am of Jonathan Meades, on the issue of dualism I prefer Socrates. What must surely be beyond doubt, however, is that, in terms of rationality, there is no compelling evidence to support materialism's glib, scornful and suspiciously certain rejection of the spirit.

Chapter Eight

Love

"Choose Love, Love!
Without the sweet life
of Love, living is a burden,
as you have seen."

– Rumi[1]

Nothing could be further from grim materialism than love. Love is the key. It is significant that Jesus' overriding commandment at the Last Supper, was that we must "Love one another." The Buddha advised us to "Love without limit."[2] Love is our greatest emotion. Even Darwin habitually enjoyed

---

[1] Jalāl al-Dīn.Rūmī (1207-1273), Tomb of Jahangir, Lahore, Pakistan. For a delightful introduction to the thoughts and love poems of this Islamic scholar and mystic please see the novel, *The Forty Rules of Love* by Elif Shafak.

[2] He also said, "Searching all directions with your awareness you find no one dearer than yourself. In the same way, others are dear to themselves. So you shouldn't hurt others if you love yourself." *Rājan Sutta: The King*

sitting with his wife to read love stories aloud. Love given and requited is a most wonderful thing, even though "the sword hidden among his pinions may wound you."[3] We have all experienced love. Love for and from our parents and family, or love for and from our children, or love for and from true friends, or love for and from a lover. In true love, where we put the good and happiness of the person loved above our own, there is an element as palpably spiritual as it is joyful. We love people, when loving them can do us no obvious material benefit. We can love people, so that joyfully we make great sacrifices for them. It is also possible to act lovingly to strangers; that is to love your fellow man and woman.

This sentiment is well caught by Leigh Hunt (1784-1859) in his poem, *Abou Ben Adhem*, which I have found rarely appeals to zealous Christians:

"Abou Ben Adhem (may his tribe increase!)
Awoke one night from a deep dream of peace,
And saw, within the moonlight in his room,
Making it rich, and like a lily bloom,
An angel writing in a book of gold:
Exceeding peace had made Ben Adhem bold,

---

[3] Kahlil Gibran, *The Prophet*.

And to the presence in the room he said,

'What writest thou?' The vision raised its head,

And with a look made of all sweet accord,

Answered, 'The names of those who love the Lord.'

'And is mine one?' said Abou. 'Nay, not so,'

Replied the angel. Abou spoke more low,

But cheerly still; and said, 'I pray thee, then,

Write me as one who loves his fellow men.'

The angel wrote, and vanished. The next night

It came again with a great wakening light,

And showed the names who love of God had blest,

And lo! Ben Adhem's name led all the rest."

Contrary to the Christian predilection for damning ourselves as worthless sinners and 'lumps of perdition,' I suggest that we should all love ourselves. Our capacity to love others is limited by the degree of our love for ourselves. If you have a loving respect for yourself you will not want to do something against your conscience which must diminish that self-love. 'All the world loves a lover', because a loving person radiates love and happiness, while an unloving person spreads negativity. "Love is generated by being loved."[4] Even the ultra-orthodox and stern Mother Teresa (1910-1997) wrote a poem including these telling lines:

"La vita è amore, godine" and "La vita è un mistero, scoprilo."[5] 'Life is love, be glad,' and 'Life is a mystery, uncover it.'

The *Upanishads* – religious and philosophical writings of about 800 to 500 BC – suggest that the truths of religion are only clear to those who have freed themselves of greed, selfishness and egoism. This condition may be achieved by living an ascetic life of contemplation, humility and self-denial. Alternatively, this seemingly almost impossible state can be achieved quite simply by opening the heart to love. If you truly love then you feel no greed, or preoccupying self-interest.

Love exists in the animal world. We are always warned against anthropomorphism. This may be correct in that, just as it is damaging to God for us to attribute to God our own human shape and unpleasant characteristics, so it is equally

---

[4] Dr Rowan Williams, Retired Archbishop of Canterbury, *Being Disciples*, page 32. Love, he writes, is "a state of openness to joy."

[5] *Un Tuffo Nell'Azzuro*, page 63.

268

unfair to animals for us to attribute to them our faulty human nature. Animals are, however, very close to us in genetic terms and, while they may be better attuned to the spiritual world than we presently are, there seems no reason why we should not have feelings approximating to theirs. I once kept an aquarium of cold water fish. Two of my fish contracted white spot disease. One was the biggest greediest fish and the other was the smallest fish. The larger was only mildly off colour and the smaller was very ill. I isolated them in a bucket of water containing the cure for the disease. When I first put food onto the surface of the bucket, the big fish, as expected, darted up and began eating. He took two mouthfuls and stopped. He then went down to the small fish and spent ten minutes nudging him gently to the surface. Only when the small fish began to eat did the big fish resume his meal. This seems like a selfless and loving act to me, when survival of the fittest would surely dictate that the big fish should have eaten the lot. Doubtless, it will be suggested that the big fish was somehow envisaging that the death of the small fish would poison his environment, but, as I watched the kindly persistence of this usually domineering fish, I saw love.[6]

---

[6] There is now research from Plannellas et al., Stirling University, suggesting that fish have emotions:

We share almost ninety-nine per cent of our genetic make-up with chimpanzees. Studies by Professor Frans de Waal[7] show that other primates tend to share the characteristics which we often view as exclusively human. Primates are clearly capable of the same love, tenderness and generosity of heart as humans. Maybe more. Unlike humans, who have evolved systems of exploitation both of the Earth and their fellows, other primates seem content to live more balanced and comfortable lives, including having more sex. In his book, *Sapiens*, Dr Yuval Harari points out that we now work much longer and less congenial hours than did our hunter-gather ancestors,[8] that our brain capacity is reducing, probably due to the reduced need for intelligent survival,[9] and

---

How Do We Know Whether Fish Have Feelings Too?, Sonia Rey Planellas, www.bbc.co.uk, 20th February, 2016.

Fish are capable of deception; for instance, small male cuttlefish assume the appearance of females to sneak past their dominant counterparts for sex with the females they are guarding.

[7] Psychologist, primatologist, ethologist and Professor of Primate Behaviour, who has written many books about chimpanzee studies, including *Chimpanzee Politics* and about primates, including *Peacemaking among Primates*.

[8] Dr Yuval Noah Harari, *Sapiens*, page 56.

[9] *Sapiens*, page 55.

that our health and height has been impaired by our new way of living.[10] The more we pause to consider our modern world the less 'sapiens' we seem.[11] Certainly studies have showed chimpanzee troops fighting minor wars and even occasionally engaging in something approaching ethnic cleansing. Other primates are not always honest. There is one famous example of a monkey who, upon seeing another find a fallen banana on the ground, falsely gave an 'I see a lion' call, so that the banana would be abandoned by the credulous finder, who immediately sprang into the trees to save himself. Despite these faults in our close cousins, anybody reading primate studies must surely pause to wonder why the God of Man is supposed to have favoured us to the exclusion of other hominids and apes.

Whilst the capacity for love in our closest living relations should not be a surprise, this capacity is not exclusive to apes. In 2016 people flocked to a Russian safari park to see the loving friendship between a Siberian tiger and a goat, which had been put into the tiger's paddock for his lunch. There are many instances of dogs and other animals helping and showing devotion to man. Humpback whales regularly

---

[10] *Sapiens*, page 57.

[11] Viewing the 1982 film, *Koyaanisqatsi* (Hopi Native American for 'Life out of balance'), should be mandatory.

save other species from attack by killer whales.[12] A conspicuous example of open-heartedness is the dolphin.[13] In 1983 at Tokerau Beach, New Zealand, a pod of dolphins rescued seventy-six pilot whales by herding them from where they had been stranded back to deep water. This is a typical incident. For instance, five years earlier another pod of dolphins had similarly saved whales at Whangarei harbour. Dolphins often save people. Many instances of this are recorded in ancient Greek literature. More recently, in 2004 a group of swimmers off New Zealand was saved from a great white shark by a pod of dolphins. The dolphins herded the swimmers into a group and surrounded them. In the Red Sea, twelve divers were lost for thirteen hours, during which time they were surrounded and protected by dolphins. In 2014 British swimmer, Adam Walker, was saved by dolphins. In some instances dolphins have been known to support drowning swimmers. Sadly, although or perhaps because mankind believes itself to have a special relationship with

---

[12] Humpback whales often swim a mile or more to save seals, sea lions, sunfish and baby whales of other types from attack with no obvious self-benefit. 31 cases of this were investigated by Dr Robert Pitman et al., *Marine Mammal Science* 2016.

[13] Dolphins and whales appear to mourn their dead. 14 instances of this are recorded in a recent edition of the *Journal of Mammalogy*.

God, we have not tended to reciprocate dolphins' loving kindness. Dolphins are destroyed by our pollution and fishing methods. In February, 2016, bathers at Santa Teresita, Argentina, found a baby dolphin in the sea. They removed the small calf for the purpose of 'selfies' and such was the prolonged and selfish demand for these, the poor thing died of dehydration. In April, 2016, the Russian Ministry of Defence purchased five mature dolphins for military purposes. Hamlet rightly said, "What a piece of work is man." It really should not surprise us that man creates such unattractive gods in his own image. On a happier note, I recently heard the story of a man surfing off Los Angeles. He came across a whale trapped in fishing nets. He went back to the beach to get a knife and returned to cut the whale free. Once free the whale began to swim away, but then returned to look at him. He had no doubt that the whale was expressing his gratitude. This story has a happy ending reflecting well on man and whale, and yet mankind still fills the oceans with plastic, discarded nets and chemicals.

Hopefully love will one day prevail. Thich Nhat Hanh[14] says:

---

[14] *Peace Is Every Step*, pages 84-85 (approved in a foreword by the Dalai Lama).

"The mind of love brings peace, joy, and happiness to ourselves and others. ... The source of love is deep in us, and we can help others realize a lot of happiness. One word, one action, or one thought can reduce another person's suffering and bring him joy. One word can give comfort and confidence, destroy doubt, help someone avoid a mistake, reconcile a conflict, or open the door to liberation. One action can save a person's life or help him take advantage of a rare opportunity. One thought can do the same, because thoughts always lead to words and actions. If love is in our heart, every thought, word, and deed can bring about a miracle. Because understanding is the very foundation of love, words and actions that emerge from our love are always helpful."

Great things can be achieved by love, which cannot be done by power or force. Virgil was the first to write, "Love conquers all" and it is true.

Aesop's fable of 'The Sun and the North Wind' is an allegory for the power of love:

The North Wind boasted of great strength. The Sun argued that there was greater power in gentleness.

"Shall we have a contest?" asked the Sun.

Below them, a man was walking along a winding road.

He was wearing a coat.

The Sun then suggested, "As a test let us see which of us can take the coat from that man."

"That will be easy for me," boasted the North Wind.

The North Wind blew fiercely. It blew so hard that the birds clung to the trees and dust flew up. The harder the North Wind blew the more tightly the now shivering man pulled his coat about him.

Then, the Sun came out from behind a cloud. Sunlight warmed the air and the frosty ground. The man on the road unbuttoned his coat.

The sun grew gradually brighter.

Then the man felt so hot, he took off his coat and sat down in a shady spot.

"How did you do that?" asked the North Wind.

"It was simple," replied the Sun, "I brightened the day. Through loving gentleness I got my way."

Tony Campolo, a conservative Baptist, tells a story of his Christian students. They had an evangelical missionary organization in the Dominican Republic. They believed that the local people were being harmed and exploited by an American company called Gulf & Western. He describes how the students tried various aggressive methods to force the company to change its corporate strategy so as to benefit the Dominican people. These well-meant confrontational methods of active protest and shareholder action completely failed. Then the students relinquished their negative protesting and met the company's executives. They discovered that, "These top executives turned out to be decent people who really wanted to do what was best for the Dominican people – not only because doing so was right, but also because it was good for business."[15] Corporate policy was changed. Where hostility had failed, loving communication succeeded in changing the corporation into a force for good.

Love, then, has four great elements:

1. It brings great joy to the lover;

2. It brings great joy to the person loved;

3. It can achieve great good both in life and the world, like Nelson Mandela's transformation of South Africa through love and forgiveness. He said, "We must use time wisely and forever realize that the time is always ripe to do right."

4. Love nurtures the soul. The soul "rejoices when we

---

[15] *Choose Love Not Power*, pp 102-103.

spend time with people we love and who love us, and when we do what we do out of love."[16]

You must have experienced love in some form. You have been able to see for yourself how love nurtures and conquers seemingly insurmountable problems. You have seen how the absence of love can lead to great harm. Hopefully you have experienced, or will soon experience, the ecstatic joy that love can bring. Does this mighty thing contain a spiritual element, or is it merely a trick by Natural Selection to improve the chances of survival and genetic reproduction? Richard Dawkins dismisses love in less than two pages for reasons primarily based on a book called *Why We Love* by an anthropologist called Helen Fisher, which book he contends "has beautifully expressed the insanity of love."[17] Dawkins' verdict of 'insanity' is based on two arguments. First, it is asserted that love is often disproportionate to what is strictly necessary to fit in with Darwinian theory. This obviously correct point about the magnitude and power of love surely suggests that it is an emotion with a peculiarly spiritual element and not just an evolutionary tool. Secondly, Professor Dawkins points out that love produces "unique brain states,

---

[16] Dr Brenda Davies, *Journey of the Soul*, page 89.

[17] *The God Delusion*, page 214.

277

including the presence of neurally active chemicals (in effect, natural drugs)." All emotion has an impact on the brain state. All actions have an impact on the brain state, such as exercise causing the release of mood-enhancing endorphins. That love produces a unique brain state suggests that it is a unique emotion. Anger is, on the whole, an unattractive emotion and it is difficult to establish a positive balance sheet for its terms of evolutionary theory. Anger produces a chemical change in the brain, primarily in triggering the release of catecholamines. Are our emotions simply a result of our brain chemicals controlling us like a puppet? I doubt it. Dawkins' contemptuous dismissal of ghosts, consciousness and love as being illusions born of our misfiring brains strikingly chimes with Dr Sheldrake's ninth 'false core belief' that scientists simply take it for granted that, "Unexplained phenomena like telepathy are illusory."[18]

Dawkins concentrates on 'love at first sight', which is really quite a rare event outside the pages of romantic novels. This he dismisses contemptuously as the irrational *coup de foudre* – sententious ... moi? Most people love, or fall in love, in a much more rational way. It is quite Dawkinsian to focus upon the most unusual and extreme manifestation of love for

---

[18] "Setting Science Free from Materialism", *Explore* 2013; 9:211.

the purpose of dismissing it. Dawkins asserts that evolutionary psychologists agree with Helen Fisher that romantic love "could be a mechanism to ensure loyalty to one co-parent, lasting long enough to rear a child together." Any analysis containing the words 'could be' is far from convincing, even if it had not already been conceded by Dawkins himself that the degree of love people feel is disproportionate to this and other evolutionary needs. Love does not necessarily have any evolutionary function. For instance, people fall in love when there is no prospect of childbearing. Same sex couples fall in love and yet in evolutionary terms this is hardly helpful. Although a man still theoretically capable of reproduction, I fell in love – not a *coup de foudre* – with a woman well beyond a conventional childbearing age. We love our special friends and quite often that friendship can give us no significant benefits in the evolutionary race. Sometimes love can involve burdensome commitment quite contrary to survival of the fittest. I have a severely disabled son. I love him very deeply, though pure evolutionary forces would surely not want to preserve him. Love can involve sacrifice, but with love there is really no sacrifice, but rather ample spiritual reward from doing things for the loved person. Also at odds with love being tied to procreation is the fact that, since the dawn of time, many men and women have had an irresistible urge to have sex without there being any love between them and equally without any intention of staying together for the benefit of a possible child.

There is a yet greater rational objection to Dawkins' dismissal of love as a mere Darwinian trick and that is the logic of Natural Selection itself. Unlike Dawkins, French atheist, André Comte-Sponville, believes in love and its part in illuminating the spiritual element in life. However, in arguing a case against the existence of God, he expresses a very poor view of humanity: "… why would God have made us so weak, cowardly, violent, avid, pretentious and overbearing? Why are there so many nasty or mediocre human beings, so few heroes and saints? Why is there so much egotism, so much envy and hatred and so little generosity and love? Banality of evil; rarity of good!"[19] This hopefully over-pessimistic indictment does cast doubt on the existence of the interventionist creator God promised by most religions, but the shortcomings of humanity do not in any way disprove the existence of a more passive force. These shortcomings do, however, disprove the materialists' attempt to use Darwinism to dismiss love. I am sorry that C-S's view of his fellow man is so bleak. It is without doubt true that all the terrible things he lists are

---

[19] *The Book of Atheist Spirituality*, page 114.

especially noticeable in the world and always have been. On the other hand, how does his perception agree with your own? Does evil-doing so outweigh love and goodness amongst your family, your friends, people in your neighbourhood, people in your country and people in other countries? We tend to notice and remember bad deeds and the consequences of evil deeds can be long-lasting. The media tend not to report acts of love with the same enthusiasm they show in covering sins and disasters. We tend to remember the bad rather than the good. Even so, Comte-Sponville grudgingly concedes that humanity has some good points, but, in arguing against God, he dismisses love even more shortly than Dawkins: "Natural selection suffices to explain our capacity for love and courage, intelligence and compassion. All these things are selective advantages that make the transmission of our genes more probable."[20] In so deploying the concept of Natural Selection as a way of dismissing love as evidence of a spiritual force in life, surely Dawkins and Comte-Sponville shoot off their own atheistical feet? If love and compassion are mere aspects of Natural Selection then the world should now be *full* of love and compassion. That is the whole point of Natural Selection: it increases the numbers of creatures carrying characteristics

---

[20] *The Book of Atheist Spirituality*, page 122.

advantageous to survival. We have had at least one hundred and fifty thousand years of evolution in a form recognizable as *Homo sapiens* and before that man's ancestors have had millions of evolutionary years. Do we see a clear increase in love and compassion with every century that passes? Even on my very much happier view of humanity, I fear not. C-S regards mankind today as "basically mediocre," but this sad view must logically refute Darwinism, if love is a 'selective advantage.' I believe in Darwinism[21] and the logic of Natural Selection demonstrates that love cannot be explained away as a purely evolutionary device. Nor, in the end, is Comte-Sponville himself so dismissive of love, because he concludes his book with these profound thoughts about love: "The absolute is not love; rather love can open us up to the absolute," and "Love, not hope, is what helps us live. Truth, not faith, is what sets us free."[22]

Being more of a materialist, Dawkins has no such happy

---

[21] According to Platonic scholars (e.g. R. D. Archer-Hind in his introduction to his edition of the *Phaedo* and R. K. Gaye in *The Platonic Concept of Immortality*, pp 207- 208) Plato, who believed in the immortality of the soul, in many ways foreshadowed Darwinism in his own physical theories (e.g. the *Timaeus*, 76D and 89B,C).

[22] *The Book of Atheist Spirituality*, page 206.

thoughts. Having purported to discount love on a dubious inference dressed in the scantiest scientific evidence possible, he poses the question, "Could irrational religion be a by-product of the irrationality mechanisms that were originally built into the brain by selection for falling in love?" Love, just like a belief in the soul, is branded as irrational by the materialists, but here Dawkins would seem to be just as mistaken and blinkered as the religionists he derides. Dawkins' bold generalisations rationally require the support of strong rational supportive evidence. Scornful assertions are not evidence. Love would seem to be a great and powerful thing and not a defective brain function. If, until given clear evidence to the contrary, we presume that love is not an irrational brain function designed by Natural Selection to trick us into preserving our offspring, then I agree with Dawkins that love and religion can be linked. Love is our clearest window into the spiritual world and makes us aware of something greater and more profound than an organism's need to replicate. Sadly, so far, religions have tended to act not as a channel to finding love, but more as a barrier between mankind and our instinctive search for spiritual fulfilment.

In seeking to link love and religion, Richard Dawkins refers to what amounts to those undergoing religious ecstasy. Again he seizes upon the most extreme example to advance his case. Ecstasy is a transporting state. Some do achieve ecstasy through spiritual enlightenment. Arnold Schwarzenegger claimed to achieve ecstasy through weightlifting in the gym, lucky man. A sad multitude seek ecstasy though drugs, including Ecstasy. Love can be a path to ecstasy as is reflected in the many songs and poems celebrating love and its many wonderful facets. You will not be surprised if I single out Nick Cave's love song, *Into My Arms*, for its lyrics:

> *"I don't believe in an interventionist God*
> *But I know, darling, that you do ...*
> *"But I believe in Love*
> *And I know that you do too ...*

There is a profound tie between love and goodness.

Epictetus, the stoic philosopher, rightly concluded, "Whoever ... understands good is capable likewise of love; and he who cannot distinguish good from evil ... how is it possible that he can love?"[23] It must be equally true that a loving person must have a functional conscience.

---

[23] 55-135 AD, *The Discourses of Epictetus*, translated by Elizabeth Carter, chapter xxii.

Love is not a trick of evolution. It is not caused by a mere change of brain chemistry, though the brain chemistry may be changed by it. It is something of great spiritual importance. It resonates with that force, which I call God; a force of love and goodness that can be felt by each of us and can give support to each of us. Not support to win a war, not a reward for a prayer of the right formula so that we may pass an exam or win a game, but rather support to be a better person, to be morally stronger, to be more positive and effective in those spiritual realms where being strong and effective is truly important; that is to leave our lives with a spirit at least as undamaged as it was when we were born.

Any conclusion on the topic of love should be left to a poet. Kahlil Gibran writes, "When you love you should not say, 'God is in my heart,' but rather, 'I am in the heart of God.'"[24]

---

[24] *The Prophet*, page 12.

Chapter Nine

Morality and Conscience

Brief consideration of the great wars and the Holocaust of the last century and the growing list of horrors in this one suggests a continuous battle between good and evil.[1]

• Slavery: according to the Wilberforce Institute in 2016 there were thirty-five million people in slavery in the world. It very conservatively estimated that there are thirteen thousand enslaved adults and children in the UK. People-trafficking is now a major part of organized crime. In 2017 slave markets began to operate openly in Libya.

• Inequality: we now have a world of financial uncertainty and austerity as a result of unbounded greed of bankers, speculators and politicians. While the rich still get

---

[1] Zoroastrianism sees existence as a battle between good and evil and other religions tend expressly or by inference to acknowledge positive evil/evil as a force. Hence Satan. Gnostics saw the world as fundamentally evil. I see evil as an absence of love.

richer, the vulnerable bear the burden. As previously mentioned, an Oxfam commissioned report found that in 2016 the richest one per cent in the world owned more than the remaining ninety-nine per cent of us put together.

● Advertising: the media and most modern films and books encourage consumerism and the spiritually corrosive delusion that the way to success and happiness is through acquiring fame, money, possessions and power. Programmes, like *The Real Housewives of Beverley Hills*, depict spiritless lives of luxury as being something to envy. A friend of mine recently attacked my dream that people should think and feel for themselves. She said, 'The trouble is most people don't think for themselves.' The objective of commercialism and religion is to make people into an unthinking flock of sheep ready for shearing.

● The Middle East: this area is now more than ever destabilized and ravaged by war inflamed by the second invasion of Iraq. This war, based on official fake news, caused hundreds of thousands of deaths and almost makes the cruelty of Saddam Hussein seem modest in comparison. I was in the United States a few months after 9/11 and I could find nobody who did not believe the preposterously fake news that Saddam was implicated in the 9/11 attacks. I repeatedly pointed out that that al-Qaeda and Saddam were the greatest enemies, but found only deaf ears.

- ISIS (Daesh): religious extremists are committing atrocities in the Middle East, including genocide of the Yazidi people. The men are murdered and the women used as sex slaves on the basis that they are spoils of a holy war and not equally human due to not being 'People of the Book'. Nineteen Yazidi women were reported as having been burned in cages in front of a large crowd for refusing sex to Islamists.[2]

- Russia is a state riddled with crime and corruption. President Putin, who works closely with the Russian Orthodox Church, has annexed parts of Georgia and Ukraine, acted with extreme violence in Chechnya – twenty-five to thirty thousand deaths – and bombed civilian areas of Syria, including hospitals. It must be conceded though that the West has provoked some of this by starting the Iraq wars, exceeding the mandate to protect Benghazi in Libya by going on to overthrow President Gaddafi – as in Iraq and Afghanistan, without any effective post-war strategy – trying to gain ascendancy in Ukraine and meddling ineffectually in Syria. Murder and attempted murder are committed on individuals in Russia and other countries – like Litvinenko in London and maybe the Skripals in Salisbury. Russian state television

---

[2] *The Times*, 8th June, 2016.

carries false propaganda – e.g. allegations that a Ukrainian fighter shot down the Malaysian airliner and that a boy was crucified by Ukrainian soldiers – but before we Westerners become too judgemental, we must remember our own false propaganda about Iraq and our support for the Mujahedeen in Afghanistan and Pinochet in Chile.

• China: this is still a repressive totalitarian state, which is gradually eradicating Tibet as a nation, is acting with aggression in the Pacific and is sustaining the inhuman regime in North Korea. Cyber war and commercial piracy are often traced back to Chinese territory. Hong Kong booksellers 'disappear'. The moral censure of the world is increasingly muted by China's power.

• The Internet: this is a very mixed blessing. There is exposure of young children to pornography and extreme violence both on the Net and in computer games, like *Grand Theft Auto* and its spawn. The pervasive commercial imperative and the dissemination of information about bomb making and eco-terrorism, radicalisation and serious crime on the 'Dark Net', the Internet Trolls and much more make me regret the invention. For the last fifty years, children have been accelerated towards maturity for the sake of their commercial market value. "Computers are like Old Testament Gods; lots

290

of rules and no mercy."[3]

• Technology: now people find their telephones more interesting than their companions, or the scenery before their eyes, or the life they could be living to the full. People these days appear to worship their mobile phones and these 'Golden Calves' of today, now elevated on 'selfie-sticks,' almost make me sympathize with the Old Testament's genocidal reaction. The poet, Goethe, visited Tivoli near Rome, in about 1787. He viewed the great cascade in the gardens of what is now the Parco Villa Gregoriana and wrote, "The sight of the waterfall there, along with the ruins and the landscape, greatly enriches the soul." When I visited the world famous Tivoli Fountain – La Fontana dell'Ovato – I noticed that six people were facing away taking 'selfies' and many more were simply absorbed by their mobile phones.[4] So spiritually dominated by these new

---

[3] Joseph Campbell (1904-1987), mythologist and seer.

[4] Venerable playwright, Tom Stoppard, said recently, "I worry about the larger question, which is whether *Homo sapiens* are on their last lap before becoming some kind of cyborg, an assimilation of technology into some kind of human being. Someone told me about a Native American who said we should be careful about all our social [media] interactions because the effect of what you say lasts seven generations, and he didn't think we had seven generations left in any meaningful way." *The Times*, 9th November, 2017.

objects of veneration are people that they cannot bear to silence them in theatres. Shower curtains are now available to avoid separation even in the bath. Indeed, many 'phone worshippers are so devout that they kill themselves and others by maintaining their devotions while driving. There have recently been more deaths by 'selfie' than by sharks. In Zimbabwe, Pastor Paul Sanyangore claims to have a direct line to God on his mobile phone.

● Gambling: this destructive addiction has become endemic in the West with rampant advertising, sponsorship and tempting online opportunities destroying those with gambling addiction and their relatives, while the poor and vulnerable squander their money on state-sponsored lotteries with ludicrously long odds against winning.

● Drugs: the cultivation, distribution and consumption of drugs corrode spiritual values in large parts of the world. Politicians, newspapers and voters cling to the costly and destructive myth that states can win a war against illegal drugs by using law enforcement.

● The environment: our wonderful world is pillaged, exploited and damaged for profit. Over one fifth of our *remaining* plant species are threatened by human action.[5] The

---

[5] *State of World's Plants* Royal Botanic Gardens 2016.

core problem, overpopulation, is usually ignored and there is a commercial incentive continually to increase our numbers, which incentive has caused China to relax restrictions on its birth rate. Dr Harari produces some stark statistics:[6] the almost seven billion humans now living together weigh about three hundred million tons, our domestic animals from cows to chickens weigh about seven hundred million tons and the remaining larger animals in the world from whales to porcupines, now weigh in at less than one hundred million tons. "When all the trees are cut down, when all the animals have been hunted, when all the waters are polluted, when all the air is unsafe to breathe, only then will you discover that you cannot eat money." (Cree prophecy).

When I look at the present state of the world I become an angry old man and I am sure that you will disagree with much of this. However, I do hope that you agree that we need more spiritual goodness. The way to this is not through fundamentalist religion or populist mass movement, but for there to be a spiritual awakening in individuals. It is not surprising that the unrest and dissatisfaction in the world feeds a craving for the comforting certainties offered by radical

---

[6] *Sapiens*, page 392.

religionists and by populist politicians harnessing prejudice and resentment. Nietzsche saw the fact that "mankind as a whole has no goals" as a central problem.[7] What is needed is for individuals to find their own moral compass and to follow it. The goal of mankind should be a loving reconnection with the spiritual purpose in life and to achieve this each of us needs individually better to develop a spiritual perception within ourselves, namely Colin Wilson's "Faculty X."

Karen Armstrong, once a Christian nun, writes of the Darwinian vision of nature as being 'red in tooth and claw' and suggests that it "could become a meditation on the inescapable suffering of life … and give us a new appreciation of the First Noble Truth of Buddhism: 'Existence is suffering (*dukkha*)' – an insight that in nearly all faiths is indispensable for enlightenment."[8] I am not particularly attacking the First Noble Truth, which I should prefer to translate as "The Truth of Suffering," but it is troubling that religions do tend so negatively to equate life with suffering. Some religions almost *revel* in suffering. Existence is not suffering. Existence is not negative, rather it is an opportunity to undergo a medley of experiences ranging from ecstasy to agony. There is great joy

---

[7] *Truth and Illusion*, 33.

[8] *The Case for God*, page 310.

to be found in life, despite the inevitability of some suffering. Most of this suffering is man-made. Despite our population explosion, the world still has more than enough food for all and yet many starve, or are malnourished. In the United States enough money is spent on slimming to feed all starving people in the world. The world has sufficient wealth for everybody to be comfortable and yet everywhere there is poverty. The cause is human greed and folly. War, terrorism, slavery, exploitation, sexual and racial abuse are all self-inflicted by man on man. Much illness is due to deprivation, lack of nutritional knowledge, consumption of junk food, fizzy drinks, alcohol and cigarettes, or environmental pollution – e.g. diesel particulates have recently been discovered in the brains of those with Alzheimer's. When human suffering is analysed, apart from unavoidable accidents and illness, our suffering is only very occasionally caused by 'Acts of God' such as earthquakes, tidal waves and hurricanes, and then only insofar as these events are unrelated to human impact on the environment. Indeed, Zeus summed it up perfectly:

> "What a lamentable thing it is
> That men should blame the gods,
> When it is their own transgressions,

Which bring them suffering that is not their destiny."[9]

Contrary to Christianity's leaning towards misery, I doubt that enlightenment is to be found by centring our meditation on suffering. Of course, it is important to develop the spiritual tools better to bear suffering and to put that suffering and all other experiences into their true context. While suffering is not something to be chosen, or revelled in, I disagree with modern happiness guru, Mo Gowdat, who emphatically states, "Suffering offers no benefit whatsoever. None!"[10] Indeed, in his own book Mr Gowdat disproves his proposition by explaining how his own suffering led him to devise a new formula for living, which both made him happy and inspired his best-selling book.

Misery is not the exclusive province of religion. The extreme materialist view of us stumbling through a brief life with no consciousness, free will, or spirit is as equally dreary. One modern atheist, Matthew Kneale, describes the wonderful gift of life as "the grim prospect of our temporary existence."[11] Having acted against conscience and damaged his spirit, Macbeth put Kneale's gloomy view of life more eloquently:

---

[9] Homer's *Odyssey*, book one.

[10] *Solve for Happy*, page 32.

[11] *An Atheist's History of Belief*, page 6.

"Out, out, brief candle!
Life's but a walking shadow, a poor player
That struts and frets his hour upon the stage
And then is heard no more: it is a tale
Told by an idiot, full of sound and fury,
Signifying nothing."[12]

Both extremes of spiritual opinion, religion and materialism, seem to dwell on the negative. St Paul, Cardinal Newman, Matthew Kneale and Richard Dawkins all seem blind to the potential joy in life. Tolstoy, who found the ideas of orthodox religion impossible to accept, made his own search for God and in this search "felt the possibility and joy of being."[13] Is it possible that one day mankind may have the goal of increasing joy and reducing misery? The way to this goal is individual spiritual awareness, but most individuals now seem more distant from spiritual insight than ever.

Rosalyn Weinman of NBC summed up rather bleakly the superficiality of our new 'virtual age': "All the stuff our parents told us didn't come true. No one cares if you're good. People only care if you're good-looking and rich." In more

---

[12] *Macbeth*, Act 5, scene 5.

[13] *A Confession*, chapter: "Seeking God."

spiritual terms, Thich Nhat Hanh wrote of the moment when the first President Bush embarked on the First Iraq War, "When he ordered the attack and said, 'God bless the United States of America,' I knew that bodhisattva[14] needed our help. ... If we get angry, countless obstacles will be set up, blocking our way. So without anger, we have to find a way to tell the president that God cannot bless one country against another. He must learn to pray better than that. ... If we want a better government, we have to begin by changing our own consciousness and our own way of life. Our society is ruled by greed and violence. The way to help our country and our president is by transforming the greed and violence in ourselves and working to transform society."[15]

Confucius said, "One who is Good sees as his first priority the hardship of self-cultivation, and only after thinks about results and rewards. Yes that is what we might call Goodness."[16] The need for individuals to cultivate spiritual awareness and personal conscience becomes ever more pressing as the existence of each of us grows increasingly anonymous. Once upon a time people lived in tribes enjoying

---

[14] Approximately, a person who seeks to open the minds of others, please see also 'bodhissata'.

[15] *Touching Peace*, pp 74-5.

[16] Confucius (551-479 BC), *Confucius Analects*, paragraph 6-22.

communal living, then they created huts and houses for family groups, then those not isolated on farms lived in villages, where everybody still to some extent knew everyone else's business and the prevailing morality moulded behaviour. Then there were towns and cities, where the individual could be freer of oversight, which was not altogether a bad thing. Now technology allows and almost compels anonymity. Forty years ago, Laurie Lee – writer and poet, (1914-1997) – who grew up and lived in a village, remarked on the way cars had driven people from the streets and how television had drawn them from the community to live in an alternative world: "At the time when women once congregated to natter about the joys and griefs that reflected the history of that small community, people now stay indoors to enjoy a second-hand history; *The Archers*, *Emmerdale*, *Neighbours*, written by manipulative scriptwriters in their city offices."[17]

When shut away in cars people often behave as if they have no social duties or need for courtesy. They tailgate, they make rude gestures, they use their horn aggressively, they risk their lives by worshipping their mobile phones and they throw things out of the windows, all of which they would not do if they were pedestrians, or if their personal responsibility were

---

[17] *Village Chistmas*

not cloaked by steel. The telephone is now used by conmen and high pressure salesmen with their telephone numbers withheld. Often, with the anonymity of a phone line people can be very rude. The Internet is riddled with examples of fraud, sexual abuse, fake news, trolls, rudeness, prejudice and aggression, which would never happen in face to face communication, or even amongst people living in a village. Perhaps the Internet is replacing religion as the natural home of the gullible, suggestible and unstable. For instance, the Internet published fake news that a pizza parlour in Washington had tunnels beneath it used by Hilary Clinton and her advisers to abuse and kill children. This ludicrous fake news led to numerous threats against the employees of the restaurant and one worshipper of the Net went so far as to attack the pizzeria with an assault rifle. The Internet is well beyond the control both of social pressure and law and the only hope is that a personal sense of morality develops in individual users. For an individual to strengthen his or her own conscience contributes to the protection of others and strengthens that person against the possibility of being abused. The conscience is a powerful thing. Not only in films and books, but also in real life and criminal history, there are many examples of people, whose sense of guilt and remorse has caused them to reform, or to confess past crimes.

I was always inclined to accept that there was somewhere a fundamental and unchanging code of morality, from which it could easily be decided whether an act was right or wrong. I had developed a belief, or been induced by religious upbringing to believe, that the path of virtue meant duty, loyalty and self-sacrifice. Despite the obvious wisdom of some Buddhist teaching, I had always tended to look askance at the Buddha – Siddhatta Gotama, 6th century BC, or for non-Christians BCE – for deserting his young wife and newly born child to seek Nirvana (*Nibbana*), a spiritual state of wholeness or completeness. Likewise when the Buddha was teaching in a forest clearing he was disturbed by a peasant, who said that he was looking for his escaped cows without which his family would be destitute. The Buddha sent the man on his way telling him that they had not seen his cows and that he should look elsewhere. He then said to his disciples that they should consider themselves fortunate to have no cows. Again, my own moral programming would have required me to jump up and to instigate a general hunt for the lost cows and so I was inclined to condemn the Buddha's inaction. It now strikes me as quite possible that the right way for me would have been to help the farmer and the right way for the Buddha was to continue his teaching.

In the same way, I was disturbed when I heard Dame

Joan Bakewell being asked if she had any regrets about her eight-year affair with the playwright, Harold Pinter, while she was otherwise happily married. She replied with obvious candour, "No, no, why would I? Why would I do that? Life is rich. You have to embrace whatever it brings. Along the way you try to accommodate and not to cause pain, but sometimes there are compulsions that have to be heeded." On the one hand this seems to be an extremely hedonistic philosophy, but on the other Dame Joan appears to be an impressive, good and well-rounded character. Certainly she seems to have led an enviably enlightened and fulfilling life. Horace asked, "Who tells what is well done, what is wicked, what is beneficial, what is not?"[18] I now realize that, by being so morally startled by Dame Joan's statement, I had fallen into the trap that I am trying to warn against. I had simply adopted a conventional set of simplistic moral principles and applied them without conscious consideration. The answer to Horace's question about the arbiter of morality is that the person to tell you in the final instance what is right is you yourself by applying your own conscience. "This above all: to thine own self be true, And it must follow, as the night the day, Thou canst not then

---

[18] Q. Horatius Flaccus (65 BC to 8 AD) "Qui, quid sit pulchrum, quid turpe, quid utile, quid non" *Ep.*i.2, 3.

be false to any man."[19]

Religion is an attempt by one or more persons to dictate to others how their conscience should work. There was a time when I should have harshly criticised Dame Joan and the Buddha for their personal decisions, but now I have at least enough sense to understand that it is not that simple. Perhaps there is even an element of philosophical truth in the lyric of Dolly Parton's *Pure & Simple*: "Anything that feels this right can't be wrong." However, we must always be alert to our conscience, because it is easy and dangerous to drown its quiet voice with self-justification and a wish to have what we want.

There is reason to doubt the existence of a fundamental morality by which acts throughout history can be judged. What is right and wrong cannot be absolutely and finally determined by religions or by rationalists, like Kant, who contended that a universal moral law could be determined by reason. About ten years ago, I began to suspect that what can be wrong for one person might not be wrong for another. I knew a man well, whose life was full of sexual encounters. I envied the variety and intensity of his sex life, but I instinctively knew that for me to live that way would do great harm. Was his way of life, I wondered, a sin for him? He

---

[19] Polonius, *Hamlet, Prince of Denmark*, Act 1, Scene iii.

seemed a pleasant man, very happy and with a superior capacity for living in the present. I noticed that the many women with whom he had affairs also seemed happy and mutual fondness remained after the dalliance had ended. Everybody involved seemed to be unharmed and indeed enhanced by these lusty flings. From what I could discern, it did not seem possible that he was ignoring the dictates of his conscience, or doing something essentially wrong for him. It gradually dawned on me that we each have our own individual moral guide within us. We should consult this unique internal moral guide, which may differ greatly from person to person, and we should not be governed by the moral dictates of scriptures, priests, or philosophers. It would be simple and convenient if a universal set of moral laws could be created and this is what religions try to do. However, it is not that easy. Later, I came upon this passage in *Demian*, where the hero is contending that there is an eternal morality and his friend, Demian, puts my idea quite elegantly: "... each of us has to find out for himself what is permitted and what is forbidden; forbidden for him. It's possible for one never to transgress a single law and still be a bastard and *vice versa*. Actually it is only a question of convenience. Those, who are too lazy and comfortable to think for themselves and be their own judges, obey the laws. Others sense their own laws within them. Things are forbidden to them that any honourable man will do any day of the year and other things are allowed to them that are generally despised.

Each person must stand on his own feet."[20] Immanuel Kant (1724-1804) thought that every person should be a judge of his own conduct, but his 'categorical imperative' was that, in coming to a decision to act, it should be considered whether the ethical reasoning to be adopted could be universally applied. In dissenting from this universality, Demian's view is daring and persuasive: moral decisions should be subjective and, while they may possibly be influenced by rationality, they should not be objectively directed by it. Applying the conscience is an internal spiritual function and not a pure operation of conscious reasoning.

---

[20] Herman Hesse, *Demian*, Chapter Three. "What I feel to be good, is good. What I feel to be bad, is bad," Jean-Jacque Rousseau (1712-1778). Pope Francis, according to *La Repubblica* (1.10.13), said much the same: "Everyone has his own idea of good and evil and must choose to follow the good and fight evil as he conceives them. That would be enough to make the world a better place." Three rules of Theosophy can be found in Mabel Collins' *The Idyll of the White Lotus*, including: "Each man is his own absolute lawgiver, the dispenser of glory or gloom to himself, the decreer of his life, his reward, his punishment." (page 149)

We should not slavishly take our personal commandments from Moses or enlightened philosophers, but should make them for ourselves. What are yours? At most I can only think of five possible personal commandments:

1. Love yourself

2. Love all sentient life forms

3. Love the environment

4. Love your conscience

5. Love the truth

The idea that we should each consult our own conscience about what is right is far from moral anarchy. Of course, people do have capacity for self-deception. Recently I read an article headed, *I Don't Feel Guilty. My Affair Saved Our Marriage.*[21] A mother of four described her brief affair with a younger man in what appeared to be an attempt to persuade her readers and probably herself that she had done

---

[21] *The Times*, 1st October, 2016.

something good, because, after a period of rampant sex had ended with her being cruelly dumped by her young lover, she had been prompted to re-evaluate her marriage. I did not get the impression that this woman had been following her own internal laws. I was pleased that all ended well, but I suspect that deep down she knows that, for her, the end did not really justify the means, especially if that end was purely fortuitous. It is quite sad how so many people try to ease their sense of guilt by denial and by encouraging others to share their sins.

Possibly relevant to the idea of personal morality is a contemporary book called *Stand Firm*. The writer, a Danish professor of psychology, Professor Svend Brinkmann, attacks self-help books, which encourage readers to concentrate on 'the self' as a way of achieving their own desires. *Stand Firm* is described as an anti-self-help book. In one way 'self-help books' are a contradiction in terms, because following the advice of some self-appointed guru is the opposite of *self*-help. Self-help books often suggest that the readers should develop a sense of personal entitlement. Professor Brinkmann cites the advice of self-help guru, Anthony Robbins, whose followers included Presidents George W. Bush and Bill Clinton: "Success is doing what you want, when you want, where you want, with whom you want, as much as you want." This way of thinking he rightly opines "resembles psychopathy or antisocial personality disorder… " Prof. Brinkmann continues, "The danger probably is that we make little gods out of ourselves. We take the exterior authority, the absolute god outside ourselves and put it into ourselves and say something is good because I like it. I'm like a little god who decides what's good and bad in life." I do not disagree with this passage, but because, at first sight, it looks so applicable to my argument, it is necessary to highlight five distinctions. First, this observation is specifically about self-help books and their egocentric advice, which is, as Brinkmann says, "devoid of ethical significance." Secondly, there is a vital difference between what Professor Brinkmann is addressing, namely encouragement of the ego in a way entwined with consumer culture, and an honest appraisal of one's own conscience from an ethical point of view rather than for the purpose of material advancement or pleasure. Thirdly, honest consideration of what you personally think right is far from being a way to worldly success and may very well bar it. Speaking for myself, I have had had many life-choices, which I could have resolved differently to my great material advantage if I had been following the advice of Anthony Robbins. Had I chosen differently I doubt that I should have been happier. Fourthly, while *Stand Firm* criticises self-help advice for paradoxically inviting people to ignore what other people, apart from the self-help guru, say, the stark choice when it comes to your own conscience is either to do what somebody else says is right, or to decide for yourself. Sometimes a person can be pressured to do something and the consensus will be that the required action is the morally right one, but it is not the majority view that should be decisive; real courage is often needed to withstand such pressure and do what is right according to one's own conscience in the face of mob morality. This is the opposite of the self-obsessed self-help credo criticised by the professor as 'psychopathic.' Lastly, *Stand Fast* relies extensively on the wisdom of moral philosophers such as Seneca and Marcus Aurelius. Their anti-consumerist message, which is that we should be at least satisfied with what we have, is properly praised. These sages stress the spiritual dangers of too strongly desiring material things. Let me add the wisdom of Lucretius as to how consumerism can make us miserable and spiritually sick: "So long as the object of our craving is unattained, it seems more precious than anything besides. Once it is ours, we crave for something else. So an unquenchable thirst for life keeps us always on the grasp."[22] Both Seneca and Marcus Aurelius

---

[22] *The Nature of the Universe*, book III, translation by R. E. Latham.

advocated resolving moral dilemmas by rigorous self-examination.[23] That the important answers are within you and that you are the final judge of what is truly right for you does not in any way mean that you have licence to pursue your desires regardless of morality and the good of others. True spiritual freedom is being able to say, 'I will not do that thing I want to do when I want, because it would be wrong.'

Does basic morality change with time and can it vary according to the nature of each person? Seventy years ago we generally obeyed ancient religious opinion that marriage is for life and in consequence to be divorced in those days was a shameful state, often involving a degree of ostracism. This, of course, did not apply to the rich and powerful throughout the ages, but it did apply to the ordinary person. I had a lovely divorced aunt who, even in the 1950s, was generally treated as a pariah. I am sure that you will find similar instances in your own family history. It was considered the correct thing for a couple to remain together however miserable and destructive their continued union might be. It was considered that one spouse should remain in the marriage even if the other was abusive, violent, or damaging the children. This strict code led to terrible suffering and much hypocrisy. This was particularly

---

[23] Please see, for instance, the beginning of chapter 10.

harsh in cases where a person had been completely deceived by their fiancé as to his/her true nature, or had married when too young, or had married under family pressure, or even under duress.

Today, and according to his reported views, Jesus would strongly disagree; the conventional moral view is that people should *not* be locked for life into a loveless, destructive and failed marriage. What good is served by married people suffering a lifetime of misery with no possible hope of respite until death does them part? Divorce gives ex-partners the opportunity to form a happy and fulfilling relationship elsewhere. There are few open-minded people who would still favour the old system of indissoluble marriage, though religions generally continue to favour continuing matrimonial misery. In Islam it might, of course, be argued that husbands have always had easy recourse to divorce – *talaq* x 3. Divorce is an example of changing morality: what was once considered morally unthinkable is now generally viewed as acceptable.

I once had a young pupil, who was a committed Christian. She stated emphatically that "To lie is a sin." I asked her if this was an invariable rule and she, like St Augustine and many Christians, was certain that it was. I asked her to imagine that she was living in Nazi Germany with Jews hidden in the attic. 'What would you say,' I asked her, 'if an SS Officer came to the door and shouted, "Are there any Jews here?"?' Sadly she refused to discuss the matter further. We did not therefore debate the example of Rahab the Harlot, who hid Joshua's spies in her house in Jericho and then lied to her own king about their presence and her knowledge of them.[24] After the destruction of her city, Rahab and her relations were exempted from the slaughter and given a home in Israel as a reward. So even in the Bible the universal immorality of lying seems far from clear. In Rahab's case the morality of her role in genocide might also be questioned. Moving away from the moral ambiguity of the Bible, it is surely undeniable that sometimes it is a moral imperative to lie, because to tell the truth would be utterly wicked. So, despite the extensive bloodletting sanctified in the Bible, most people would say that killing is wrong. However, it is not difficult to imagine circumstances, in which many rational people of conscience would think it right to kill. Certainly most nations' laws recognize self-defence as a justification for killing. Whilst there are pacifists who would follow their principles by refusing to exercise self-defence, it becomes an even more difficult question when the potential victims are, say, one's own children. To stand aside and not to resist the

---

[24] *Joshua* 2:1-4

killing of innocents would be a very testing moral challenge. The answer is surely that it is for every person to ensure that their own conscience is well tuned rather than mindlessly to apply a simple set of moral rules as an absolute statement of right and wrong. We must take personal responsibility and not defer to the opinions of long dead humans like Saints Paul and Augustine, who took it upon themselves to speak for God.

William Blake, who thought the Biblical God – "Nobodaddy" as he called him – to be overfond of "war & slaughtering" and sending people to hell, summed up the risk of religion replacing conscience in these four lines:

> "THE GOOD are attracted by Men's perceptions,
> And think not for themselves;
> Till Experience teaches them to catch
> And to cage the Fairies and Elves." [25]

That is, good people must not slavishly follow the rules of religion, but should reconnect with their own spiritual selves.

Religions set out rigid moral rules. These rules are not open to exceptions, nor by and large do they change with the

---

[25] *Motto of the Songs of Innocence and Experience.*

times. Temporal rules of law do change with the times, albeit with dragging feet. As society changes there is no way that civil laws can entirely resist evolution. Likewise, if there can be no room for exception, laws, whether of state or morality, will often be unjust and cruel. What is worse, religion can replace, or distort, a person's conscience.[26] Most people who have been reared from birth in a particular religion tend to apply the moral guidance of that religion to their lives, rather than refining an individual conscience. This early moral structuring can have a subconscious influence, even over those who believe that they have begun to think for themselves. Thinking for yourself does not mean that all that is good in religions, philosophy or other learning should be rejected. I know a lovely agnostic, who describes himself as "infused with Christian sensibility and traditions." Questioning childhood values can be challenging. In his semi-

---

[26] "Men who live by laws and rules are parasites. Others shed their strength to bring these laws out of nothing into the light of day, but the law-abiders live at their ease – they have conquered nothing for themselves." David Lindsay, *A Voyage to Arcturus*, chapter 19. John Gray considers religionists: "What those who follow these traditions want most is not any kind of freedom of choice. Instead, what they long for is freedom *from* choice." *The Soul of the Marionette*, page 7.

autobiographical novel about Catholicism, Rory McGrath recalls, "I remember thinking when I was about 14, 'I hope God doesn't find out I'm an atheist.'"[27]

Conscience *can* be a painful master and the simple substitution of a ready-made set of values is potentially much more comfortable. Guilt about offending against religious principles can override clarity of thought about what is truly right. Perhaps it because criminals have weak consciences that prisoners are more readily converted into religious fundamentalists? Further, or alternatively, it could be that it is particularly attractive to do wicked things, when given divine sanction. It is to be noted that the 2016 Islamic bombers of Brussels were established criminals.[28] Salah Abdeslam, said to be the last surviving terrorist of the Muslim atrocities in Brussels and Paris – 13th November, 2015 – was reportedly described by his Belgian lawyer thus, "He is a little moron from a world of petty criminals – more of a follower than a leader, with the brains of an ashtray." Abdeslam, he added,

---

[27] *The Father, the Son and the Ghostly Hole*.

[28] The man, who drove a lorry into families celebrating Bastille Day, 2016, was also a petty criminal and a general failure as a human being. Likewise, the murderer, who attacked Parliament in March, 2017, in the name of Islam, turned out to have been a complete loser with a serious criminal record.

had not read the Qur'an, but "had read its interpretation on the Internet." On the other hand, Abdeslam's French lawyer, who was taking over his case, is quoted as saying, "He's a boy who's falling apart and has obviously had an awakening of conscience." Both lawyers were probably correct. A young man, whose moral vacuity is reflected in his early terrorist brutality, having easily been groomed by those offering the moral certainty of a God grateful for violence, but later prompted by the aftermath of his violence to perceive that what he had done was in fact wrong. It is natural for those who are lacking a developed conscience and spiritual character to be potential sponges for religion. Some conversions are not altogether for the worse. For instance, notorious and very violent British criminals, including Arthur White, have become 'born again Christians'. It would seem though that their conversion from extreme drug-fuelled violence and dishonesty to extreme Christianity has, in their case, made them better men.[29] Even a second-hand moral code is better than none, always provided that the effect is to reduce and not to inspire violence. It would still have been better if these men had been shown love as children and if their capacity to think

---

[29] *Tough Talk* by Arthur White, Steve Johnson and Ian McDowall.

316

morally for themselves had been nurtured *before* they began committing their terrible crimes.

Founders as well as followers can be of questionable moral fibre. I have raised doubts about Abraham and St Paul. Joseph Smith, the man who created Mormonism by claiming to have copied the Book of Mormon from plates of gold presented to him by an angel – oddly, they contained extensive passages from the *original* Bible – had been tried and possibly convicted for fraudulently taking money to find lost treasure by gazing psychically into a mirror. His antics in purporting to transcribe the Mormon Bible from the golden plates, upon which only he could look, were denounced by his own wife as false pretences.

Today spirituality and idealism seem to be diminishing. This, according to religionists, is due to lack of religion. The conservative Baptist, Tony Campolo writes of the USA: "The Religious Right puts a strong emphasis on family life, and improvements in this area are desperately needed. Its condemnation of the decline of ethical standards that made our society decent is very timely. Their indignation over the relentless imposition of secular humanist values on the American consciousness is much needed."[30] This is

---

[30] *Choose Love Not Power*, page 97.

evangelical myopia. I have never heard of humanists seeking to challenge family values, or advocating an unethical lifestyle. The British Humanist Association website suggests that, "Humanists tend to think for themselves about what is right and wrong, based on reason and respect for others. They find meaning, beauty and joy in the one life we have, without the need for an afterlife and look to science instead of religion as the best way to discover and understand the world. Importantly for pastoral care, humanists believe people can use empathy and compassion to make the world a better place for everyone." This does not sound like an evil philosophy hostile to family or ethics, though it may be one less intent on preserving unhappy marriages at all costs. What religionists hate about humanism is its denial of God and its emphasis on following the individual conscience[31] rather than obeying a set menu of ethics derived from ancient texts. Probably Mr Campolo is correct to suggest that ethical standards are currently declining. This may be attributable, in part at least, to the impact of religions, their excesses and the vacuum left as ever more people reject them. One does not have to be

---

[31] Jean-Paul Sartre stressed that existentialist-humanism reminded "man that there is no legislator other than himself and that he must, in his abandoned state, make his own choices ...", *Existentialism is a Humanism*, page 53.

religious to be good. The enemy is not humanism, or atheism, or Freemasonry,[32] but commercial materialism made rampant by the 'virtual world' with its tendency to reduce spiritual awareness in individual people.

One contemporary atheist writes, "Frankly, do you need to believe in God to be convinced that sincerity is preferable to dishonesty, courage to cowardice, generosity to egoism, gentleness and compassion to violence and cruelty, justice to injustice, love to hate. Of course not!"[33] This statement of the obvious misses an obvious point: religions have tended to foster just those negative things. Today this is reflected in religiously motivated violence, intolerance and extremism affecting great parts of the world. Religion is not the only culprit. Nationalism and extreme 'idealistic' political movements, such as Maoism, Stalinism, Nazism and the Khmer Rouge, have also caused wars, terrorism, repression and destruction. They have all leant towards the negative side of the list. There is a common thread in extreme religions and political ideologies, which is that each of these moral

---

[32] According to the website of The Royal Hanover Lodge, Freemasonry is based on development of self-knowledge, with emphasis on love of fellow creatures, charity and striving for truth. This sounds good.

[33] A. Comte-Sponville, *The Book of Atheist Spirituality*, page 22.

distortions involves an obligatory belief system with a concomitant assumption that those not sharing it are hostile inferiors. Whether resisting pressure from fascism or religious extremism, the message remains the same for all: think for yourself and listen to your own conscience. Our kindly atheist would not consider shooting families on a Tunisian beach or massacring Muslims in Burma. Why do religionists and political fanatics do these things?

Our Western World is now dominated by amoral commercial forces amassing wealth and power, just as it was once dominated by the Christian Church with the same aims. There is a spiritual void in the world and many human beings lack the individual force of will and conscience to cope satisfactorily. This may well account for the success of religious groups such as Mormons, Jehovah's Witnesses, Moonies, or Islamic extremists, who bother to make personal contact with individuals. Advertisers bombard us all with messages of material greed, but religionists are the only ones directly contacting lonely people with a spiritual message promising salvation. In 2015 some British Muslim girls ran off to join ISIS in Syria and the sister of one of them was surprised, because she declared that her errant sister "used to watch *Keeping Up with the Kardashians*." We have created a new Golden Calf to worship, this time in the form of a spiritually empty edifice of fame, money and power. It is not surprising that some people are so easily drawn by religious zealots away from this spiritual desert to radical religion with promises of spiritual comfort and an amazing certainty of God's will.

Conscience

Do you have a conscience? Of course, you do. It is an inner touchstone, which tells you whether you are doing right or wrong. We sometimes find our conscience uncomfortable and override it for pleasure or convenience. For instance, a person may try to trick the conscience by contriving a grievance against a spouse to justify committing adultery. Whatever the ruse we use to self-deceive, the conscience will prick. Our acts, words and thoughts are not watched by God, but they are watched by ourselves and justly assessed by our conscience. Some people are capable of ignoring their conscience to such an extent that the pricking of it becomes hardly perceptible. Sadly they refuse to see the injury that they do to themselves by reducing their self-esteem and their capacity for happiness. It is commendable that, despite the preference for misery shown by St Paul and his successors, the American Declaration of Independence emphasizes "the pursuit of happiness." Happiness is not to be caught through buying a bigger car but by living a good life. Leading atheist and cosmologist, Lawrence Krauss, says, "We become good people in general by looking at the consequences of our actions and thinking rationally about them."[34] In rational terms, this is the operation of conscience and you do not need to believe in God to examine your actions and to act well. To act well often takes courage. Once, when I was a student living in a hall of residence an injured bird was found in the grounds. The bird was clearly beyond saving and was suffering terribly. A group of students stood around twittering with ineffectual concern. Another student, who was a member of the rifle club, fetched his weapon and killed the bird. The mob turned on him quite irrationally for his courageous and compassionate act. He was a better man than I, but at least I was able to assist him in facing down this misplaced anger.

Although we instinctively know that we try to trick our conscience, there is now scientific research to support this knowledge.[35] Scientists have concluded, "Because people

---

[34] *The Life Scientific*, BBC Radio 4, 31.5.16.

[35] Kouchaki and Gino, "Memories of unethical actions become obfuscated over time", *Proceedings of the National Academy of Sciences*, May, 2016.Harvard and Northwestern University.

value morality and want to maintain a positive moral self-image, but often act dishonestly when facing the temptation to behave unethically, they are motivated to forget the details of their actions so that they can keep thinking of themselves as honest individuals." Here again is our propensity for cognitive dissonance. Unless suffering from a psychological affliction, people can only cheat themselves on a fairly shallow level. This is reflected in the way we invent euphemisms for our sins; so for instance an affair, which is sometimes a brutal betrayal, can be called 'a fling', 'a dalliance', 'a liaison', 'hanky-panky', or 'a carry-on'. Despite our best efforts to comfort ourselves, deeper inside we are still aware and discomforted by having acted wrongly. We cannot truly fool ourselves, but we can so regularly override our conscience that its voice becomes no more than bat squeak in the dark.

I have met many criminals and it seems that every wrong a person does against conscience diminishes that person's capacity for happiness, while every act of goodness increases the capacity for happiness. I stress 'capacity for', because we have all known many good people, who have not been well treated by life. Even then I would say that their capacity to bear misfortune is strengthened by their goodness. You do not have to wait to die to experience heaven and hell. Acting against your conscience will eventually put you in a world without happiness. It is like fighting your way ruthlessly forward to participate in a great feast only to find that the food is made of wax. I have never come across a bad person, who was happy. Some pretend to be happy and others delude themselves, but have you ever come across a person who has lost touch with their conscience and yet been truly happy?

"People who do wrong, wrong themselves. People who act unjustly, act unjustly to themselves injuring their nature ... For if we have lost even the consciousness of doing wrong what reason can we find to carry on living?"[36]

After the Buddha's death, the concept of 'nirvana' became more like paradise after death, but the Buddha himself viewed nirvana as a state of bliss achievable during life. Lacking the Buddha's spiritual powers and devotion, we may fall short of perfect nirvana in life, but we can still increase or reduce our capacity for joy by the way we behave. In regard to happiness, I respectfully disagree with Dr Harari, who

---

[36] Marcus Aurelius, *Meditations*, chapter one. Aristotle, in Book 10 of his *Nicomachean Ethics*, considers that pleasure will at best provide fleeting happiness and that the way to sustained happiness is through living a good and moral life.

suggests that our level of happiness is regulated at 'level X.'[37] If we strengthen our spirit we may become happier. If fifty years ago, the overall happiness of humanity was at level X, it seems painfully clear that the general happiness now registers X minus minus. Statistically, depression in young people is escalating rapidly. The number of suicides in the USA presently far exceeds the total for deaths by violence of all other types put together.

Pliny the Elder's simple observation, "God is one mortal helping another," is quite moving. However, we do not have to be religious, or to read about Scrooge's experience in *A Christmas Carol*, to appreciate the link between doing good deeds and capacity for happiness, because this proposition is also supported scientifically. For example, it has been scientifically demonstrated that doing good works and acting generously reduces blood pressure,[38] increases self-esteem,[39]

---

[37] *Sapiens*, page 435.

[38] Sneed and Cohen, "A Prospective Study of Volunteerism and Hypertension Risk in Older Adults", *Psych Aging* 2013 June; 28(2) 578-586.

[39] Thoits et al., "Volunteer Work and Well-being", *Health Soc. Behav.* 2001 Jun 42(2): 115-131.

reduces depressive symptoms,[40] reduces cortisol levels,[41] increases life expectancy[42] and, indeed, makes people happier.[43] There is a large body of scientific evidence supporting what we all already instinctively know about these links from our own experience. Is this connection between goodness and happiness to do with the spiritual element in us, as even Darwin himself wondered, or is it merely a trick of evolution? If it is purely evolutionary then it seems odd that so many modern people are bad and sad and that perception of spiritual joy is diminishing in the world. The link is probably a spiritual one rather than evolutionary, but, even if it is not, there is still every reason for us all to act generously according to our conscience. In following our conscience it is important to resist attempts by others to impose religious or temporal codes created by ancient and modern 'know-it-alls' in place of our own honest perceptions. Many of my friends, who have

---

[40] Morrow-Howell et al., "Effects of Volunteering on the Wellbeing of Older Adults", *Psych Sci. Soc. Sci*: 2003 May; 58(3): s137-145.

[41] *Scientific American*, 23rd October, 2010.

[42] Poulin et al., "Giving to Others and the Association between Stress and Mortality", *AJPH*, vol. 103, issue 9 (September, 2013).

[43] Professor Sonja Lyubomirsky, reported in *Health News* 24.1.13, "Acts of Kindness Can Make You Happier".

discarded their various religions, still say that they tend subconsciously to feel guilty when they are acting contrary to their childhood teachings. In this respect I bitterly take issue with the spiritually slavish message in *Proverbs* 28:25-26: "... he that putteth his trust in the Lord shall be made fat. He that trusteth in his own heart is a fool ..." Our own heart is the true guide. In this matter, at least, I agree with Nietzsche that it is necessary to progress from the 'moral conscience' – a simple conscience based on faith – to an 'intellectual conscience', which entails questioning one's personal existence and relationship to the world, the universe and everything. We should not weakly settle for the comfort of believing in a received morality, instead we should bravely look into ourselves to use our consciences to discover what is truly right and wrong: "You should become the one that you are."[44] Whether we have conscience as a gift from God, or as a key part of our spirit, or by way of Natural Selection – these concepts are not mutually exclusive – we should follow our conscience and our heart and not the dictates of some fellow ape, who has taken it upon himself to lay down God's law. The Buddha is reported to have said, "Believe nothing, no

---

[44] Friedrich Wilhelm Neitzsche (1844-1900) *Du sollst der warden, der du bist.*

matter where you read it or who has said it, not even if I have said it, unless it agrees with your own reason and your own common sense."[45]

Socrates – almost the Buddha's contemporary – believed that he had a Daemon, or voice within him, which counselled him against doing an act which would be wrong. I have experienced such a voice myself on occasions. When I raised this with one of my closest friends, who is very far from a 'tree-hugger', I was surprised to hear that he also has on occasions experienced a clear inner voice suggesting that he should avoid some act he was considering and always with a moral context. I suspect that we all have this inner voice, if we care to listen to it.[46] All of us, unless afflicted with some mental distortion, feel the prick of conscience, which, unlike the Daemon, is an everyday experience. On one occasion my inner voice went beyond right and wrong and urged me not to take up my second stint in a motor racing event. I told myself that it was just because I had driven badly in my first effort,

---

[45] Some scholars challenge the accuracy of this translation from *Kalama Sutta*.

[46] "She listened to her inner voice, and to nothing else besides. Which of us others is strong enough for that?" David Lindsay, *A Voyage to Arcturus*, chapter 19.

but although I drove well the second time another driver made a mistake and caused me very serious life changing injuries. I wish I had listened. The Stoics believed that each of us is assigned a type of Daemon by God, as a guardian of the soul and that all virtue and happiness comes from acting in concert with this guardian. Whether the voice is internal or not, Socrates, my friend and I would all agree that the inner voice never encourages the doing of anything wrong or negative.

Confucius, also approximately the contemporary of Socrates and the Buddha, placed emphasis on *ren*. '*Ren*' means humanity, goodness, empathy and Confucianism suggests that we each have *ren* within us and that it is our life's task to refine and strengthen our *ren*. The more developed a person's *ren* the greater the capacity for personal peace and happiness, but also the greater peace in the world. There seems little practical difference between *ren*, Socrates' Daemon and what we call conscience.

Arthur Miller's play, *All My Sons*, is primarily about conscience. It is a morality tale about a man who makes a fortune by manufacturing substandard aeroplane parts during the Second World War and then frames his partner and best friend to avoid being convicted himself. Despite his huge wealth, his life becomes totally hollow and eventually his damaged conscience makes him lose everything of real importance. There is one particularly haunting line: "The compromise is always made. In a peculiar way, Frank is right … every man does have a star. The star of one's honesty. And you spend your life groping for it, but once it's out it never lights again."

The true aim of a good life is to avoid that act which your conscience tells you not to do. That is the way to be happy, or at least to retain the capacity to be happy. With every act against our conscience our star shines a little less brightly. I am less convinced, however, that we can ever really extinguish our star, or be unable to relight it with sufficient spiritual effort. I have seen bad people become good, I have seen good people do bad things, but I have never seen a good person turn truly bad. One conspicuous example of a person moving from the dark side was Emperor Ashoka, who ruled most of the Indian subcontinent from 268 to 232 BC. Ashoka began his reign with incredibly bloody wars and repression based on the widespread torture and killing of his own people. Gradually he began to perceive that this was wrong and eventually he adopted Buddhism. He moved across the moral spectrum from being one of the cruellest monarchs in history to sending out missions to encourage peace and philanthropy. On a more modest level, I remember a judge at Portsmouth, who was well-known as miserable, spiteful and obstructive.

Lawyers would groan aloud, when discovering that their case was before him. Then one day he transformed and became kind, constructive and just. His last years on the Bench were happy ones both for him and for all those he helped.

The conscience is either part of the soul/spirit, or it is the necessary partner to it. The conscience tells us what is right and what will damage our soul. Have you ever met anybody who has lived an evil life, but whose spiritual life force still shines out of them? "If only our eyes saw souls instead of bodies how very different our ideals of beauty would be."[47] One happy day we may be governed and guided by people of conscience, but currently in terms of Natural Selection it seems that a weak conscience is an advantage in progressing to power and wealth. Happily there are exceptions. The most obvious exception is Nelson Mandela, the one-time believer in violence, whose great capacity for love and forgiveness in his later life ensured a peaceful transition of power in South Africa. Sadly some of his successors have compromised their consciences all too frequently. I doubt that former President Jacob Zuma's star is shining very brightly these days. Another politician possibly touched by love is Mikhail Gorbachev. One quote attributed to

---

[47] H. H. The Dalai Lama.

Gorbachev is: "I believe in the cosmos. All of us are linked to the cosmos. So nature is my god. To me, nature is sacred. Trees are my temples and forests are my cathedrals. Being at one with nature." So, when the USSR was crumbling, Gorbachev was faced with the choice whether to ensure a peaceful transition even at great risk to himself, or to react with repressive violence. He made the loving choice. Sadly some of the comments attributed to Gorbachev in relation to Putin's present foreign policy seem less encouraging. When our leaders do loving acts wonderful things result, but usually their acts are not those of love and the world changes for the worse.

Shortly after the Second World War and having spent several years in a Japanese prison camp, the great sage, Sir Laurens van der Post, pondered on the way that the Western World had, for a century and a half, worshipped reason and yet had produced bigger and fiercer wars. To van der Post, reason was an essentially masculine thing, which in its pure form, untempered by spirituality, had conspicuously failed to serve humanity well. His conclusion was that, "What needs our understanding and friendship at this restricted moment in time is this other side of life, so brutally locked out of our awareness that it can only draw attention to itself indirectly, humbly and secretly in the joylessness of the results around us.

In this nightfall of the spirit... "[48] For van der Post this alternative spiritual side was essentially 'unconscious and female,' which is much what in the East is called *yin*. Rationalism and scientific scepticism, which materialists see as 'reason', are at least as rampant as they were before the World Wars and the present state of our world still starkly reflects the way in which the spiritual and intuitive part of individuals has been suppressed. Despite, or maybe because of, the advance of technology most people's lives are increasingly joyless. The misguided message of materialism is equally joyless.

I witnessed a practical example of the triumph of instinct over reason. Our son contracted viral pneumonia at the age of five. Just after my wife and I had ended our hospital visit, his condition declined. We were recalled to the hospital, because he was dying. When we arrived back we could see him lying in his intensive care cot surrounded by life-support systems and monitors. As these tubes and wires were manifestly keeping him alive, reason dictated that they should not be disturbed. However, to the horror of the medical staff, my wife stepped in and picked him up so that everything fell away. Although *in extremis*, limp and breathless he recognized

---

[48] *Venture to the Interior*, preface.

his mother and giggled. I am certain that without that intuitive moment he would have died. *The Horse Whisperer* is a beautiful story of a young girl and her horse, both left physically and emotionally disabled by being hit by a truck. So extreme are the horse's injuries that rationality conclusively demands that he be put down. The mother, a powerful left-brained business woman, intuitively senses that the recovery of horse and daughter are inextricably linked.[49] Rationalism must be tempered and even challenged by our intuitive instincts. By reason of religious misogyny and male philosophers' veneration for logic, intuitive thinking has been derided for thousands of years. Intuitive thinking is at least as important as logic.

Fifty years on from van der Post's observations, physicist, Dr Fritjof Capra, reached much the same conclusion: "At present our attitude is too *yang* – to use again Chinese phraseology – too rational, male and aggressive. Scientists themselves are a typical example. ... I believe that the world view implied by modern physics is inconsistent with our present society, which does not reflect the harmonious

---

[49] Nicholas Evans, "There were such moments, he knew, when the world chose thus to reveal itself, not as it might seem to mock our plight or our irrelevance, but simply to reaffirm for us and all life the very act of being."

334

interrelatedness we observe in nature. To achieve such a state of dynamic balance, a radically different social and economic structure will be needed: a cultural revolution in the true sense of the word. The survival of our whole civilization may depend on whether we can bring about such a change. It will depend ultimately, on our ability to adopt some of the *yin* attitudes of Eastern mysticism: to experience the wholeness of nature and the art of living with it in harmony."[50]

This view expressed by a modern physicist informed by Eastern mysticism is in its essence strikingly similar to the ancient wisdom of Native Americans as revealed in this Ojibway prayer to the Great Spirit:

> *Look at our brokenness*
> *We know that in all Creation,*
> *Only the human family*
> *Has strayed from the Sacred Way.*
>
> *We know that we are the ones*
> *Who are divided*
> *And we are the ones*
> *Who must come back together*

---

[50] *The Tao of Physics*, pages 339-340.

To walk in the Sacred Way.

Grandfather, Sacred One,
Teach us love, compassion, honour
That we may heal the earth
And heal each other.[51]

Important though it is, reason alone cannot return us to the sacred way, or to any form of joyfulness. The Ojibway do not pray for machines to kill and process buffalo more efficiently, or for more scientific rationality. What impulse has taken so many of us from the path of love, compassion and honour? Why should anybody not choose a moral and loving life? Many individuals have lost their way due to their upbringing and the force of commercial materialism. A strict religious upbringing with a set of rules to obey without scope for intuitive questioning cannot help. Not surprisingly the *Bhagavad Gita* – Hindu scripture – enjoins believers to follow "scriptural commands," but crucially it also requires the believer to apply to this obedience "an intuitive

---

[51] Wa-Na-Nee-Che and Brid Fitzpatrick, *Great Grandfather Spirit*, page 1.

understanding."[52] At the other extreme materialists deride intuition[53] and mysticism. True happiness does not come from adopting a myth, or from accumulating wealth, or from applying pure reason. We have a spiritual component to be nurtured during life and which in some form survives death. Maybe those of us believing this are suffering a misfiring in the brain, as Dawkins suggests. Passing over the question of how materialists have such supreme confidence in their own brain function, dualist thinking is benign. If we, who believe that reason must be tempered by some input from our spiritual side, are indeed suffering from a 'God Delusion,' then no real harm can be done by such a kindly misfiring. Regardless of the truth about the existence and nature of the spirit, a moral and loving life brings great benefit both to the person living it and to the countless others touched by it.

Another truth caught by the Ojibway in their prayer is

---

[52] Book XV1: 23-24.

[53] Book XI of the *Bhagavad Gita* is devoted to the importance of intuition: e.g. self-realization is referred to as an "intuitive realisation" which is "the king of sciences, the royal secret, the peerless purifier, the essence of dharma [our righteous duty]"

that mankind is just one part of the totality of living things[54] and, far from being a superior part, we are the segment most in need of amendment. Likewise, Dr Harari concludes that we *Homo sapiens* are not at all special, save in our destructive potential: "Humans are the outcome of blind evolutionary processes that operate without goal or purpose."[55] Whilst our ancestors may be forgiven for not fully understanding this, surely today it is clear that our evolution to date, when we have become 'too clever for our own good,' has been a process just like the process creating all other life forms. If this is so, then God did not create us specially. It is equally improbable that in our evolved state we turned out by chance to be in God's image. However, as so many Native Americans sensed, this does not mean that humanity is necessarily without a spiritual element, or that there is no God. The key

---

[54] Anne Conway (1631-1679), English philosopher, saw all living things as endowed with a spirit; referring to all living things she opined that "whole creation, is but one only Substance or Essence in Specie." (*The Principles of the Most Ancient and Modern Philosophy*, chapter 6.4) For all creatures ranking on an infinite staircase of future lives depended on goodness in life. Plato saw souls climbing, or sometimes descending, a ladder according to and retaining the benefits of moral training in life.

[55] *Sapiens*, page 438.

338

qualification is not being human but being alive. All living things share a life spark. All living things have a spirit. The *Divine Life* fills all things. We humans are not supremely special in spiritual terms and we are only exceptional in one respect: unlike our fellow life forms we have managed to wander far from the 'sacred way.' It is by reason of being alive and not by reason of being *Homo sapiens*[56] that we have a spiritual dimension. Each human has the capacity, if that individual chooses to use it, to find the true path by using the evidence of the senses and conscience. Unlike other life forms, we do have the ability to illuminate this evidence by considering the experience and spiritual ideas of others ranging from Socrates to the Ojibway. Unfortunately the current trajectory of humanity seems set to take us ever further from the sacred way.

---

[56] Sadly the widely believed report, that 85% of Conservative Christians in America polled that they would disown their child if found to be *Homo sapiens,* is a hoax.

Chapter Ten

The God Conclusion

When Einstein was asked if he believed in God, he replied, "First tell me what you mean by God, and then I'll tell you if I believe in him." Leading atheists, like Dawkins and Hitchens, expressly acknowledge that they cannot prove the non-existence of God. This concession is probably over-generous in its generality. The claim that it cannot be proved that God does not exist is equally subject to the Einstein test. What form of God is said to be beyond disproof? If what is meant by God is an entity which actively intervenes in the world and in the affairs of men, then it seems that quite a powerful body of proof can be amassed to dispute the existence of such a God. If God is defined as an omnipotent, infinitely wise and just overseer, then great injustices and sufferings past and present tend strongly to refute such a concept. If God is said to have spent a week creating the world just over six thousand years ago, the evidence against this God is overwhelming. God in such forms is more than Russell's 'teapot in space', because God is defined so specifically that if he existed in any of those forms there would be clear evidence of his existence and his benign influence.

What God is not is relevant to what God is. God may be, but may not necessarily be, the creator of the Universe. God could be part of that creation. God may be Voltaire's "clockmaker", or part of the clock. If there is a God, then God is very different from the one portrayed in most religions. Where do we begin to look for evidence of God? Not in contemplating the universe, but looking inside ourselves.

"Nothing is sadder than those people, who go around all of creation and as the poet says, 'search the bowels of the earth' and peer intently into the minds of others without once realizing that all they need to discover is their own inner spirit and to nurture it sincerely."[1]

Marcus Aurelius is right in identifying our own inner spirit as the key to spiritual discovery. As a dedicated seeker for spiritual truth himself, he missed the sad fact that many

---

[1] Marcus Aurelius, *Meditations*, chapter three: "We listen for guidance everywhere except from within," Parker J. Palmer, *Let Your Life Speak: Listening for the Voice of Vocation*

people, rather than seeking in the *wrong* place, are not seeking at all. A lack of interest in spiritual development can be due to the adoption of a set of rigid religious guidelines taken 'off the peg'. Talking of religion, Jesus said much the same as Aurelius, "... The kingdom of God cometh not with observation: Neither shall they say, Lo here! or, lo there! for, behold, the kingdom of God is within you."[2] Tolstoy wrote a book called *The Kingdom of God Is Within You*, in which the great man found God in love and espoused pacifism. He was struck by how profoundly the Orthodox Church's blessing of Russian armies on the way to war contradicted Jesus' message of peace and love. Blessing of armies was, in his view, a blasphemy. The importance of looking to one's inner core is generally recognized. For instance, Yajnavalkya, Vedic sage of Hinduism, talked of the *altman*, which is our deepest inner core: "This Self within *Brahman* [the All] is this *altman* of

---

[2] *Luke* 17:20-2. Despite his love of Rolls Royces, Bhagwan Shree Rajneesh, Acharya Rajneesh (Osho 1931-90) created ten 'commandments' as a matter of amusement, three of which seem particularly true: "(1) Never obey a commandment unless it's coming from within yourself, ... (3) Truth is within you, do not search for it elsewhere, (4) Love is prayer ..."

343

yours,"[3] although it must be conceded that he did not encourage the seeking out of our *altman*.

In advising us to look within ourselves, Aurelius implicitly catches another truth. We are encouraged by religions to believe that God takes an interest in every minute part of our lives. Just like the absurd idea that God created us in his image, this is to get things the wrong way round. Humanity naturally finds it tempting to believe that the doings of we advanced apes are of infinite interest to God. That spiritual force to which, for the want of another name, I refer as God, is not interested in the minutiae of our lives. Rather it is for us to interest ourselves in God. We cannot do this by blind faith, or by formal worship, or by following archaic mumbo-jumbo like religious rules for dress or diet. It is by discovering and nurturing our own inner spirit that we become better attuned to that universal force. We nurture our spirit by acting lovingly, mindfully and by attending to our conscience. Hermann Hesse wrote, "I do not consider myself less ignorant than most people. I have been and still am a seeker. I have begun to listen to the teachings my blood whispers to me ... Each man's life is a road towards himself. Each of us is

---

[3] Yajnavalkya (7th or 8th century BC), *Brhadaranyaka Upanishad*, 4.5.15.

able to interpret himself to himself alone."[4]

By seeking and becoming better attuned to the 'Great Mystery' we become spiritually stronger. It is a virtuous circle. In consequence, we can better love ourselves and thereby increase our capacity to love others. We can enlarge our potential for true happiness, just as, by acting contrary to the small voice of the spirit within us, we can diminish our capacity for love and happiness. Contrary to Paul's passion for self-denial, neither pleasure nor passion is intrinsically wrong, let alone sinful. However, it is important to ensure that the loud temptations of pleasure and passion do not deafen us to the sometimes quieter and less welcome voice of conscience. Excesses like drug and alcohol abuse can drown the conscience, muffle its voice and damage the spirit.

Atheists ridicule religion and, having to their satisfaction rationally refuted religion, they mistakenly believe that God has also been disproved. It is possible to approach this in the other direction and to suggest that God is the spark of truth that has led both to the creation of so many religions

---

[4] (1887-1962) the introduction to *Demian*. This is much like the sage advice of Joseph Campbell that we should look into ourselves to "follow our bliss" (what is spiritually right for us) and to ascribe our own meaning to our own lives (please see his *The Power of Myth*, especially page 120).

and their longevity. From cave paintings and prehistoric spiritual artefacts it is clear that mankind has always been aware of a spiritual element and has historically created rituals relating to the spirit. This evidence of prehistoric and almost ubiquitous recognition of the spirit suggests that there is something mystical beyond mere existence. It may even support John of Damascus's suggestion that "the awareness that God exists is implanted by nature in everybody."[5] At all times and in all places, including islands and other isolated areas, separate groups of people have clearly believed in a spiritual, or mystic, element in life and have often responded by formulating rituals and religions. Religions can be utterly absurd and repugnant. The Aztecs believed in three top gods, including a hummingbird wizard and plumed serpent, which required regular sacrifices of human blood and hearts to feed them and yet this religion lasted as long as the Aztec nation. In comparatively modern times, in western civilization, the Carthaginians and Phoenicians probably engaged in religious rituals involving child sacrifice. Just because religions often evolve into quite distorted forms does not mean that there was no element of truth originally inspiring and underlying them. Why have religions sprung up everywhere and why have they

---

[5] *De fide Orthodoxa*, 1, 1. PG 94,789.

persisted despite their manifest absurdities and often cruel consequences? The answer is either that human beings have, throughout almost our entire time on Earth, suffered a catastrophic misfiring of brain modules, or that there really is something to life beyond a mere set of chemical reactions and bodies obeying the laws of physics. The history of religion suggests that there is an element of truth at the core of all religions relating to the dualistic spiritual side of people. If there were no element of truth at all within a religion, or within any proposed system for guiding human behaviour for that matter, it seems impossible to conceive that it could be widely established let alone perpetuated so extensively in both time and space. Religions in their evolved and distorted state may be absurd and may indeed 'poison everything,' but the reason for their creation, power and longevity is that there is a kernel of spiritual truth within the mass of religious nonsense. The faithful are, to plagiarize *Corinthians*, 'looking through a glass darkly,' but they are still glimpsing something true and supremely important.[6] New religious converts tend to be filled

---

[6] "A deeper principle must be at work" and "… important psychological truths can be found in the rubble [of religion]." Sam Harris, *Waking Up*, pages 9 and 7. Leo Tolstoy found truth and falsehood in religion. He asked, "Where did the truth and falsehood come from? Both were contained in the so-called holy tradition and

with light, love and joy. So powerful is this feeling that they yearn to tell others. These feelings are not illusory; rather they reflect the wonder of a first glimpse of the spiritual element in life. It is for them a first step on the spiritual path, but the formulaic belief system of most religions may also mean that it is their last. As religions themselves evolve, so the glass becomes darker, but there is still a glimmer of spiritual truth, which attracts us, not least because other avenues of spiritual development have been closed to us by reason of those religions themselves. "The Truth, in the matters of religion, is simply the opinion that has survived."[7] That is why I have tried to challenge the surviving opinions. However, it seems probable that there is a Truth underlying religions, their duration and predominance.

Is there a good reason for the past power of religion, or are all religions hollow myths? Dr Yuval Harari in *Sapiens* places great emphasis on the importance of 'myth'. He argues that the key to humanity's big jump from small bands of hunter-gatherers to large groups capable of working together to eradicate other related hominids was an ability to share myths, or fictions. He points out that much in the modern

in the scriptures. Both the falsehood and the truth had been handed down by what is called the Church."

[7] Oscar Wilde (1854-1900), *The Critic as an Artist*.

world is mere fiction, like laws, national borders, currency etc., all of which depend on general recognition to have any practical function in reality. The most obvious common myths enabling large numbers to cooperate would be 'A has the function of a king', or 'B is empowered by our constitution', or 'C's guidance is divinely inspired.' These myths, he argues, gave our ancestors enough in common to allow and encourage them to work with each other, even though they were essentially strangers. The jump from small groups to large numbers working together is called by Dr Harari the 'Cognitive Revolution'. As it was a revolution based on myth it was essentially the triumph of cognitive dissonance, or a massive cognitive failure. The importance of myth in promoting unity was recognized by an Italian prime minister in 1912, when he attacked the possibility of historical accuracy discrediting "beautiful national legends."[8] Presently anger runs high amongst Hindus in India, protective of the purity of their myths, over the release of a film retelling the partly mythical story of 14th century Queen Padmavati. According to an epic poem, she was besieged in a fortress by the Muslim sultan of Delhi, who was obsessed by tales of her beauty. She chose to

---

[8] David Gilmour, *The Pursuit of Italy: A History of a Land, Its Regions and Their Peoples*.

burn herself on her husband's pyre, rather than submitting to the sultan. The reaction to an alternative version, including Internet threats and an attack on the set, has so far culminated in an offer by Suraj Pal Amu, a senior official of the ruling BJP party, of one hundred million rupees for the murder of the leading actress, Deepika Padukone. Religious violence results, in part, from a determination to preserve myth at all costs.

There was undoubtedly a time when mankind moved away from hunter-gatherer groupings. Natural selection would not have favoured cognitive dissonance until the ability to cooperate in large numbers made survival more likely. So in a small tribe Ug tells Og that he has seen a tiger. When Og was a child his father told him that there were no tigers. If Og's core belief about tigers makes it impossible for him to consider the possibility that Ug's warning is true he may well be eaten. His survival depends on what is really true, rather than belief. After the cognitive revolution, Ugson and Ogson live in a small nation. Ugson tells Ogson that their king is appointed by God. Even though Ogson has good intellectual reason to doubt this, it is now to his advantage to share the myth, because truth may kill him. Did a tendency to cognitive dissonance arise from the need to work in greater groupings, or did it trigger the leap? Either way, this leap seems to have broken our link with nature and spiritual awareness. I suspect that the ability to work more materialistically in greater groupings relates to another cause. The *Sapiens* of the last century was a book called *The Origin of Consciousness in the Breakdown of the Bicameral Mind*. The word 'bicameral' in this snappy title means separate function of the two halves of the brain. The main theory of the writer, Julian Jaynes, is that we came late to consciousness, but the aspect of his theory which seems quite persuasive, is that at some time in the past – possibly about 1200 BC, around the Mediterranean – a series of natural disasters obliged man to change his brain function. Before man had lived in reasonable harmony with nature, but now that freak accidents of nature were threatening his existence, man was obliged to rely more on his left brain for technical solutions. The practical benefits derived from this use of the material side of the brain led to the dominance of the left brain. Certainly it is clear that when, in more recent times, left-brained Europeans came across nations of right-brainers living in balance with nature the right-brainers had to adapt their brain function or be destroyed. Maybe subjugation of the right brain makes us more inclined to swallow myths and the theories of Jaynes and Harari are two sides of the same coin.

Overall Dr Harari is scathing about the damage we have done, but at one point his left brain appears almost seduced away from his damning analysis: "Cognitive dissonance is often considered a failure of the human psyche. In fact, it is a vital asset. Had people been unable to hold contradictory beliefs and values, it would probably have been impossible to establish and maintain any human culture."[9] Cognitive dissonance in any guise is a grave human failing as the destructive history of *Homo sapiens* surely demonstrates. To hold two conflicting beliefs in one's head without trying to resolve them is unforgivable. To hold a false belief and to deny conflicting evidence is just as bad. Dr Harari himself makes out a powerful case for viewing as disastrous both for our world and for ourselves the great change by which we moved from comparatively happy hunter-gatherers to the dominant species. If this move was, as he suggests, facilitated by cognitive dissonance, it underlines the importance and urgency of seeking truth above belief. It is significant that the dystopia, so graphically described in Orwell's *1984* – features of which are now recognizable in our world – was centred on cognitive dissonance in the form of 'doublethink': "*Doublethink* means the power of holding two contradictory beliefs in one's mind simultaneously, and accepting both of them. ... The process has to be conscious, or it would not be

_____

[9] *Sapiens*, page 184.

352

carried out with sufficient precision, but it also has to be unconscious, or it would bring with it a feeling of falsity and hence of guilt."[10] We must escape cognitive dissonance before our fictions snuff out our spiritual awareness – and any life on Earth more complex than cockroaches and moss.

Religion has certainly functioned to unite large numbers in a willingness to trust each other enough to cooperate. This reasoning well explains why religions and rulers favour the myth of an interventionist God overseeing our actions and ensuring that we conform to religious and civil rules. However, while it is undeniable that religion would be amongst those concepts capable of that function, it is doubtful that the spiritual awareness at the heart of religion can be wholly attributed to the need to band together in groups of more than a hundred and fifty. Religion may well have been part of the 'Cognitive Revolution,' but was spirituality purely a fiction born of that revolution? Probably not. First, *Homo sapiens*, well before the era of large groupings, showed an inclination to spirituality and ritual. Dr Harari appears to agree with "most scholars" that animism – belief in the soul/spirit – was common amongst hunter-gatherers long before the

---

[10] *1984*, part 2, chapter 9.

'Cognitive Revolution.'[11] Far from doubting the argument in *Sapiens*, I suggest that the fact that animism *was* common amongst most of the small groups of our ancestors, long before the developmental leap based on the capacity to create myths, supports the view that animism is based on what humans actually sensed and not derived from their capacity to create myths. Early humans commonly believed in the spirit, because they perceived evidence for the spirit. Now fewer humans perceive this truth, because they are distracted by the modern fictions that they require a new car or a designer handbag to be truly happy. More recent studies of surviving small groups of hunter-gathers show them to have spiritual awareness and religious practice clearly unrelated to a move to larger groupings.[12] Secondly, archaeology appears to show that Neanderthals, who were never able to function in larger groups, also had burial rights, ritual and an appreciation of the mystical. Thirdly, if the need for a common fiction was the driving force, it is not difficult to think of uniting myths, which could have been more easily imagined by our ancestors, than complex abstract concepts of spirits and gods. Fourthly, while these groups of our ancestors were making the leap from

---

[11] *Sapiens*, page 60.

[12] *Sapiens*, page 58.

small bands to large cooperatives of unrelated individuals, they were doing this separately throughout most of the world and yet all 'religions' tend to have striking commonality at their heart. Dr Harari notes that at the time Europeans invaded Australia there were up to six hundred separate tribes of aboriginals, all of which had a separate religion.[13] That each tribe had a ritualized form of spiritual awareness suggests that religion has roots in something beyond a need to bond into greater groupings. Again this universality of religion containing common threads seems to suggest that there is some genuine perception of spiritual truth prompting and informing it.

Lucretius – born about 100 BC – disagreed. This great observer and scientist even presented a treatise on atoms, so he was a very advanced thinker for his time. He also wrote about religion, "Let us now consider why reverence for the gods is widespread among nations. What has crowded their cities with altars and inaugurated those solemn rites that are in vogue today in powerful states and busy resorts? What has implanted in mortal hearts that chill of dread which even now rears new temples of the gods the wide world over and packs them on holy days with pious multitudes? The explanation is not far to

---

[13] *Sapiens*, page 50.

seek. Already in those early days men had visions when their minds were awake, and more clearly in sleep, of divine figures ..."[14] He also suggests that awareness of celestial phenomena caused men to ascribe to the gods the control of the scheme of things ranging from the movement of the planets to the weather. "Poor humanity," he adds, "to saddle the gods with such responsibilities and throw in a vindictive temper!" He foreshadows Spinoza and Einstein in concluding, "True piety lies rather in the power to contemplate the universe with a quiet mind."

Lucretius's first explanation is unconvincing. Assume a group of prehistoric people, who have not yet had any religious or spiritual ideas. What a complex leap of abstract thought it would be for these primitive people to construct from dreams a wholly fictional concept of hidden divine beings. Also, the dream explanation would need satisfactorily to explain how people throughout time and everywhere in the world, whether on isolated islands or in distant forests, came to create such extraordinarily odd beliefs in a divine being or force, which belief systems do have so many common features. If we discount an intervention by something like von Däniken's *Chariots of the Gods* and the great monolith in

---

[14] Book V, 1130-1196.

2001 A Space Odyssey, then what explanation is there for so many religions to arise and endure other than that there is a strong spark of truth at their core? This spark we instinctively sense, despite those religions themselves being, over time, distorted to absurdity by those wanting control. Nor should dreams be dismissed. Quite possibly dreams can sometimes provide a helpful bridge to the mystical.

Lucretius' second explanation for religion, namely a need to account for the movements of the cosmos and of nature, seems no more persuasive. The wonders of the universe could be a reasonable justification for speculating that there is something more to life than physics alone can explain. Lucretius himself notes the unanswerable questions posed by the creation and infinity of the universe. These matters at least encourage consideration of the possibility of some hidden force, which is at least as much beyond our understanding as questions like 'what preceded the Big Bang?' and 'what is outside the universe?' The Big Bang brings us to Aristotle's concept of the Prime Mover.[15] Aristotle argued with seemingly impeccable logic that every movement has a cause. If each movement is traced back to its origin there will

---

[15] Aristotle (384 to 322 BC),"ὃ οὐ κινούμενος κινεῖ,ho ou kinoúmenos kineî" – that which moves without being moveable. (*Metaphysics* XII, 1072a)

inevitably be a first and single cause. That initial cause, for which there is no earlier cause, is the Prime Mover. That Prime Mover he saw in metaphysical terms as God. He suggested that the Prime Mover was itself infinite and incapable of change and therefore it must be pure and good, because otherwise there would be the possibility of change by improvement. He saw 'love' as being a significant part of this goodness and capacity to instigate the first move. God was, according to him, "complete reality." Aristotle's logic was adopted by St Thomas Aquinas (1225-1274 AD) as the basis of the first two of his five arguments for God. Darwin, like Aristotle, was greatly impressed by consideration of what he referred to as "The First Cause" and how it is possible to account for the origin of the Universe.[16]

Unlike Darwin, evolutionary biologist, Dr Dominic Johnson, feels able to dismiss religion as a delusion born out of evolutionary benefits: "Humans the world over find themselves, consciously or subconsciously, believing that we live in a just world or a moral universe, where people are supposed to get what they deserve. Our brains are wired such that we cannot help search for meaning in the randomness of

---

[16] Autobiography, page 93. Likewise Leo Tolstoy, *A Confession*, chapter: "Seeking God."

life."[17] It would certainly be very comforting to think that we live in a just world. However, when there is so much cruelty and unfairness all around us it would seem very difficult to believe that justice prevails. If we in the pampered West find it difficult to see life other than as inexplicably random, it is almost inconceivable that ancient and primitive peoples living in times of war, famine, plague, high child mortality, slavery, religious persecution, or widespread poverty might have even begun to consider the world as just. I doubt if the majority of people living today believe that our world is moral and just. Likewise, it would be wonderful to find some meaningful pattern in the chaos of life, but we are either the masters of our own destiny, or we are not. One cannot have just a limited portion of free will. You can have neither free will nor any meaningful input into your destiny, if life is ordered and just. This modern Dr Johnson himself acknowledges the challenge posed to his theory by the strikingly unjust and capricious nature of the deities recorded in the scriptures of many religions; the injustice and capriciousness of the Old Testament God has been reviewed at length, but other once popular gods, like Zeus (Jupiter) and Thor, contradict any

---

[17] *God is Watching You; How the Fear of God Makes Us Human*, 2016.

suggestion that their devotees believed in an ordered and just world. That gods are created in such a cruel or arbitrary image does not accord with the theory that religion is being primarily motivated by a hardwired belief in a just and explicable world. To preserve his theory of religion being an evolutionary way of denying the randomness of life, Dr Johnson contends these unjust gods are 'exceptional outliers', but this is a clearly untenable view. Poor Job is afflicted and Abraham is favoured by God in the scripture of all three monotheist religions. To suggest that spiritual awareness is really an illusory product of hardwiring for the purpose of evolution is a bold claim requiring compelling proof. If belief in God is hardwired then people are to be congratulated for creating secular societies whether in the late Roman Republic, where religious ceremony continued in form only, or in the nominally Communist bloc countries of the last century. Likewise, many belief systems, which are loosely described as religions, such as Taoism, Confucianism and Buddhism, do not, in their more basic forms, depend upon a belief in God. In evolutionary terms do we benefit from the fear of divine retribution from a capricious God, or was Christopher Hitchens right in suggesting that we do not need religion to be good? I agree with Hitchens that belief in a vengeful God is not essential to good moral conduct. Fear of God is certainly not the beginning of wisdom. There is a stark choice here: either we are hardwired to delude ourselves into believing in the existence of God, or we are not hardwired and what mankind perceives is true. Again, atheists raising these arguments do not explain how they have escaped the hardwiring they perceive in others. There is absolutely nothing wrong in our tendency to seek for spiritual truth underlying and even possibly making sense of our lives and the world. What is very wrong is to create fictions either to comfort, or to control. 'Perception', say the materialists, is unreliable. Science proves that a thing is colourless and the appearance of colour really relates to which colours on the spectrum of visible light are absorbed and which reflected. Accordingly, the materialists suggest that we wrongly perceive a red car as red, because its colourless paint merely reflects red light. I say that the car is red and that science has simply refined our meaning of 'red' by allowing us to understand the way colours appear to the eye. Our perception that the car is red is still essentially true and what better ways of finding spiritual truths do we have than by using our own perceptions and applying our powers of reason and intuition to them? Without proof to the contrary, it seems more rational for us to presume that our perception of spiritual reality is not a mere evolutionary trick. In summary, the theory that we are hardwired to religious belief for evolutionary reasons is unconvincing, because:

• Confounding the argument that Darwinian theory refutes God is Darwin's own declaration that "a man may be an ardent theist [a believer in a God, or gods] and an evolutionist."[18] Darwin had serious concerns about Christianity, especially after the death of his daughter, but he was not an atheist. Darwin never quite declared himself to be a 'theist' and it is sad to note that the relevant passage in his autobiography was taken shockingly out of context by Cardinal Pell in a debate with Richard Dawkins in 2012. Contrary to Pell's claim, nothing in Darwin's book suggests him to be a believer and even if Darwin had declared himself a

---

[18]Also, "I have never been an atheist in the sense of denying the existence of God" and "agnostic would be the most correct description of my mind." (*The Victorian Church*, 2, 2) Later he wrote, "When thus reflecting I feel compelled to look to a First Cause having an intelligent mind in some degree analogous to that of man; and I deserve to be called a Theist." However, he later suggested that his feelings had cooled and concluded, "I cannot pretend to throw the least light on such abstruse problems. The mystery of the beginning of all things is insoluble by us; and I for one must be content to remain an Agnostic." (*Autobiography*, pp 92-93)

theist, this would have been very far from an endorsement of Christianity. My point is that Darwin, the father of evolution, expressly affirmed that evolution was not inconsistent with belief in God;

• Dr Johnson, like Richard Dawkins, is an evolutionary biologist and so he is hard-wired to see matters in evolutionary terms, just as a priest would see them in religious terms;

• As Dr Johnson acknowledges, religions, in which the divine beings or the divine process are unfair and arbitrary, are inconsistent with the theory that religion has an evolutionary role in creating a fairer and more explicable world. Most religions appear to describe divine beings and processes strikingly *lacking* in fairness and consistency. I should like Dr Johnson to show me a religion that really makes life's events seem more explicable and just;

• This evolutionary theory depends upon the premise that we need religion to act well and to produce a cohesive society, but religion is not a prerequisite for either and, indeed, historically religionists have not been conspicuously good or constructive and religions have tended to be divisive, repressive and destructive;

• Religion has tended to impede scientific, medical and technological progress, which does not look very evolutionary. It would be delicious irony if religion springs from evolution, when Christianity bitterly opposed the concept of evolution, executed evolutionists in the 17th century, aggressively resisted Darwin and still clings to Creationism and Intelligent Design;

• Religion has tended to create and perpetuate prejudice and subjugation and to resist the introduction of more humane laws, which again is not evolutionary unless, say, it is better in evolutionary terms for the function of women to be restricted to minor and menial roles. For the potential of half the population to be radically limited does not jump to the eye as very helpful in evolutionary terms;

• There is no scientific evidence for 'hard-wiring', or for misfiring of brain modules, or for the claim of universal delusion, and the most obvious explanation for our tendency to perceive a spiritual element in life is surely that there is such an element.

John Gray doubts the evolutionary thread in materialist argument: "These 'new atheists' [Richard Dawkins, Daniel Dennett, Sam Harris and others] are simple souls. In their view, which derives from rationalist philosophy and not from evolutionary theory, the human mind is a faculty that seeks an accurate representation of the world. This leaves them with something of a problem. Why are most human beings, everywhere and at all times, so wedded to some version of religion?"[19] This can be put the other way too. Insofar as atheists attribute all spiritual evidence to a misfiring of the brain, they are themselves relying on the use of the same organ they so disparage in formulating and communicating their own claims, which claims, despite their air of rationalist superiority, are mere speculation lacking hard scientific underpinning. They perceive themselves as the favoured few, free from delusion, but why?

We rightly have great trust in science. However, the general belief that science has all the answers is quite mistaken. The greater part of the universe is composed of dark matter and dark energy. Both dark matter and dark energy are still scientific mysteries. For those of us with bad backs, science has confirmed what we would in any case have suspected, namely that if God created man he could have done a much better job. Science has produced some of the answers, but the more our knowledge grows, the more we realize we do not know. One of the good things about science is that it discovers new questions, which, but for advances in our scientific knowledge, we would not have been able to ask. These are Rumsfeld's 'known unknowns' leaving all those "unknown unknowns" still to identify. Religion has long

---

[19] *The New Statesman*, 20th January, 2016.

opposed science and its logical implications. Astronomers Copernicus and Galileo, were persecuted. Copernicus died shortly after his astronomical book was banned by the Church, but Galileo was tried by the Inquisition and compelled to recant the truth about the Sun being the centre of the Solar system. Leading scientist Michael Servetus (1511-1553) was burned at the stake, though this was primarily for denying the Trinity. Scientist Giordano Bruno (1548-1600), was burned at the stake for agreeing with Copernicus. Unfortunately for Lucilio Vanini he was ahead of his time in suggesting that humans had evolved from apes. In France in 1618, his fellow apes hanged him after his tongue had been cut out. Scientific advance used to be very much despite religion, which in itself underlines the lack of evolutionary benefit in religion. In relation to the unknown unknowns, the Father of Gravity, Isaac Newton (1642-1727), who was interested in all other aspects of life, including alchemy, said, "I do not know what I may seem to the world, but as to myself, I seem to have been only like a boy playing on the seashore and diverting myself now and then finding a smoother pebble or a prettier shell than ordinary, whilst the great ocean of truth lay all undiscovered before me."

Could God really want us to restrain our search for knowledge? Could God really want horrible things to be done to searchers for knowledge? Of course not, and yet some religious leaders and fanatics unaccountably believe that their deities require cruelty and suppression of knowledge. Such nonsense was rightly rejected by Socrates: "So God cannot be the cause of all things, but only good things. Of evil things he is not the cause."[20] It is symptomatic of the corrosive power of religions that devotees have throughout the ages committed acts of unspeakable evil in the name of their deities, just as they smugly ascribe earthquakes and tidal waves to their God's/gods' supposed displeasure, which displeasure tends to coincide with their own. What seems to escape them is that by crediting destructive acts to their own God/gods they are surely themselves committing a blasphemy of a monstrous and irrational type. How could the misguided individual, who shot a lorry driver and drove the stolen lorry into the Berlin Christmas market killing and injuring sixty-eight innocent people, have possibly thought that his conduct could in anyway honour his God? Despite the bloody example set by the Old Testament God, Judaism regards the shedding of human blood as 'diminishing the divine image.'[21] This should surely be the logical conclusion for all religions. However,

---

[20] Book 2 of Plato's *Republic*

[21] Mekhilta on *Exodus* 20:33 Belkin.

sympathize though one may with the problems faced by modern Israel, this precept does not seem to have been very rigorously applied either in the bombing of the King David Hotel, or the recent bombardment of Gaza.

It is easy to debunk many religious certainties and by and large they discredit themselves. It is easy to reject Dawkins' "old man in the sky with a long white beard." It is easy to reject claims of a Superman God, who will intervene to open seas, smite enemies and give wealth to those who worship him in precisely the right way. It is easy to reject the personal God, who, as we are assured by religion, takes an active interest in the small details of our personal lives. Great egotism is surely required for the faithful to believe that God is fascinated by them and their individual doings. Likewise, contrary to most religions, there is no reason beyond our own vanity to suppose that God has any human characteristics and especially not the form of a human male. In Islam, the Mu'tazalia movement held a powerful position in the eighth and ninth centuries. Mu'tazilites believed that what was good could be determined by reason and that God had no human characteristics, but was simply an essence.[22] They may have been right, despite subsequent changes in Islamic theology. Today, Raser Aslan, a Muslim writer, advocates the importance of believers seeing God in a strictly non-human way. He says, "If you dehumanize God in your consciousness and if you see God as all creation then it is impossible to denigrate other human beings. If you see God in human beings you cannot dehumanize people. If you see God in nature you cannot abuse and exploit it."[23] Aslan suggests that, because God is necessarily "a cognitive concept", we wrongly tend to give God our human form and character. As the great Baruch Spinoza – Benedictus de Spinoza, 1632-1677 – said, "I believe that, if a triangle could speak, it would say, in like manner, that God is eminently triangular, while a circle would say that the divine nature is eminently circular. Thus each would ascribe to God its own attributes, would assume itself to be

---

[22] In the same way, Mandaeism, which is probable the only Gnostic sect to survive Christianity, which it substantially predates, sees God as supreme formless Entity. Mandaeism has been driven out of Iraq, where it was centred, by reason of the last Iraq war.

[23] BBC Radio 4, 24.11.17, talking about his book, *God: A Human History*.

like God, and look on everything else as ill-shaped."[24] Spinoza was excommunicated by his own Jewish community for deviating too far from Jewish scripture in his original thinking about God. Whatever God is, he is not centred on mankind. If God exists in some form then that form has probably existed at least twenty-one billion years since, or before, the Big Bang. It seems possible to be reasonably certain about what God is not.

God is not:

- in human form
- an active interventionist
- fascinated by the detail of our lives
- cruel, capricious, or wanting to be feared
- capable of encouraging or approving human cruelty, violence, or killing
- responsible for 'Acts of God'
- the immediate creator of the Earth – though God cannot yet be excluded as the creator, or initiator, of the Universe
- concerned with being worshipped, flattered, or

---

[24] Also in Montesquieu's *Persian Letters*, "Were triangles to invent God, they would give him three sides."

370

believed in

- a tool to be exploited by those seeking wealth and power

What then is God, if anything? This is a question best avoided by those, wise like Socrates, who saw his own wisdom as being his superior perception of his own total ignorance. Plato puts these words into the mouth of Timaeus in this account of a Socratic discussion of the nature of God: "Now the maker and father of this All it were a hard task to find, and having found him, it were impossible to declare him to all men."[25] In his *Natural History*, Pliny the Elder thought it "a mark of human stupidity to seek to discover the shape and form of God." St Thomas Aquinas was much of the same opinion nearly a thousand years later: "Man's utmost knowledge of God is to know that we do not know him. For then alone do we know God truly, when we believe that he is far above all that man can possibly think of God."[26] A Baptist friend of mine was doing good works in Romania, when a little girl asked him, "What is God made of?" He sensibly replied, "I don't know. What do you think?" I am self-

---

[25] *The Timaeus of Plato*, 28c, R.D. Archer-Hind edition.

[26] *De Potentia*, 7.5 ad 14.

evidently far less wise than he, because I venture to suggest that God is a universal – or almost universal – force, energy, or essence.

I am in good company, because aliens told a prospective candidate for the US Congress, Bettina Rodriguez Aguilera, that "God is a universal force."[27] More down-to-earth, the Stoics sometimes defined God as an intelligent fiery spirit, without form, passing into whatever things it pleases.[28] Many 'Native Americans' traditionally see this force as Wakan-Taka (the Great Spirit). The spiritual world is sometimes referred to as the "Great Mystery". It is possible that my concept of God very roughly approximates to the Chinese *Tao* – especially in Confucianism with its emphasis on love – the Buddhist's *Dharmakaya* and the Hindu's *Brahman*.[29] In the East, God is often seen as a 'cosmic soul' and in the West, Plato's 'Form of the Good' is something like my concept. Doing some real injury to Plato's philosophy through brevity and passing over Aristotle's criticism, 'the Form' was superior, detectable

---

[27] *The Miami Herald*, 16th October, 2017.

[28] *The Moral Discourses of Epictetus*, translated by Elizabeth Carter, Introduction, page xiii.

[29] The Upanishads suggest that Brahman is essentially passive, being "the unchanging reality amidst and beyond the world," which "cannot be exactly defined."

372

through mathematics and it created harmony, coherence and unity; "the truly good … binds and holds everything together."[30] Plato believed the 'Form' emanated a force, but I wonder if perhaps the force is the 'Form' itself. Spinoza saw God as a force lying behind all things in creation, but a force which does not intervene in the affairs of men. This is much the same view that was taken by deists like Voltaire and Thomas Paine. Rather like the spiritual completeness sought in Buddhism, Spinoza's conviction was that a love of God could give a person serenity and freedom from passion so that that person would be "… hardly troubled in spirit, but being, by a certain eternal necessity, conscious of himself, and of God, and of things, he never ceases to be, but always to possess true peace of mind,"[31] Despite claims to the contrary, Albert Einstein resisted all blandishments to embrace the Biblical God, but Spinoza's non-interventionist God did receive his endorsement: "I believe in Spinoza's God, who reveals himself in the orderly harmony of what exists, not in a God who concerns himself with the fates and actions of human beings." Those of a philosophical bent can read Spinoza in depth, or the morality-based reasoning of Immanuel Kant, to

---

[30] *Phaedo*, 99c.

[31] VP42S.

consider their philosophical arguments purportedly proving the existence of God. For my part I have never been convinced by philosophy. I am unimpressed by the suggestion that Schrödinger's cat is in a state of being simultaneously alive and dead.[32] It is either alive or dead and its condition can be determined by the practical step of looking in the box. Leading mathematician, Sir Roger Penrose, puts it more bluntly, "His [Schrödinger's] point was, that's a load of bollocks." Surely a tree falling in the forest makes the same noise regardless of whether there is anybody near enough to hear? So I have little time for philosophical party tricks like Saint Anselm's *a priori* argument that the definition of God itself logically proves that God exists. I am a lawyer and not a sophist and I prefer to look at the practical evidence.

In consideration of the evidence of God's existence, the poet Shelley wrote a pamphlet called *The Necessity of Atheism*, for which he was sent down from Oxford University.

---

[32] Schrödinger postulated a sealed box containing a cat, a vial of poison and a radioactive source. There is a possibility that a particle emitted by the source will smash the vial killing the cat. Since the existence of the particle is only said to exist upon observation, this means that the vial and the life of the cat are equally subject to observation leaving the cat in a state of being alive and dead simultaneously until observed.

His argument is that we should each rely upon our own senses and give comparatively little weight to historical reports by other people claiming their own experience of God. It is clear from the first three sentences of his argument that he was not a true atheist, but rather that he simply rejected on evidential grounds the religious concept of an interventionist God: "There Is No God. This negation must be understood solely to affect a creative Deity. *The hypothesis of a pervading Spirit co-eternal with the universe remains unshaken [my italics].*"[33] He also recognized "The miracle of life." As to the nature of God as created by religions he makes some telling points, "If he is infinitely good, what reason should we have to fear him? If he is infinitely wise, why should we have doubts concerning our future? If he knows all, why warn him of our needs and fatigue him with our prayers? If he is everywhere why erect temples to him? If he is just, why fear that he will punish the creatures that he has filled with weakness? ... If he is all-powerful, how offend him, how resist him? If he is reasonable, how can he be angry at the blind, to whom he has given the liberty of being unreasonable? If he is immovable, by what right do we pretend to make him change his decrees? If he is inconceivable, why do we occupy ourselves with him? IF HE

---

[33] Percy Bysshe Shelley (1792-1822) *The Necessity of Atheism.*

HAS SPOKEN, WHY IS THE UNIVERSE NOT CONVINCED? If the knowledge of a God is the most necessary, why is it not the most evident and clearest?" [his capitals].[34]

Like Shelley, my argument is practical and not philosophical. Unlike Shelley, the purpose of this book is not to persuade you to adopt a particular view. My purpose is to invite you to cast off the fetters of the indoctrination forged by upbringing, family, religion, education and the media and, in the case of atheists, by an over-reaction to the absurdities they perceive in religion. The purpose is to encourage free thought about the *possibility* of a spiritual element to life. Although our own direct experience and perception are fundamental, each person can explore and assess this spiritual element by reference to the ideas and morality of other people and other belief systems, even including religions, which can contain truth and wisdom. The possibility and nature of this spiritual element should above all be explored by reference to evidence, our own senses, instinct and intuition, our personal reason, our experience and conscience. There is no place for blind Faith. It is not necessarily through intellectual and philosophical

---

[34] Based on *Système de la Nature* by Paul Henri Thiry and with translation of Shelley's French by Amazon.

thought, but through experiences such as a special moment with a loved one, a wonderful sunset, a powerful poem, a moving piece of music, an unexpected act of kindness, a moment of revelation, that we may begin to glimpse that there is something more in our lives than can be prosaically explained and that this something is special and beyond the material.

I met a lovely left-brained atheist on a bus in Monaco. His view was that religion is a construct to 'allow men in pointy hats to control others.' He declared, 'Show me the evidence and I will believe.' By evidence, he clearly meant something so concrete that his left brain would understand it. Quite unprompted he stated with great force that the 'warm feelings' he sometimes experienced were not sufficient to convince him. He clearly associated these warm feelings with spiritual experience and his intellect was over-emphatically rejecting the experience of his senses. Ghosts, spiritualism, near death experience were to his mind all fraud, hysteria, delusion, or coincidence.

We all have 'warm feelings.' Music can give us a momentary sense of something wonderful, even religious music like Thomas Tallis' *Spem in alium*, plainsong, chanting by Native Americans, or Vedic Mantras. Who could not feel a spiritual charge when listening to Braat chanting the *Gayatri*

Mantra, even if not understanding Devanagari? Translated, part of this chant seems particularly apt:

> "I pray to thee,
> To illuminate my intellect and dispel my ignorance,
> Just as the splendorous sunlight dispels all darkness.
> I pray to thee to make my intellect serene
> And bright with enlightenment."

Spiritual enlightenment is surely part of life's purpose, whether or not there is a God. I have already suggested that the questions of God's existence and true nature are less important than the question of whether there is a spiritual element within us. "Behind our existence lies something else that becomes accessible to us only by our shaking off the world."[35] However, to try to live up to the title of this book, the time has come for me to attempt the impossible task of coming to a conclusion about that 'something else'. My diffident suggestion is that God is a passive spiritual force, which is, in essence, life-enabling, wise and above all loving. Followers of the Kabbalah may say that my perception of God simply

---

[35] Schopenhauer, *The World as Will and Representation*, translated by E. F. J. Payne.

merges the penultimate Sephiroths – 'emanations of God' – and that I am blind to Kether, the Creative Godhead. They may be right, but I am not claiming great enlightenment beyond the conviction that there is a vital spiritual element in living things. In respect of the Creative Godhead, Mo Gawdat, whose devotion to mathematics enabled him to rise in Google, sets out a strong arithmetic argument based on pure mathematical probability that the development of forms of life, which have appeared on earth, has significantly outstripped any reasonable mathematical chance of having randomly done so in such a limited period –albeit millions of years.[36] His argument is that evolution cannot satisfactorily be explained by mathematical probability and that, applying the pure logic of arithmetic, the course of the development of life has been impossibly swift. He concludes, "This story *demands* the presence of a designer – which, unfortunately, is an entity that has been taken over and disfigured by religious institutions to the point where we would rather deny its existence than belong to the madness waged in its name."[37] He may be right that, whether or not God is the 'clockmaker', there is a force which moves forward the clock's hands. Even if there was no

---

[36] *Solve for Happy*, pp 305-331.

[37] *Solve for Happy*, page 324.

simplistic Biblical creation of the world, quite possibly this force does have some interrelationship with the general evolution of living things. This makes sense, if, like Socrates and Shelley, we see a vital link between life and spirit.

It is in part due to my own ignorance that I am able to presume to make the practical argument that each person should undertake a spiritual quest for themselves and that the most important discovery is that we, as living things, have vital spiritual spark within us. My spiritual naivety allows me, like the small boy who knew no better than to point out that the Emperor was wearing no clothes, to challenge the absurdities in our religions and the closed-mindedness of many religionists and materialists alike. The Ophites, who were a branch of the persecuted Gnostics, believed that the serpent in the Garden of Eden, far from being evil, was an instrument of divine goodness, because it was through the agency of the serpent that we derived the knowledge needed to develop our spiritual selves and by doing so to save our souls. Providing that this is an allegory, I absolutely agree. Through knowledge – our intellect, personal experience, intuition, conscience and consideration of the wisdom of others – we can and should work to protect our souls. The most important part of this knowledge is to know yourself.[38] It is impossible to succeed in the quest for spiritual knowledge by unquestioningly borrowing a second-hand belief system, as to do so is to abandon the quest.

> "I count religion but as a childish toy,
> And hold there is no sin but ignorance."[39]

John Gray makes an elegant analogy between, on the one hand, Gnostics, who believed that the world was essentially evil and that only through knowledge could evil be perceived and escaped, and, on the other hand, materialists, who believe that increasing our knowledge is crucial even though we are mere biological mechanisms. Gray, referring primarily to materialists, I presume, suggests that they yearn for "a type of knowledge to make us other than we are."[40] I

---

[38] "To know yourself is to understand balance.

Without balance you cannot stand upright

And your heart will not mend." (Wa-Na-Nee-Che)

"Yesterday I was clever, so I wanted to change the world. Today I am wise, so I am changing myself," Jalāl ad-Dīn Muhammad Rūmī (Persian poet and mystic, 1207-1273).

[39] Christopher Marlowe (1564-93), prologue to *The Jew of Malta*.

[40] *The Soul of the Marionette*, page 165.

agree with him that we should not try to escape from ourselves through knowledge. Nor should the knowledge we gather be limited by the materialists' own scornful prejudices. They appear to favour the material type of knowledge fitting us for materially productive tasks in our modern world, which knowledge tends to suppress our instinctive sense of the spiritual well of joy within us. "Civilized man (and woman) has developed the left brain until it completely dominates and overawes the right."[41] Accordingly we have lost much of our intuition and awareness of the spiritual aspects of living. When in Nyasaland, Sir Laurens van der Post approached a shopping street and heard laughter seeming to "come from some sure, inviolate source within where one felt they were unfailingly refreshed ..." He found in the street a minority of Europeans and "oriental" tradesmen, who were lifeless and joyless – like so many we see about us today – but the native Africans were animated, joyous and producing the laughter, which had so captivated him. He then entered an office and was met by an 'educated' African, who, in contrast with his countrymen outside, had the "self-conscious gloom which higher education inflicts, almost without exception, on an instinctively happy

---

[41] Colin Wilson, *Afterlife*, page 47.

people ..."[42] In *Sapiens* Dr Yuval Harari cites comparatively recent anthropological research into hunter-gatherers in Peru called the Aché. The Aché were observed to smile and laugh constantly, to be extraordinarily generous and to hate domineering people.[43] Most children are instinctively happy and yet somehow we tend to lose this instinct as we 'mature' and are loaded with material information. Look about you at the many people you pass in our Western world and sadly you will see very little joy amongst them. Spiritual knowledge on the other hand helps us to a clearer self-understanding and a surer link with joy. Only in this way can you, as Joseph Campbell put it so well, "Follow your bliss." Our spiritual battle ground is within us.

"We're so engaged in doing things to achieve purposes of outer value that we forget the inner value, the rapture that is associated with being alive, is what it is all about."[44]

Neither technological learning nor religious knowledge can give us this 'rapture.' Perhaps Gray is correct in suggesting that the spiritual battle can be won by "accepting

---

[42] *Venture to the Interior*, chapter 8.

[43] Dr Yuval Noah Harari, *Sapiens*, page 59.

[44] Joseph Campbell, *The Power of Myth*.

the fact of unknowing." Similarly, Karen Armstrong suggests that, "A modern theology must look unflinchingly into the heart of a great darkness and be prepared, perhaps, to enter into the cloud of unknowing."[45] This awareness of ignorance is very much a Socratic posture, but knowledge can help us better to perceive and understand the extent and nature of our 'unknowing.' It is probable that our knowledge will never fully explain the Great Mystery, but it is essential at least to know that there *is* a Great Mystery. We have been spoiled by religions, which so confidently presume to explain the Great Mystery by providing full particulars of God and his wishes. There is no reason to suppose that we shall ever have a detailed knowledge of these matters, because the essence of spiritual development during life is to find the path towards eventual enlightenment. There is every reason to view with grave suspicion any person providing a comprehensive analysis of God.

I am lucky enough to have had a small number of wonderful friends, some of whom are religionists, some

---

[45] *The Case For God*, page 267.

humanists[46] and some atheists. They are open-minded, tolerant, forgiving, generous-hearted and loving. Despite their lack of conscious spiritual inquiry they are still in tune with the God force. The force is with them. Does this mean that atheist-existentialist, Sartre, was right when he declared that, "Existentialism ... affirms that even if God were to exist, it would make no difference – that is our point of view"?[47] In one way he is certainly correct, because God does, as Sartre suggested, leave each of us to be conscious of what we are and to be solely responsible for our own existence. In another way he is probably wrong, because whilst it is possible to lead a perfectly good and spiritual life without believing in God, it is a distinct benefit to have some spiritual perception.

There is no absolute need to have faith in God. First, as already suggested, it is improbable that God has any interest in what individual humans believe. Secondly, you do not have to have mere faith, because there is evidence to be found. If you seek the force that is God you will find that force without

---

[46] 'Humanist' in the modern sense. At about the time of the Reformation, 'humanist' meant a Christian who was inclined to believe men and women were essentially good and not mere 'lumps of perdition'.

[47] Jean-Paul Sartre (1905-1980), *Existentialism is a Humanism*, page 53.

385

much difficulty. Finding the force is easy and can be done without trying and even by accident, but knowing what you have found is more challenging. I would say that self-declared atheist, Dr Sam Harris, linked with this force when as a young man he sat on a couch with a friend under the influence MDMA/Ecstasy and felt selfless love for his friend and then boundless love giving him a geometric appreciation of spiritual things.[48] Likewise when he sat on the famous 'Mount' by the Sea of Galilee and he felt a blissful stillness and sense of all things being one.[49] Dr Harris and I might argue whether the source of this type of revelation is internal, external, or a bit of both, but it makes no practical difference. I suspect that in the essentials we do not disagree at all, but rather that there is simply a difference in terminology.[50] Contemporary atheist, Comte-Sponville, is open-minded enough to record, "Other individuals, every bit as sincere as I am, seem to have experienced a presence, a love, a communication, an

---

[48] *Waking Up*, pp. 3-5.

[49] *Waking Up*, page 81.

[50] "An impersonal God is no God at all, but merely a word wrongly used, a misconception ..." Arthur Schopenhauer (1788-1860), *Parerga and Paralipomena*, chapter 1: Fragments for the History of Philosophy. Translated by E. F. J. Payne.

exchange ..."[51] This is just about it. It may be different for those especially sensitive or adept, but there is certainly no blinding light on the road to Damascus. Sensing the God force is a period of peaceful resonance, during which we can better perceive our spirit and its 'oneness' with something greater. We can better distinguish between what is truly important and what is not. Tolstoy ends *A Confession* with an account of a transforming dream, in which he was able to "look into the infinite" and was, as a result of this contact with something greater, left with a profound feeling of being "glad and tranquil." I suspect that everyone has these experiences, but that different people perceive them differently.

As already mentioned, André Comte-Sponville, although an atheist, believes in the spirit. He has personally experienced a number of these periods of being at one with something greater, which he describes as "Infinite peace! Simplicity, serenity, delight." He provides great detail of his experiences and comments on them.[52] He refers to Michel Hulin's book, *La mystique sauvage: Aux antipodes de l'esprit*,

---

[51] A. Comte-Sponville, *The Book of Atheist Spirituality*, page 100. He rather mars this open-mindedness by adding the dismissive rider, "More power to them, if it helps them live" and then by preening himself on his own spiritual tolerance.

[52] *The Book of Atheist Spirituality*, pages 154-160.

which contains a number independent and yet strikingly similar accounts from witnesses of these experiences of oneness: 'the now, the infinite and loss of self in being one with this absolute thing.' Albert Camus[53], as he points out, describes this experience in his books, *The Stranger* and *The Wrong Side and the Right Side*. What is this force, which so many people experience and sense to be greater than themselves, if not a divine force, even if atheists prefer not to use the term 'God'? Even the Quakers are now debating whether to remove references to God from the new edition of *Quaker Faith and Practice*, because "spirit" and "the mystery" are generally their preferred ways of describing the power they sense. Making a spiritual connection through silence and stillness is at the heart of Quakerism.

A similar sensation to that described by Comte-Sponville and others was experienced by Robert Graves, when a schoolboy tranquilly sitting on a roller behind a cricket pavilion: "I remember letting my mind range rapidly over all its familiar subjects of knowledge; only to find this was no foolish fancy. I did know everything. ... I ... held the key of truth in my hand, and could use it to open the lock of any door.

---

[53] Albert Camus (1913-60) also wrote *The Myth of Sisyphus*, a philosophical work, in which he found a world without God to be depressingly pointless.

Mine was no religious or philosophical theory, but a simple method of looking sideways at disorderly facts to make perfect sense of them."[54] Sadly for Graves this experience faded for him as it does for us all. Practitioners in meditation[55] and in other great wisdoms of the East do not have to rely so much on chance for these experiences, but the extensive evidence of these almost accidental experiences is particularly important, because those experiencing them have no pre-existing belief system or expectation. There are similarities between these experiences and those reported by those near death. One of those, who had undergone a near-death experience, studied by Dr. R. A. Moody recalled, "It was like I knew all things ... I thought whatever I wanted to know could be known."[56]

Lucretius clearly had experiences of 'oneness': "As soon as your reasoning, sprung from that god-like mind lifts up its voice to proclaim the nature of the universe, then the

---

[54] An autobiographical passage in "The Abominable Mr Gunn," *Collected Stories*, page 90.

[55] Martin Heidegger suggested that meditative thinking was the way to experience *Sein* ('the Being') and that it was necessary first to dismantle any pre-existing faith in a personal God. Regrettably, given the similarity of Heidegger's argument to my own, his reputation is somewhat tarnished by his involvement with Nazism.

[56] *Reflections on Life after Life*.

terrors of mind take flight, the ramparts of the world roll apart, and I see the march of events throughout the whole of space. The majesty of the gods is revealed and ... All their wants are supplied by nature, and nothing at any time cankers their peace of mind. But nowhere do I see the halls of Hell, though the earth is no barrier to my beholding all that passes underfoot in the space beneath. At this I am seized with a divine delight, and a shudder in awe, that by your power nature stands thus unveiled and made manifest in every part."[57]

Some Christians, particularly in the fourteenth and fifteenth centuries, created a new theology based on this direct and personal contact with God. A leading representative for this movement was the hermit and mystic, Richard Rolle (1290-1349). He talked of his personal experience of God. On the first occasion of this direct contact he was "surprised" by the warming of his heart. He was filled with love giving him "great and unexpected comfort." He observed that once over the initial shock of this sensation, "I realized that it came from within, that this fire had no cause, material or sinful, but was the gift of my Maker, I was absolutely delighted and wanted

---

[57] *The Nature of the Universe*, book III, translation by R. E. Latham.

390

my love to be even greater."[58] Sadly, he was emotionally and intellectually confined by his rigid Christian preconceptions and so Rolle's experiences of the 'fire of love' did him little good. He remained an unhappy hermit who, in practice, was as unloving to his fellows as he was to himself.

Dr Brenda Davies, consultant psychiatrist, spiritual healer and possessor of advanced spiritual wisdom, sums up this transcendent experience as "living in love with God" and she further describes it: "Sometimes it occurs spontaneously and without warning, perhaps when listening to music, or reading poetry, walking in a forest or even watching a film that inspires us. Sometimes it happens during meditation, or even at times of illness or crisis. We can also learn to have this experience at will. ... we feel ourselves gently bump the supreme superconscious and we feel it reach out and embrace us. Suddenly we're home, we flow into the Spirit and become part of it again. ... we're nurtured, loved, cherished, re-energized."[59]

Perhaps the last word should be given to the person with arguably the greatest claim to scientific rationalism. I refer to Einstein and not Dawkins. Einstein famously wrote: "The

---

[58] *The Fire of Love* (*Incendium Amoris*).

[59] *Journey of the Soul*, page 35.

391

most beautiful thing we can experience is the mysterious. It is the source of all true art and science. He to whom the emotion is a stranger, who can no longer pause to wonder and stand wrapped in awe, is as good as dead – his eyes are closed. The insight into the mystery of life, coupled though it be with fear, has also given rise to religion. To know what is impenetrable to us really exists, manifesting itself as the highest wisdom and the most radiant beauty, which our dull faculties can comprehend only in their most primitive forms – this knowledge, this feeling is at the center of true religiousness."[60]

There are thousands more examples of people experiencing this kind of transcendental link with the spiritual. Practitioners of many of the religions and other spiritual disciplines in the East will probably feel great surprise that I am highlighting something which for them is commonplace in their spiritual lives. Doubtless materialists would seek to dismiss this as another example of how brain cells misfire, but this widespread experience is a fact and it is for the sceptics to produce proof that this 'evidence of the senses' suggesting spiritual connection is merely a delusion produced by defective brain function. Their 'intellectual' scorn is based not

---

[60] *Living Philosophies*, paragraph 14. I should note in fairness that in the same short statement of his conclusions about life he rejects the concept of a soul.

on any actual evidence of 'misfiring,' but on a false certainty that these facts cannot be true, because they contradict their own materialist faith. They reach this certainty using a brain, which they believe prone to serious misfiring in others. Probably their right brain is not firing at all.

As Comte-Sponville demonstrates, not all atheists are in denial. Many, like him, accept a spiritual element and he accepts that many people experience love during these short periods of resonance. He makes an excellent point about the force he senses at these times of transcendence, "That *I* can love *it* is a good thing – indeed, the best there is. But why should *it* love *me*?" This observation is strikingly similar to Gibran's suggestion that to feel love means "I am in the heart of God." Here seems to be a key truth. This force can give us spiritual benefits, but only if we are capable of finding and making something of it. Contrary to the promise central to most religions, this force does not seek us, but rather we must seek it. If there is a fire, you can approach it and use it to keep warm, or to cook. However, unless you are most unfortunate, the fire does not come to you. Although the fire may give you great benefit, it has no interest in you. Again, by and large, C-S and I appear to be in agreement as to the essentials. He recognizes the supreme importance of the spirit and the way our spirit can be at one with a force he calls "the All," which is essentially what *Brahman* means. He calls this eternal thing "the All" and Spinoza, Shelley, Davies and I call it "God." Plato envisaged an infinite 'Universal Mind,' of which every finite mind like ours is a minute part. Some spiritualists refer to *the Logos*. The descriptive title of this omnipresence is not really important and perhaps terms like 'God' and 'soul' have become too enmeshed in religions any longer to be particularly helpful in spiritual analysis.

Why do I suggest that God is an *almost* universal force? There seem to be places where the force of God is particularly strong, whether you call them a convergence of ley lines, sacred places, or otherwise. There are places where particularly bad things have been done, which seem comparatively cold and empty. This empty cold feeling I see as a reduction of the force of God, or at least a restriction in that location of our capacity easily to come near that force. Putting it another way, in these places "the current of higher energy" is disturbed. Some might say that this is simply another trick of the mind, because if you visit the site of an extermination camp, or the scene of a great tragedy, then you are probably already primed to feel an inner revulsion. However, it works in reverse. First we feel the sense of cold disturbing emptiness and then we discover that there was indeed an historic and tragic reason for it.[61] Animals, such as dogs and horses with no historical knowledge, are sensitive to the negative spiritual fields of places, where dreadful things have happened. Is this negativity caused by evil? Science teaches us that there is no such thing as positive cold. Cold does not exist in science, because it is simply a result of lack of heat. Likewise, darkness is simply lack of light. So those people who act brutally are like places lacking spiritual warmth. They are not possessed by evil, but are simply lacking in spirituality and love. How often it proves to be the case that those people who do bad things, politicians who grasp for power, and the greedy obsessed with wealth, have lacked love in their childhood. We say that an act is evil and the perpetrator is evil for having done it, but this is the same as saying your fingers are cold, or that you could not see because of the dark. If there is no positive evil and acts, which we describe as evil, are really acts where love is absent, then "the All" must contain only love and goodness. Though it causes me acute discomfort to do so, on the non-existence of evil I

---

[61] Dr Brenda Davies describes how she viewed a house for sale. With no prior knowledge she was aware of a temperature change and a sense of anguish. It turned out that a deranged son had murdered his parents and then committed suicide (*Journey of the Soul*, page 222).

appear to agree with none other than the awful Augustine, leading advocate of 'original sin' and 'scriptural authority.'

There are many recognized ways to seek to relate to God; these methods include quiet contemplation, visiting one of those quiet and special places in nature so venerated by Native Americans and Maori, mindfulness, meditation, yoga, love, acting in tune with conscience and nature, a Native American Energy Balancing Ceremony,[62] re-birthing, sitting in places of worship and, of course, prayer. The one thing that stands out is that relaxation is a key to spirituality. If a person relaxes deeply "the left and right halves of the brain seem to merge together, and he experiences a sense of peace and serenity, the 'all is well' feeling."[63] Now we are programmed almost to fear doing nothing; it is wrong to have 'time to stand and stare.' Research has shown that the majority of men and twenty-five per cent of women prefer to apply electric shocks to themselves, rather than to spend a tranquil fifteen minutes with their own thoughts.[64] "The mind is designed to engage

---

[62] Towards the conclusion of which, "There is deep peace within you. You feel free and full of love, understanding and compassion." Wa-Na-Nee-Che and Bríd Fitzpatrick, *Great Grandfather Spirit*, page 156.

[63] Colin Wilson, *Afterlife*, page 59.

[64] Wilson et al., University of Virginia, *Science*, 4th July, 2014.

with the world," said lead researcher, Dr Timothy Wilson. "Even when we are by ourselves, our focus usually is on the outside world. And without training in meditation or thought-control techniques, which still are difficult, most people would prefer to engage in external activities." This craving for continuous stimulation is an addiction of the left brain and we must return to our right mind.

Prayer has the potential to still the mind. In many religions, including the big three monotheistic ones, prayer is the conventional way to communicate with God. What is the purpose of prayer? If it is to persuade God to smite your enemies, or even to ease suffering of those at a distance, it is not going to be effective. The late great Dr Oliver Sacks (1933-2015), neurologist, became sceptical about religious claims for prayer, when young. To investigate prayer he planted two rows of radishes and then devoutly prayed to God to bless one row and to curse the other. When fully grown, the rows were indistinguishable and young Sacks had proved his point. Richard Dawkins reviews research done into one thousand eight hundred and two heart patients in six hospitals, which was reported in the *American Heart Journal*.[65] Three churches directed their prayers to specific patients and there

---

[65] *The God Delusion*, pp 86-88.

was no difference between outcomes for those for whom they prayed and those unmentioned in prayers. This is yet more evidence against an interventionist God. Another research project into healing by prayer showed profoundly inconclusive results.[66] Those of us, who have prayed for specific outcomes, will know just how rarely the desired outcome occurs. My score was probably nil for about two thousand prayers, before I stopped praying in the conventional Christian way.

However, it is not necessarily the case that prayer is pointless. The very action itself may benefit the person praying. I once met a Christian woman who, being dissatisfied with the simplistic evangelical guidance given to her as a girl, had begun her own journey of spiritual discovery. She looked about for new sources of enlightenment. As a result she agreed that members of an extreme Christian sect could visit her at home. She later felt uncomfortable about this invitation and prayed. Suddenly she pictured in her mind, "2 *Tim* 2:14." She thought this might be a Bible reference even though she had no recollection of a 'Tim' in the Bible. She went to her Bible and discovered that it was a reference to "The Second Epistle of Paul the Apostle to Timothy." She was astounded to find

---

[66] John A. Astin, et al., "The Efficacy of 'Distant Healing': A Systematic Review of Randomized Trials", *Annals of Internal Medicine* June 6, 2000; vol. 132 no. 11 903-910 [1].

that this passage contained the words, "… they strive … to the subverting of the hearers." When her visitors arrived she politely told them that she had changed her mind. They demanded to know why and she explained. Their response was that such things do not happen, which seems to be more than a bit inconsistent with their own religious thinking. Was this woman's experience a result of some subconscious response to her anxiety, or was it a tapping in to a universal consciousness, or was it a message from God, or was it a reply from guardian spirits,[67] or was it something else? Whatever the exact answer, the point is that this is a practical example of how individuals can derive personal spiritual benefit from prayer and meditation.

Despite my fundamental opposition to the rigid certainty of religion, it seems clear that very often solace and occasionally spiritual insight can be derived from ritualistic and communal worship. Somebody I know had a distinct moment of spiritual revelation while at her synagogue, which assisted her in overcoming her depression. Many practical examples exist of prayer and meditation benefitting the individual not in terms of winning the lottery, but in terms of

---

[67] Dr Brenda Davies describes how prayer allows spirits to give her ideas, or inspiration, or energy. Please see, in particular, chapter 7 of *Journey of the Soul*.

spiritual welfare. For those of a more scientific inclination there is also research suggesting clear benefit from prayer. One study of heart patients showed that meditative praying by the patients themselves with a rosary, or reciting yoga mantras at specific rates, significantly increased beneficial baroreflex sensitivity.[68] The *Scientific American* of 23rd December, 2013, previewed research[69] suggesting that prayer assists cognitive function and the individual's ability to resist temptation. Prayer, contemplation, mindfulness, acting with love and in sympathy with conscience all give clear benefit to the individual doing the praying. This, I believe, is because these are ways of resonating with the benign force, even if there is no conscious intent to do so. So, by praying, or by being a loving person, you may not be able directly to intercede for the recovery of a loved one, but you may derive from the process strength to cope, or even possibly the inspiration to investigate an alternative treatment or to cause the treating specialists to review the treatment, or you may at the very least be able to reduce that loved one's suffering, when through the strength of your love you do not reflect back the pain that their suffering

---

[68] Bernardi et al. (2001) Effect of rosary prayer and yoga mantras on autonomic cardiovascular rhythms: comparative study, *BMJ* 323(7327): 1446-9. (doi:10.1136/bmj.323.7327.1446).

[69] Reported in the *Journal of Experimental Social Psychology*.

causes to you. The Confucian view of ritual is similar. Before Confucius, the Chinese set great store by ritual honouring of their ancestors. Apart from custom there was a belief that these precise rituals, involving special vessels with offerings of food and wine to the spirits of the ancestors, could attract real benefits by avoiding the anger of these spirits and maybe enlisting their aid. Confucius venerated these and other rituals more than his contemporaries, but his view was that their primary importance was in developing the spiritual goodness of those performing the rituals. The common thread is that one way or another people should be mindful of what is right and good. Confirmed humanists and dogmatic atheists, who, with an attuned conscience, act in a loving way, are at one with the force of God whether they like it or not.

It is doubtful whether Christianity, after St Paul had finished reinterpreting it, was ever well attuned to love and personal conscience. It is now faltering as a force in the world. I agree with the new Bishop of Woolwich that our world is "spiritually deficient in many ways."[70] Probably Christianity has taken too many wrong turns to cure these deficiencies. The Roman Emperor Julian tried to turn back the Christianity,

---

[70] The Right Rev Woyin Karowei Dorgu, upon his consecration in April, 2017.

which his predecessor, Constantine, had unleashed. He was so benign in his attempts that Christians angrily denounced his clemency for denying them martyrdom. Julian found the task impossible despite all his imperial power. The time has come to turn back the tide both of religion and materialism in their fundamentalist forms, both of which in different ways can poison our capacity to sense personally the presence of something spiritually important beyond mere existence. Unlike the Emperor Julian, I am not seeking to reinstate the pagan gods of the ancient past. I have tried to warn of the danger arising from individual people losing personal touch with the all-important spiritual side of their lives. Rather than worshipping a God in our own image, or being obsessed with Mammon,[71] or accepting the beguiling simplicity of materialist atheism, I am asking each person to think for him/herself and to apply his/her own conscience, instinct and intellect

---

[71] "I am a Millionaire. That is my religion." George Bernard Shaw (1856-1950) *Major Barbara*, Act 2. In addition, Sam Polk recounts how he was a rich and miserable Wall Street success, when he was saved by spiritual counselling by a guide of Cherokee heritage. Now he is happy running a charity bringing good nutrition to the poor. "If you have a life focused on self and accumulation, no matter how wealthy you get, there is just no satisfaction at the end of the road." *For the Love of Money: A Memoir*

rigorously. With absolutely no need for faith, each of us should consider attuning ourselves to that spiritual force which runs through everything and within us. Leading atheist Sam Harris asks, "Is it possible to find lasting fulfilment despite the inevitability of change? Spiritual life begins with a suspicion that the answer to such questions could well be 'yes.'"[72] From this statement it is clear that it is not necessary for Dr Harris and I to fight over whether there is a God and how to define spiritual forces – not least because he is an expert in martial arts. The essential point, agreed on by many atheists like Harris and Comte-Sponville, is that spirituality is of incalculable importance to each of us. Although I make a case for something, which I define using the word 'God,' my conclusion has no great importance compared to the vital need for individuals to open themselves to the spiritual dimension in life.

In respect of my presumptuous attempt to argue the case for the existence of God, Marcus Aurelius said it all: "To seek the impossible is madness, but the foolish will always try."[73] I have tried enough and before I become too trying I shall end my attempt in the hope of following this equally good bit of

---

[72] *Waking Up*, page 17.

[73] *Meditations*, chapter two.

Aurelian advice: "Stop talking about what a good person should be and just be that person."[74]

---

[74] Marcus Aurelius, *Meditations*, chapter one.

An Afterthought on Free Will

"Si può fare, si può fare   *You can do it, you can do it*

puoi prendere o lasciare   *You can take it or leave it*

sipuò crescere e cambiare   *You can develop and change*

continuare a navigare."[1]   *To continue to chart a course.*

I had completed this book, when I experienced an irresistible urge to write a short postscript on free will.

In the main text I longed to digress. I yielded to this temptation in devoting too much space to refuting the irritating claims of Christian evangelists. On the other hand, you will be pleased to know that I resisted a strong inclination to review in depth the history and theology of John the Baptist – *also* called 'Messiah' – and to speculate on what would have happened if his greatest proselytiser, Apollos, had been a better salesman than Paul. I yearned to consider free will in greater depth, but, either 'controlled by a product of prior events' or freely

---

[1] *Si può fare*, by Angelo Branduardi.

exercising my own will, I decided that it would unduly interrupt the flow of the main argument.

Deniers of free will often suggest that it is a fear of facing the stark truth that we are mere toads under the ploughshare of fate, which compels us to cling to our illusion of free will. Most of those denying free will confess to an inclination to believe in free will themselves, which inclination they seemingly have the will to resist. We come back to the Dawkins dilemma. If we perceive that we have free will why is this perception not of itself some evidence that we do indeed have it? What compelling evidence is there that we are mere automata suffering from a fundamental illusion?

In the body of this book I suggested that one of the great attractions of religion is that it spares believers from the trouble of having to decide moral questions for themselves. Religionists find that they can in this way somehow lighten the burden of exercising their free will. Personal will can be delegated to control by scripture and priests. Weighing decisions for ourselves, especially in the moral and spiritual realm, can be difficult and painful. Doing what we ourselves decide is right can sometimes require great courage. Facing the fact that we have failed to do what was right can be a torment, if we are honest with ourselves. Just as abdicating our moral conduct to the dictates of a religion can seem comforting, so those denying free will may find comfort in the lack of personal responsibility. Lack of free will must mean freedom from blame. If we have no choice, then in a perverse way, we have an anarchic freedom to do what we think we want to do without responsibility, while conscience is effectively irrelevant as we have no conscious will upon which it can act. John Gray reviews one of Kleist's essays, which suggests that the automatism of a puppet is not slavery and he concludes, "The idea that self-awareness may be an obstacle to living in freedom is not new."[2] Dr Sam Harris, perhaps the leading denier of free will, claims that shedding a belief in free will has "improved my ethics"[3] and has "increased my feelings of freedom."[4] Belief in free will is not therefore of itself comforting, so we – the majority – can at least be satisfied that we have no incentive to deceive ourselves about our possession of free will. It is intellectually neat to see ourselves as Dawkinsian automata, because it frees us both from the need to grapple with the possibility of a spiritual element in life and from having to accept responsibility for our actions.

Dr Harris limits the possible location of free will to the

---

[2] *The Soul of the Marionette*, page 6.

[3] *Free Will*, page 45.

[4] *Free Will*, page 46.

conscious mind. He notes that, in this, he differs from Daniel Dennett, who thinks that unconscious thought is still our thought.[5] I still think in terms of the conscious and subconscious mind. The subconscious is a repository for memories,[6] learned facts and experience. It can do great things ranging from initiating wonderful works of art to solving difficult crossword clues as we sleep overnight. Life would become unbearable if each time we had to make a decision we had consciously to review all the relevant possibilities and pertinent facts. We take a short cut to decisions by relying in great part on our instinct and intuition. The more trivial the decision, the greater the short cut we tend to take. We could not drive a car with only our conscious mind. If we were consciously to consider and will every action – I must change gear; now I must move my left leg so that it depresses the clutch-pedal; I have done that so now I move the gear stick;

---

[5] *Free Will*, pp. 20-22.

[6] Dr Harris contends that he has "forgotten most of what has happened to me over the course of my life ..." *Waking Up*, page 84. Of course he has not forgotten, because most of it is stored in his subconscious mind. It can be retrieved by prompts, such as experiencing related smells, reminiscing, visiting old haunts and, of course, hypnosis. What Dr Harris is saying is that his conscious memory is limited.

which way should it go? – we should soon crash. The subconscious, though, is our servant and not our master. Subconscious thought is obviously a type of thought and I am unable fully to discern why Dr Harris excludes the unconscious as an element in our free will, save of course that if you do not exclude the role of the unconscious mind then the argument against free will becomes almost impossible to make. For the disbeliever in free will, night follows day: I believe there is no free will and therefore it must be that subconscious/ unconscious thought cannot be part of free will.

Dr Harris, who, according to his views, must have had no choice in writing his books, relies heavily on research by Benjamin Libet and others.[7] In 1983, using EEG,[8] Libet and his colleagues recorded findings, which they said demonstrated that activity in the brain's motor cortex –referred to as 'readiness-potential' – can be detected three hundred milliseconds before a person is conscious of the intention to move. From this and associated research Dr Harris concludes that we have no free will, because the decision to move comes as a *fait accompli* delivered to the conscious mind. I

---

[7] Libet et al., "Time of conscious intention to act in relation to onset of cerebral activity (readiness-potential): The unconscious initiation of a freely voluntary act", *Brain* 106(3): 623-642.

[8] An electroencephalogram for recording brain activity.

respectfully disagree for the following reasons:

1. Libet and his colleagues themselves expressly stated that their research did not necessarily refute free will, primarily on the basis that the conscious mind has the opportunity to veto the proposed action. So when we are waiting to cross the road we may be consciously thinking about the theological meaning of life, or what to eat for supper, but the subconscious mind is considering the traffic. We may feel an impulse to cross, but sometimes our conscious mind decides that the approaching lorry is coming too fast and vetoes stepping into the road;

2. The modest conclusions of the research itself have come under scientific criticism. For instance, Daniel Wenger, psychologist, points out that we really do not know what the 'readiness-potential' noted in the research actually means and that the cortex activity may have nothing to do with the action.[9] He points out that while the use of a compass is important in steering a ship the compass itself does not

---

[9] "The Illusion of Conscious Will", *MIT Press*, page 55, please see also Alfred Mele, *Effective Intentions, the Power of Conscious Will* and an excellent article on www.informationphilosopher.com entitled *Libet Experiments*.

actually steer the ship;[10]

3. I view with some suspicion research which depends on the pushing of buttons in reaction to the subject being conscious of being conscious. "There are many criticisms and rebuttals, with debate raging about how and if the experiment is relevant to the freedom of our everyday choices. Even supporters of Libet have to admit that the situation used in the experiment may be too artificial to be a direct model of real everyday choices."[11] Dr Harris' theory is based on the 0.3 second lag between brain activity said to indicate the intention to move and the moment of awareness physically recorded by the subjects. Interestingly, in 2018 Nissan announced successful results of its 'brain-to-vehicle' technology. Using sensors placed on the heads of drivers Nissan's computers were able to detect a driver's intention from brain waves, and technology proved to be between 0.2 and 0.5 seconds faster than the drivers in implementing the intended action. Though the computer was quicker in carrying out the driver's intention, the intention itself was the intention of the human subject. The point is that the delay is between the moment of will and the performance of the

[10] "The Illusion of Conscious Will", *MIT Press*, page 317.

[11] *Why do We Intuitively Believe That We Have Free Will?*, Tom Stafford, www.bbc.com, 7th August, 2015

action so willed. A time delay between the formation of intention to act and the actual performance of the action is hardly surprising and does not begin to refute free will;

4. It would seem that the moment of decision occurs in the conscious mind, but even if the subconscious mind were part of our capacity for free will then the fact that a possible decision originates in the unconscious mind a moment before it is consciously considered would not in any way refute free will;

5. The theory that *irresistible* intentions 'created by a product of prior events' jump unbidden into our conscious minds and so control us, does not accord with our practical experience of thinking and acting.

Dr Harris asserts that we suffer from the "false assumption" that we could have acted differently in the past.[12] To him criminals are merely 'poorly calibrated clockwork' and did not exercise free will in choosing to commit their crimes. In particular, he cites a usually unpleasant case of two men, who raped and murdered a family. The fact that these

---

[12] *Free Will*, page 6.

men had themselves been unloved and abused does to some extent explain their conduct and may even make us slightly less condemnatory, but before and during their crime they must have made a series of conscious decisions. Unless they were mad, they must have known that what they were doing was wrong, or at the very least was generally regarded as wrong. Even on the Libet theory, as the ideas came into their conscious minds, they could have drawn back from such evil. That their consciences had been so weakened by their life experience that they ignored any moral sense in pursuing their evil desires does not mean they lacked free will. If you have an inclination to act badly in a particular way you can work both to strengthen your consciousness of that weakness and to develop methodology of resisting. We all have a conscience.[13]

· Recently in England a family of gypsies were given heavy sentences for enslaving men with learning difficulties and using them to build driveways. The sentencing judge told the convicted slave masters that they had deprived their

---

[13] Even Sam Harris appears to accept this insofar as he refers to the possibility of feeling guilty if he had a glass of beer too early (page 19). He recognizes the importance of 'character' (page 49) and yet we all contribute to the development, or distortion, of our own character. In our character can be found input from our spirit and our conscience.

victims of their free will. If we do not have free will it is difficult to see how there can be slavery at all. If a slave never had free will, of what exactly is the master depriving him? If the master has no free will then he is surely above condemnation however brutally he treats the slave. It seems clear that slavery is so abhorrent for the very reason that it steals another person's free will. It seems equally clear that slavers have the capacity to review their behaviour and to amend. I agree with the late Maya Angelou, whose life experiences could so easily have left her resentful and twisted, that, "The wonderful thing about human beings and staying alive is that we have a chance to change. That is the most exciting of all our possibilities."[14] We are capable of changing ourselves, or being changed by therapy, knowledge, meditation, good example, guidance, or even religion. I have already referred to violent criminals, who have reformed.[15] I once came across a case of a man who, when a child, had suffered a life of cruelty in the 1950s. This culminated when his wicked stepmother forced him to kill his pet with a hammer. As she turned her back on the scene he did the same

---

[14] Maya Angelou, *Colin Johnson/Maya Angelou*, BBC Radio 4, 24.8.16.

[15] *Tough Talk* by Arthur White, Steve Johnson and Ian McDowall.

to her. I can see compelling reasons why this boy should have been treated with mercy by the legal system, although typically he was ruthlessly tried, convicted and given a life sentence for murder. However, he probably did make a decision to strike out, however much we may sympathize. The law does theoretically allow for the conscious mind being affected, or driven by extraneous matters, as in the formal legal concepts of provocation, diminished responsibility, automatism and intoxication.

Subsequently, I represented a man, who had pederastic inclinations. Because he was conscious that this weakness was wrong, he successfully resisted it. For the purpose of blackmail another man drugged him and placed him in the same room as a stupefied youth with the result that there was a sexual assault. I failed ignominiously in my attempt to persuade the House of Lords that my client was, in these compelling circumstances, not sufficiently responsible for his actions to be convicted of indecent assault due to his higher mind being impaired by the drugs slipped into his drink.[16] I strongly agree with Dr Harris, who shines from the pages of his books as a good, intelligent and humorous person, that "Our system of justice should reflect an understanding that any

---

[16] R v Kingston [1994] 3 *WLR* 519.

of us could have been dealt a very different hand in life."[17] Sadly the legal systems in the UK and the US seldom do so in practice. That a person's exercise of his will may be adversely affected by past experience should be better reflected in legal systems, but, other than in cases of insanity, I cannot agree that criminals have no free will. There may be extenuating circumstances, but we are all responsible for our actions and we can all change for the better.

Chance ordains that life does not always change for the better. Certainly the dinosaurs would have agreed at the moment when a wandering asteroid – six miles in diameter – smashed into Mexico sixty-six million years ago wiping out seventy-five per cent of life on earth. This is a perfect example of the randomness of life and the absence of any divine master-plan. Dr Harris considers that the randomness of life denies the possibility of free will. He suggests that we did not pick our parents, place of birth, or gender. Oddly Dr Douglas Baker, Dr Brenda Davies and various concepts of reincarnation suggest that we do in fact do just these things. The spirit, it is said, chooses its new existence for the purpose of its future development. A great artist may choose to return as visually impaired to balance his spiritual development.

---

[17] *Free Will*, page 54.

Whether this is right or not, the fact that events in life are random does not mean that we have no free will to cope with them. If events were predestined then for that very reason free will would be impossible. If events were fixed by fate, by divine will, or developed according to a rigid mathematical formula, there would be no practical purpose for free will. It seems almost certain that events are random. Randomness surely goes hand in hand with free will. I suppose that you could say that the asteroid deprived the dinosaurs of free will by killing them, but this is only true on a most trivial level.

Free will and self-knowledge also share a bond. Self-knowledge is recognized by Dr Harris as important. He writes, "Getting behind our conscious thoughts and feelings can allow us to steer a more intelligent course through our lives (while knowing, of course, that we are ultimately being steered)."[18] If we have *any* control over our course through life, then we have free will. Just as a one degree deviation in course of a ship crossing an ocean can drastically alter its destination, any ability we have to use our own will to adjust our path must be capable of radically changing our course through life. If we can make any adjustment to our path then we have free will. Either we are Kleist's puppet, or we are not. The maid in the

---

[18] *Free Will*, page 47.

old tale could not be, as she claimed, 'just a little bit pregnant' and we cannot have just a little bit of free will. Prisoners have their lives regulated and controlled, but within the limitations imposed upon them they still have free will. That our genetic make-up and our past experiences in life may affect our decisions is clearly true, but do they control us so that we have no free will? If they do then how can self-knowledge help at all? The fact that self-knowledge and spiritual development do help us to steer a fair course through life means that we do have free will.

Dr Harris asks, "Am I free to do *that which does not occur to me to do?* Of course not."[19] Surely the point to be taken from this statement of the obvious is that we have the free will to widen our horizons and to discover the possibility of doing or refraining from doing something, which but for that greater knowledge would for us have remained a part of the Great Mystery. Dr Harris appears to agree, because he writes in another book, "There is little question that how one uses one's attention, moment to moment, largely determines what kind of person one becomes. Our minds – and lives – are largely shaped by how we use them."[20]

---

[19] *Free Will*, page 19.

[20] *Waking Up*, page 31.

Amen to that!

Bibliography

The Bible
The Qur'an
The Complete Works of Shakespeare
The Internet

A

Adam, Alexander "Roman Antiques"
Armstrong, Karen "Buddha"
Armstrong, Karen "The Case For God"
Aurelius, Marcus (translated by Meric Casaubon) "Meditations"

B

Baker, Dr Douglas "The Opening Of The Third Eye"
Booker, Christopher "The Neophiliacs"
Brinkmann, Professor Svend "Stand Firm,"
Brown, Ellen "Forbidden Medicine"

C

Campolo, Tony "Choose Love Not Power"
Capra, Fritjof "The Tao of Physics"
Chalke, Steve "The Lost Message of Jesus"
Clarke, Roger "A Natural History of Ghosts"
Comte-Sponville, André "The Book of Atheist Spirituality"
Curtis, Edward S. "Prayer to the Great Mystery"

D

Davies, Dr Brenda "Journey of the Soul"
Dawkins, Professor Richard "The God Delusion"
Dennett, Daniel "Consciousness Explained"
De Hamel, Christopher "The Book. A History of the Bible"
De Montaigne, Michel Eyquem "The Complete Essays"

De Waal, Professor Frans "Chimpanzee Politics"
De Waal, Professor Frans "Peacemaking Among Primates"

E

Epictetus (translated by Elizabeth Carter) "The Moral Discourses of Epictetus"

F

Festinger and Others "When the Prophecy Fails"
Foster, Paul "The Apocryphal Gospels"

G

Gaye, R. K. "The Platonic Conception of Immortality"
Gawdat, Mo "Solve for Happy"
Gibran, Kahlil "The Prophet"
Gosse, Edmund "Father and Son"
Graves, Robert "Goodbye to All That"
Gray, John "The Soul of the Marionette"

H

Harari, Dr Yuval Noah "Sapiens"
Harris, Dr Sam "Free Will"
Harris, Dr Sam "Waking Up"
Hesse, Herman "Demian"
Herodotus (translated by Aubrey De Sélincourt) "The Histories"
Hitchens, Christopher "God Is Not Great"

J

Johnson, Paul "Socrates"
Jones, A. H. M. "The Later Roman Empire"

K

Keller, Timothy "The Reason for God"
Kneale, Matthew "An Atheist's History of Belief"

L

Lindsay, David "A Voyage to Arcturus"
Lucretius (translated by R. E. Latham) "The Nature of the Universe"

M

Monroe, Robert A. "Journeys Out of the Body"
Montaigne, Michel de (translated by J. M. Cohen) "Essays"

N

Newman, Cardinal John Henry "Apologia Pro Vita Sua"
Nixey, Catherine "The Darkening Age"

P

Plato "The Republic"
Plato "The Symposium"
Post, Sir Laurens van der "Venture to the Interior"

R

Roland, Paul "Ghosts"
Rowling J. K. "Harry Potter"

S

Sacks, Rabbi Jonathan "The Dignity of Difference"
Sartre, Jean-Paul (translated by C. Macomber) "Existentialism is Humanism"
Shaw, George Bernard "The Complete Prefaces"
Sheldrake, Dr Rupert "Setting Science Free from Materialism"
Shelley, Percy Bysshe (Amazon Version) "The Necessity of Atheism"

T

Tolstoy, Leo "A Confession"
Tich Nhat Hanh "Peace Is Every Step"
Tich Nhat Hanh "Touching Peace"

V

Vidal, Gore "Julian"

W

Wa-Na-Nee-Che and Bríd Fitzpatrick "Great Grandfather Spirit"
White, Arthur and others "Tough Talk"
Williams, Dr Rowan "Being Disciples"
Wilson, A.N. "Jesus"
Wilson, Colin "Afterlife"

Wilson, Colin "Poltergeist"
Wilson, Colin "The Occult"

Index

About the Author

Charles S. Taylor was born in London after the Second World War. He grew up on the south coast of England and went to University in the north. He won a number of glittering prizes, including the oddly named, "Prince Delphus Adebayo Odubanjo Prize in Law."

He spent 40 years as a barrister. During this time he saw much of the best and worst of people. He learned how to assess and apply evidence and how to detect and expose inconsistent statements.

His interests include: gardening, tennis, Italy, Italian and, of course, The Great Mystery.

He has had the opportunity to meet many amazing people and to listen to the wisdom of sages, ranging from ghost hunters to Nelson Mandela. While admiring the courage and enthusiasm of Professor Richard Dawkins, he found the materialism of "The God Delusion" to be as delusional as some of the religious absurdities so rightly scorned.

When rejecting religion we should not reject the Spirit.

438

Proudly published by Accent Press

www.accentpress.co.uk